Surpassing Standards
in the Elementary Classroom

Studies in the
Postmodern Theory of Education

Joe L. Kincheloe and Shirley R. Steinberg
General Editors

Vol. 330

PETER LANG
New York • Washington, D.C./Baltimore • Bern
Frankfurt am Main • Berlin • Brussels • Vienna • Oxford

Lee R. Chasen

Surpassing Standards in the Elementary Classroom

Emotional Intelligence and Academic Achievement Through Educational Drama

PETER LANG
New York • Washington, D.C./Baltimore • Bern
Frankfurt am Main • Berlin • Brussels • Vienna • Oxford

Library of Congress Cataloging-in-Publication Data

Chasen, Lee R.
Surpassing standards in the elementary classroom: Emotional intelligence
and academic achievement through educational drama
in the elementary classroom / Lee R. Chasen.
p. cm. — (Counterpoints: studies in the postmodern theory of education; v. 330)
Includes bibliographical references and index.
1. Language arts (Elementary) 2. Social sciences—Study and teaching (Elementary)
3. Emotional intelligence—Study and teaching (Elementary)
4. Academic achievement. I. Title.
LB1576.C455   370.15'2—dc22   2008043859
ISBN 978-1-4331-0307-0
ISSN 1058-1634

Bibliographic information published by **Die Deutsche Bibliothek**.
Die Deutsche Bibliothek lists this publication in the "Deutsche
Nationalbibliografie"; detailed bibliographic data is available
on the Internet at http://dnb.ddb.de/.

The paper in this book meets the guidelines for permanence and durability
of the Committee on Production Guidelines for Book Longevity
of the Council of Library Resources.

© 2009 Peter Lang Publishing, Inc., New York
29 Broadway, 18th floor, New York, NY 10006
www.peterlang.com

Printed in the United States of America

I dedicate this book to my mother, Louise Chasen,
for making such a great choice.

CONTENTS

FOREWORD

The world today needs more creativity, and creativity arises from the integration of imagination, intuition, and emotional sensitivity with language and reason (Pink, 2005). The natural vehicle for this kind of integration is experiential learning, and for more than straight-ahead motor skills, for skills that involve human interaction, the natural vehicle for that kind of learning is improvisational drama, role playing (Blatner, 1995).

While many people tend to associate drama with the performance of scripted and rehearsed plays, in fact that is only one of many ways drama can be done. By enacting problem situations through role playing or sociodrama, students can more effectively learn-by-doing. Pioneers in education from the late 19th and early 20th century advocated a more experiential approach to teaching, and drama is the most natural vehicle for integrating the mind-body-social network in this way.

I have been a physician and child/ adult psychiatrist who has found role playing (in its original format of psychodrama, invented in the mid-1930s by J. L. Moreno, M.D.) to be a particularly effective form of psychotherapy (Blatner, 2000). Beyond that application, though, I've discovered that these methods are most useful in other settings—business, community building, personal development, and of course all types of education.

When two media are "hybridized," observed Marshall McLuhan (a theorist of communications in the mid-1960s), there is a great release of cultural energy. He was referring to the explosion of new forms coming out of the mixing of cinema and radio to produce television, but this observation would apply today also to the mixed media of computers and further, to the mixing of participatory education and drama. *Drama should be recognized as a medium of communication*, one that brings together not only a presentation of the problem, but also considers the hidden psychological dimensions, what is not outwardly spoken (the voice over technique), the possibility of role reversal (to build empathy), the opportunity of skill building through re-play and re-hearsal, the intrinsic motivation generated by the context of play, and other factors.

Lee Chasen, the author of this present book, has built on the substantial developments in the fields of drama in education over the last fifty years so that once again a more dynamic approach may be offered instead of the still-prevalent and deadening pedagogy of rote memorization. This book thus serves as another component of the paradigm shift that is needed in contemporary education.

—Adam Blatner, M.D.

References

Blatner, A. (1995). Drama in education as mental hygiene: a child psychiatrist's perspective.
Youth Theatre Journal, 9, 92-96 (March, 1995).

Blatner, A. (1997). Applications in education (Chapter 13), in *The Art of Play: Helping Adults Reclaim Imagination and Spontaneity*. New York: Brunner/Routledge.

Blatner, A. (2000). *Foundations of psychodrama: history, theory, & practice*. New York: Springer.

Blatner, A. (Ed.) (2007). *Interactive & improvisational drama: varieties of applied theatre and performance*. Lincoln, NE: iUniverse.

Also webpage supplement: http://www.interactiveimprov.com/whydramawb.html

Blatner, A. (2008). Expanding communications through psychodrama (webpage supplement), retrieved from http://www.blatner.com/adam/pdntbk/expandcommunicatpd.html

Pink, D. H. (2005). *A whole new mind: why right-brainers will rule the future*. New York: Riverhead.

ACKNOWLEDGMENTS

My first and foremost expression of gratitude is offered to all the children who enter our program prepared to hate it. Thank you for daring me, through your masks of skepticism and cynicism, to reach out and provide you with something that might be meaningful to your life. I see your desperation and will continue to hold the grown-ups accountable and work for your healing.

I so appreciate Doreen Montefusco, Jenny Shore, Stefanie Schaller, Kate Nodarse, Krista Granieri and the rest of the Kid Esteem staff, interns and volunteers, for supporting our mission with all your great work, heartfelt support and general silliness. Tremendous thanks to the editors at Peter Lang, Chris Myers, Shirley Steinberg and especially Sophie Appel who showed such kindness and patience throughout this process.

Rosalie Franzese and Kelly Markham Mahon are two exceptional teachers who were such a pleasure to work with. Thank you to my family, mother, father, sister, nieces, nephews, cousins, all my in-laws, dear friends and colleagues, for all your words of support and encouragement.

Finally, the happiest expression of gratitude and acknowledgement belongs to my wife and co-creator Marianne and our four children. I love our vision and all the struggles that come with it. Kids, your interest and participation make it all such a joy.

The Great Disconnect

The profound dysfunction of American education was epitomized for me a number of years ago by my daughter's school-sponsored fifth-grade trip, a three-hour cruise on a party boat complete with a DJ, food. and activities, that commemorated the children's graduation from elementary school and the culmination, I suppose, of all they had learned.

Our district is average and middle class, with the same aspirations for excellence that thousands of other districts share. My children's teachers and school officials are good and smart people with the best of intentions. What occurs in this district occurs, I have no doubt, in any seemingly progressive district that upholds high performance as an authentic standard.

I am positive that many times and within various components of the curriculum between kindergarten and fifth grade, the students "learned" about nutrition, the food pyramid, endangered animals, local marine life, the threat of pollution, and the dangers of substance abuse. These important lessons notwithstanding, as students, teachers, and parents boarded the boat, eager to celebrate and honor six years of education, we were initially met by mountains of donuts, chips, and junk food, replete with processed sugars, preservatives, chemicals, and dyes, ready for our immediate consumption at 9AM.

As the boat sailed out of port into more open waters, the plastic leis, balloons, and party hats the students and teachers were adorned with to add to the celebration casually blew overboard as we merrily chugged along, leaving a trail of colorful plastic dancing into the waves of the environmentally sensitive Great South Bay, and eventually, perhaps, into the throats and stomachs of the endangered turtles and marine animals living there that the children had diligently studied. Teachers, students, and parents laughed together as these enticingly deadly objects flew out of their hands, off their heads, and into the water.

Meanwhile, parents, teachers, and the principal started dancing with the children to what was deemed to be a family-friendly mix of songs. The DJ even made a somewhat apologetic announcement to the students as the music started, that he would be spinning a "cleaned up" play list, as per the principal's direction. Yet, for the next three hours, the DJ played songs, as the principal and his graduates smiled and danced along, which encouraged us, over and over again, to take off all our clothes, smoke pot, drink a six-pack, and engage in sexual activity. I suppose this was considered to be OK because there weren't any curses in the songs, although an occasional "ass" and "damn" slipped out from time to time.

Yes, this was a party, and we should have fun at these types of celebrations, but what does this experience say about how, why, and what we learn? Shouldn't we live by or model or at least pretend to uphold the curriculum we so dutifully promote that instructs our students to eat healthy, protect the environment, just say no, and abstain? Shouldn't the information we methodically dole out in our classrooms day after day, year after year, be presented as whole and relevant to everyday life at every opportunity we have? Otherwise, what type of connections are we, or are we not, facilitating? How many other contradictions and disconnects are we unknowingly promulgating on a regular basis during our 180 or so days with the children? Do we believe in what we teach or are we just "getting through" the curriculum to appease institutional demands? Does the system "set us up" to give gratuitous lip service to the notion of meaningful connection while ultimately manipulating us to participate in the ongoing severing of these connections in order to serve the more corporate interests of a culture defined by commercial consumption?

Most of the people who were on that boat are good, smart, and well-intentioned, and some teachers did express discomfort with at least the inappropriate messages that were implied by the music. It seems though that even our most progressively minded teachers and administrators are ultimately compromised by the vapid demands of an institutionalized and uninspired approach to the curriculum that methodically shuts down any meaningful digestion and internalization of the academic information that we force feed to our students. Whatever message or information we are responsible for facilitating, we need to present it, process it, and stand by it as whole and relevant to our students' lives. Otherwise, the information we spend so much time on and effort dispensing over so many years is, as I witnessed on that boat, ultimately meaningless.

These contradictions and disconnects are grotesquely highlighted by the uniquely American spectacle of students who increasingly end up using semi-automatic weapons in a desperate and tragic effort to create meaningful experience. Antisocial acts of violence and aggression, substance abuse, even everyday activities such as watching television, eating, shopping, and video game playing have become the distorted and addictive waste products of misguided attempts to satisfy the need for meaningful encounter.

The journey to restructure our classrooms and instructional approaches and mend this great disconnect in our education system so that students may be empowered by information that is truly meaningful and applicable to their lives will be a long and hard one, but it is a journey that is critically necessary to take.

PART I

Empowering Thought and Feeling

CHAPTER 1

An American Education Identity Crisis

For decades, concerned American educators have worked to establish instructional practices that can empower the emotional and social development of students. School districts and state education departments across the country have pursued such ideals through initiatives such as *Character Education, Citizenship, Values Clarification, Self-esteem, Social Skills,* and *Conflict Resolution.* While these institutionally sponsored programs have come and gone with varying degrees of success and support, our instincts and humanistic sense of what "a good education" should be continue to push us to further articulate and approach instruction with the goal of generating more substantial, meaningful, and relevant experiences in our classrooms.

Research from the field of neurobiology has now confirmed that these instincts, initially conceived from a social perspective, actually engage critical and necessary processes that facilitate optimum brain functioning, cognitive development, intellectual engagement, and academic success. This reality, amplified by the ongoing violence and antisocial behavior that continues to plague our students and our culture, provides a synergetic foundation for realizing the decades-long quest to improve the quality of American education.

Presently and historically, American education typically ranks nearer to the bottom of lists that indicate success with academic performance and achievement (Trends in International Mathematics and Science Study, 2003; UNICEF, 2003; Progress in International Reading Literacy Study, 2007). We do manage to come out on top though with regard to violent crimes committed by and against youths (FBI, 2006; U.S. Department of Education, 2008; Centers for Disease Control and Prevention, 2008), illegal drug use among teenagers (National Drug Intelligence Center, 2008), the amount of mood-altering and antipsychotic drugs prescribed for our children in response to the growing violence (American Medical Association, 2000; Associated Press, May 5, 2008), and the ever-increasing high school dropout rate (EPE Research Center and America's Promise Alliance, 2008).

The narration of this national drama and the ongoing failure of the American education system began in earnest, perhaps, with the Soviet launching of the *Sputnik* satellite in 1957. Headlines such as *Educators Upset over Soviet Stroke,* insisting that the United States "wake up to the dangers of educational neglect" (Fine, 1957a, p. 1, 11), and *Satellite Called Spur to Edu-*

cation, trumpeting the notion that "education as usual can no longer be accepted in this country" (Fine, 1957b, p. 1, 3), pushed a sense of collective anxiety with regard to poor academic achievement into the national consciousness. We came to realize that something in our educational system wasn't working as well as it should.

Half a century and billions of dollars later, the nonstop drip of low scores, unmet standards, and failed initiatives continues to echo around sensationalized television news segments with urgent titles such as *America's Failing Education System* (CNN, November 3, 2003) and *Education Crisis in America* (FOX, November 23, 2003). How does this happen in a country that prides itself on being the best, number one, and the leader of the world?

A comic strip by a political cartoonist attempts to illustrate the problem with American education by comparing it to education in Finland. The main character, a duck that works as a reporter, points out that Finland's schools placed first in an international survey of educational excellence even though they spend less per student and have close to thirty kids per class (Tinsley, April 27, 2004). The author is apparently trying to make the point that, in order to fix our schools, we need not focus on costly "liberal" ideas like more funding and fewer students per class. If Finland does it that way, why can't we?

The unintended irony here is that Finland, like many other countries seen as having exceptional educational systems, comes from a tradition of Social Democracy, which promotes a more liberal, communal culture, facilitating, perhaps, more efficient and effective functioning in groups. While the author of the comic strip may or may not be right about how we allocate our resources, the Finnish approach to social structure and management, which lends itself to success in their education system, is probably one that the author, who aligns himself with political conservatives, would least likely prescribe for America.

We need to construct a philosophical and practical approach to education in our country that reflects who we are as Americans. We need to direct our resources toward development of an education system that reflects and empowers values emerging from the unique history, traditions, and culture of the American experience if we are going to realize the opportunity for excellence and achievement ingrained in our national identity.

CHAPTER 2

Grounding an Integrated Approach

A cornerstone of American identity is often epitomized by the spirit of individuality. Unique emotional experience is perhaps one of the most distinct ways aside from DNA that individuality can be expressed and understood. The lesson plans presented in this book are grounded in the concept of *emotional intelligence*, a term popularized by social psychologist Daniel Goleman in 1996. The skills of emotional intelligence facilitate an individual's ability to identify and express emotion in a manner that alleviates emotional distress while enhancing cognitive processing.

Educational Drama—a learning approach using role-play, improvisation, creative thought, story making, expressive language, gesture, puppetry, masks, costumes, set building, and enactment—provides an ideal vehicle for integrating cognitive and emotional processing and engaging critical learning processes. While educational drama has been an established and documented field for over half a century, these activities, because of their relatively unconventional nature, are rarely included in a mainstream approach to classroom instruction.

The *Literacy Express* teaches reading and writing by integrating emotional intelligence skills facilitated through educational drama activities. The approach emerged from research for a doctoral dissertation at New York University conducted by Reading Specialist Rosalie Franzese and myself. Potential links between emotional intelligence and literacy skills were studied for at-risk first and second graders participating in a pilot program. Established literacy assessments used in the research study showed a significant increase in reading and writing scores for most students, while rating scales and parent interviews documented enhanced emotional intelligence skills for the students after participating in the fifteen-week language arts program (Chasen, 2003).

Our findings indicated that the program did not merely increase emotional intelligence skills and literacy scores. Rather, we found that integrating the two within one approach created an interactive learning paradigm, in which each domain, cognitive and affective, traditionally thought of as separate entities, informs and empowers the other in an intricate dynamic that mirrors developmental processing. Subsequently, the instructional techniques, although unconventional, generated greater interest and investment in gaining knowledge and acquiring new skills. Understanding this important dynamic furthered our intent to create practical, comprehensive lesson plans that can integrate cognitive and emotional development and facilitate greater student achievement.

The program *Building Communities, Character and Social Skills*, an approach to social studies that integrates emotional intelligence skills through educational drama activities, was piloted by my wife, certified teacher Marianne Chasen, and myself in a suburban third-grade classroom taught by Kelly Markham. During the twelve-week program, we noticed high achievers excelling while more challenged, inattentive learners became dramatically more engaged in and responsive to the learning process and curricular concepts. These exceptional teachers, Rosalie Franzese and Kelly Markham, who share our vision for transcending more limited conventional approaches to instruction, welcomed us into their classrooms. We were concerned though that our unconventional techniques might be a tough sell in an institution that, in spite of itself, seems to place insurmountable obstacles on the path toward establishing new, progressive approaches to classroom instruction.

We knew that, at first glance, it might be difficult for education professionals to understand how our approach could comprehensively cover the "meat and potatoes," the mechanics of reading and writing, deciphering flow charts, applying map skills, analyzing time lines, and solving word problems, for example, of academic standards and requirements. Our concerns regarding "the sell" of our approach turned to excitement as we began reviewing the *New York State Learning Standards* program, which includes key goals such as *creative thinking, problem solving, visioning, responsibility, integrity, team work, reasoning, interpersonal skills, leadership,* and *self-management*. These concepts comprise the driving force that motivates our students to find success with curricular standards and requirements, and they are the seemingly intangible elements that inspire them to surpass those standards.

Moreover, many of the established standards emphasize reflection on the "how" and the "why" of the curriculum, in addition to the "who, what, when, and where." In the district where we piloted our social studies project, we were delighted to find a call for educational experiences and outcomes that included *ability to communicate feelings, personal character and ideas, moral and ethical sense of values, pride, self-understanding, self-awareness, self-worth, respect for others, awareness of the processes of group relationships,* and *creative self-expression* in the *Educational Philosophy* section of the teachers' *Handbook* published by the district. In our estimation and experience, these goals are hard to come by when we rely on conventional vehicles of instruction that limit individual expression.

So, while we were initially concerned that we might be seen as trying to fit a square peg in a round hole, we came to discover, upon further investigation, that our peg wasn't actually square. We had the round one; the one that, according to the directives and goals identified and documented by the established educational institutions, would provide the right fit.

CHAPTER 3

Emotional Intelligence
Foundation for Cognitive and Social Development

Emotional intelligence, as stated earlier, indicates an ability to be aware of and express emotional states of being, using self-identified language, in a manner that assists with the task of fulfilling individual needs and solving problems, be they personal, social, or intellectual.

From a social perspective, increasingly violent and deadly tragedies across our country and in our schools—highlighted by events at Columbine High School and Virginia Tech University—darkly illustrate the need for proactive models that can teach emotional management skills to children. Alcohol and substance abuse, drug addiction, divorce, family and gang violence, physical and sexual abuse, suicide, all kinds of bullying, and the glamorization of commercial culture as the answer to these problems are only some of the regular, mainstream occurrences that indicate what Goleman identified as an increasingly dangerous "collective emotional crisis" (1996, p. xi).

Violence from stabbings, beatings, and other abuse kills American children at a rate greater than that is any other Western nation, according to the federal Centers for Disease Control (CDC) and Prevention. The CDC also published in 2008 their findings that about 1 in 50 infants in the United States are abused or neglected. Our inability to appropriately process and express intense emotions such as anger, rage, sadness, and fear in a manner that is self-aware, empowered, and satisfying lies at the desperate heart of these and other antisocial acts and behaviors. All statistics, including news reports and government studies (FBI's 2007 Uniform Crime Report), show this to be a crisis that continues to grow.

In addition to these more pressing social issues, problems that arise from the everyday stresses of family life, such as getting ready for school, managing homework and other daily tasks, would be greatly alleviated with a simple model for conflict resolution. How many families get bogged down in these frustrations, running in the same circles day after day, with no protocol for emotionally intelligent discourse, resulting in distracted children being sent off to school on the wrong foot, with fallout from aggression, anxiety, and a host of unresolved emotional issues that negatively affect school performance? These realities, along with newly emerging problematic social encounters such as road rage and Internet aggression, make a strong case for teaching the skills of emotional intelligence that can assist in managing daily life routines.

Certainly, social crises and quality of life concerns such as these are reason enough to implement a skills-based emotional intelligence curriculum in our schools. What is perhaps even more compelling is that neurobiologists who study brain function have made it clear that emotional intelligence skills play an imperative role in cognitive development and intellectual achievement. By tracking patterns of biochemical brain activity, researchers have shown that cognitive functions do not and cannot operate properly without engaging a methodical approach to processing emotion (Damasio, 1999).

Damasio found that an organism couldn't relate to objects, events, or concepts in the environment, and construct knowledge about them, without initially processing a response from its biological regulatory systems, and accurately registering it within its emotional perceptions (p. 26). Self-awareness of its emotional state provides the organism with the necessary information and constructs for building a knowledge base. This neurological evidence demonstrates that the absence of emotional processing poses a real problem for cognitive functioning, and without "well-targeted and well-deployed emotion...reason cannot operate properly" (p. 42), establishing emotion as "integral to the processes of reasoning and decision making" (p. 41). The age of reason, which sought to subtract emotion from intellectual discourse four hundred years ago, has now come full circle. We need to include emotional processing skills as a central component of an instructional approach that can optimize cognitive development and empower academic success.

The concepts and skills of emotional intelligence are relatively easy to understand and simple to facilitate. Our cultural misunderstandings and taboos with regard to emotion and its expression, though, can make such facilitation seem impossible to implement in a systematic manner. It is understandable that teachers would be resistant to or feel incompetent with the notion of teaching emotional intelligence skills. Emotions cause fights. Emotions disrupt the class. Emotions, even happy ones, can get out of control. Lecturing students and setting up charts about their behavior and the need to control their emotions seem to distract from the curriculum, not add to it. We need to understand the concept of emotional management and control in a different light.

The true facilitation of emotional intelligence skills does not make teachers responsible for promoting, censoring, controlling, or changing any type of emotional content expressed by a student. Rather, it teaches a set of skills that support students toward engaging and identifying a greater range of emotional awareness and expression, without prejudice or judgments that certain emotions, such as anger, are "bad" or undesirable. We need to learn how to teach emotional intelligence skills in a manner that empowers students, teachers, and classrooms toward new levels of academic and social success.

When we ask our students to vote on whether they think getting mad is a *good* or a *bad* thing, usually, 80 percent or more vote that it's *bad* to get angry. I ask the students to imagine that as they are getting on their school bus or walking to school, a bully who is a couple of years older starts grabbing at their backpacks and spilling the contents onto the ground as their parents watch from afar. I ask them to tell me how their parents would feel toward the bully if they witnessed such an event. The students, of course, respond that their parents would be mad, and I illustrate how that would be a good thing! Their parents would use their anger as a positive tool that would empower them to stick up for the children, do the right thing, and hopefully solve the problem. Through this hypothetical example, the students come to understand that anger, or any emotion, is not in itself a "bad" thing.

Along these lines, Salovey and Sluyter (1997), social scientists who originated the concept of emotional intelligence, note that the concept is *not* about "the institutionally sanctioned requirement of behaving 'well' or 'nicely'" (p. 15). They explain that teaching emotional intelligence does not "dictate the outcome of a person's emotional behavior but rather encourages a process of personal investigation that can occur in the context of the person's own politics, ethnicity, religion, and other characteristics" (p. 16). It is not about imposing values or controlling students. It is about facilitating skills that generate individual values and self-control. The process guides students to be empowered as well as responsible. It teaches them to process and verbalize their experiences through self-identified language, examples of which will be demonstrated throughout the lesson plans in parts II and III.

Salovey and Sluyter (1997) define emotional intelligence as "the ability to perceive emotions, to access and generate emotions so as to assist thought, to understand emotions and emotional knowledge, and to reflectively regulate emotions so as to promote emotional and intellectual growth" (p. 5). They establish four levels of skills for emotional intelligence. A summary of these levels is listed here:

1. *Perception, Appraisal, and Expression of Emotion*
   Ability to identify emotion in one's physical states, feelings, and thoughts. Ability to identify emotions in other people, designs, artwork, and so on, through language, sound, appearance, and behavior. Ability to express emotions accurately, and to express needs related to those feelings. Ability to discriminate between accurate and inaccurate, or honest versus dishonest expressions of feeling.

2. *Emotional Facilitation of Thinking*
   Emotions prioritize thinking by directing attention to important information. Emotions are sufficiently vivid and available that they can be
   generated as aids to judgment and memory concerning feelings. Emotional mood swings change the individual's perspective from optimistic
   to pessimistic, encouraging consideration of multiple points of view.
   Emotional states differentially encourage specific problem approaches
   such as when happiness facilitates inductive reasoning and creativity.

3. *Understanding and Analyzing Emotions; Employing Emotional Knowledge*
   Ability to label emotions and recognize relations among the words and
   the emotions themselves, such as the relation between liking and loving.
   Ability to interpret the meanings that emotions convey regarding relationships, such as that sadness often accompanies a loss. Ability to understand complex feelings: simultaneous feelings of love and hate, or
   blends such as awe as a combination of fear and surprise. Ability to recognize likely transitions among emotions, such as the transition from anger to satisfaction, or from anger to shame.

4. *Reflective Regulation of Emotions to Promote Emotional and Intellectual
   Growth*
   Ability to stay open to feelings, both those that are pleasant and those
   that are unpleasant. Ability to reflectively engage or detach from an emotion depending upon its judged informativeness or utility. Ability to reflectively monitor emotions in relation to oneself and others, such as
   recognizing how clear, typical, influential, or reasonable they are. Ability
   to manage emotion in oneself and others by moderating negative emotions and enhancing pleasant ones, without repressing or exaggerating
   information they may convey. (p. 11)

Researchers from the fields of social science and neurobiology have made
it clear. Our public school systems need to respond to the "desperate need for
lessons in handling emotions" (Goleman, 1996, p. 231). The concepts and
skills of emotional intelligence are relatively easy to implement, as will be
demonstrated in detail, even though they may appear complicated and cloudy
as a result of cultural perceptions and misunderstandings.

If we, as teachers, don't learn how to integrate and anchor the academic
curriculum with the skills of emotional intelligence, we ignore an important
resource that naturally empowers the intellectual and social growth of our
students. If we don't take the opportunity to tap into this resource and tran-
scend the limits of the conventional classroom, our increasingly disabled cul-

ture will continue to be misinformed by a fragmented and misguided curriculum. We need to overhaul our approach to intellectual engagement and classroom instruction and place emotional and social development at the core of a revitalized curriculum.

CHAPTER 4

Synthesizing Thought and Feeling Through Educational Drama

Educational drama, as stated earlier, uses forms and techniques associated with dramatic interaction to engage and empower critical learning skills. As an instructional approach, educational drama establishes and maintains a personal connection between the student and the curriculum, while facilitating a number of specific processes that are key to development and sorely missing from mainstream instructional practices.

While traditionally considered as merely an extra-curricular outlet not necessarily germane to the academic curriculum, the connections that educational drama facilitates are significant and noteworthy. It figuratively, as well as literally, brings the curriculum to life by asking students to respond to seemingly irrelevant concepts and materials from a personal and meaningful understanding that is unique to each student's life. Students are naturally more invested in the process, because the process is naturally more invested in the individual experiences of the students, connecting them to an otherwise detached curriculum in a manner that is fun, creative, and child-centered.

Along with and because of this initial connection to the concepts and materials of the curriculum, the educational drama paradigm is able to directly activate and facilitate fundamental learning processes that are key to development. In order to gain an understanding of the significance of educational drama as a critical teaching and learning tool, the concepts of symbolic representation, cognitive/affective integration and multimodal learning will be briefly illustrated.

Symbolic representation, which allows information to exist and be perceived within different contexts, most notably real and not real, is at the core of all developmental processing. Historically, humans, since the time of the caveman, have used art, ritual, and performance as symbolic representations of events and experiences in order to gain objectivity, understanding, and mastery over those events and experiences. The forms of drama allow the student to represent information within a symbolic context, the real and the not real, and function as if the pretend or fantasy, the not real, is actually occurring, with simultaneous awareness that the events being dramatized are fictional and not real. He or she is able to shift perception and move between these different contexts in which the information resides, generating a dynamic in which information can be accessed, organized, and appropriately applied. This dynamic mirrors key operations described in classic theories of both cognitive and socio-emotional development.

Piaget's (1951) concept of reversibility, central to his theory of cognitive development, refers to a similar perceptual movement between states of awareness, allowing individuals to link polarized contexts of information in order to generate development of new knowledge. Erikson (1968) also describes a key perceptual movement that occurs within his model of social-emotional development, an alternating focus between polarized states of information and experience that the individual needs to perceive and move between in order to link the disparate states of information and experience, facilitate understanding, and resolve intrapersonal conflict.

It is within this fundamental operation of movement and alternating focus, where polarized contexts of information interact and link to facilitate knowledge and development, that educational drama functions as a significant and indispensable teaching and learning tool. Through the forms and activities of educational drama, students construct symbolic representations of meaningful experiences relative to the shared theme or topic of the classroom. These experiences are established and perceived by the students within the different contexts, the real and the not real, that are supported by the dramatic forms. Dramatic enactment instructs the students to move more skillfully and purposefully between the different contexts, linking the polarized or disconnected sources of information. By providing such forms and techniques that mirror and reinforce this natural developmental process of movement between contexts, students become more able to shift perception and construct the links that generate new sources of knowledge.

It is within this same model of developmental movement that educational drama can be understood as an essential facilitator of emotional and cognitive integration, shifting and integrating perceptions between the two interconnected domains traditionally thought of as separate entities. For over half a century, before the advent of sophisticated neurobiological and social science research, contributors to the field of educational drama have described it as an essential structure for learning that actively engages and integrates cognitive and emotional processes to facilitate a deeper, more comprehensive intelligence (Slade, 1954; Way, 1967; Bolton, 1979; Courtney, 1980; McCaslin, 1980; Neelands, 1984; Wagner, 1998).

During dramatic enactment, participants are often called upon to identify and express emotion, symbolically represented within different contexts as described earlier, in order to respond to an objective set of shared events or concepts. As with Damasio's organism, the individual registers a response from his or her emotional state in order to relate to the event or concept and construct knowledge about it. The student is instructed and motivated by the shared nature of the drama to create objective knowledge that is at the same time personally meaningful. Acquired objective knowledge, in response to the shared, collective experience, can then assist in constructing skills toward managing and expressing subjective emotional experience and content. Educational drama facilitates the integration of emotional and cognitive processes by providing specific forms and techniques that engage students in an organic process of perceptual movement between subjective and objective realms of emotional and cognitive information, mutually enhancing each domain while deepening personal and intellectual understanding and growth.

This function of educational drama as a "developmental unifier" (Courtney, 1995, p. 44) can also be understood in the context of what Damasio (1994) identified as the "convergence zone" (p. 242), an area of the brain that is not exclusively supportive of object images nor subjective images of the self, rather, it is a "reciprocally interconnected...third-party neuron ensemble" (p. 242) that responds to each one of those areas, mediating perceptual relationships between the contexts, sorting the subsequent cognitive meanings that are created by such mediation, and estimating potential action that may need to be taken by the organism as a result of the newly acquired cognitive meanings. This is precisely where the processes of educational drama reside, operating in that critical convergence zone of the brain, strengthening students' ability to mediate relationships between contexts of real and not real, reality and fiction, self and role, thought and feeling, objective information and subjective experience, unique interpretation and collectively shared meaning as well as other complex intra- and interpersonal developmental poles.

Constructivist learning theorists refer to this movement as a "dynamic dance," in which the individual strives for "equilibration...[through a] process of self-regulated behavior balancing two intrinsic polar behaviors" (Duffy & Jonassen, 1992, p. 13). The structure and process of educational drama provide direct access to these polar contexts and then assist in teaching the steps to the dance, instructing students how to choreograph a unique approach using their own personal rhythms that can most efficiently facilitate equilibration and empower emotional and cognitive development.

The possible steps of this dance are further illuminated and made tangible by the multimodal nature of learning that occurs in the educational drama paradigm. By engaging the "whole person" (Way, 1967, p. 2), the techniques facilitate access to many of the individual learning strengths and strategies that students rely on, supporting them to work with, rather than

against, their unique cognitive abilities. The techniques encourage exploration and response from a range of multiple intelligences, including linguistic,
logical-mathematical, musical, bodily kinesthetic, spatial, interpersonal, and
intrapersonal, identified by Gardner (1983, 1999). During dramatic enactment, students are articulating, expressing, studying, estimating, measuring,
calculating, strategizing, comparing, composing, moving, connecting, containing, constructing, projecting, and interacting with aspects of individual
and subjective experience in order to purposefully relate to the shared objective context of the classroom topic or theme.

So, the structure, forms, and operations of educational drama truly serve
as an organic conduit for basic cognitive and developmental processing. Besides providing forms and structures that directly access, activate, and facilitate connection with the curriculum and essential learning processes, children
naturally adore it. This, of course, makes sense since the activities mirror and
enhance their own natural tendencies and desires for pursuing knowledge
and deepening understanding. It is a user-friendly approach, emerging from
our natural childhood instinct to play act and pretend as a primary learning
strategy. It focuses on the whole experience of the participant so that essential processes for cognitive development may be engaged and integrated, empowering the student in all realms of intellectual and social development.
Students we've worked with in previous years still approach us and ask
whether we can "please do it again." One boy asked us to return to his classroom and simply said, "I miss it."

In spite of all this positive reflection, it makes sense that teachers would
be uncomfortable with using educational drama techniques in their classrooms, just as they might be with the notion of integrating emotional intelligence skills. Students would be moving around physically in such an
approach. The classroom space would need to be redefined and renegotiated.
Outcomes would be unpredictable. All this is true. It is important to understand though that the structures, forms, and techniques of educational drama
contain elements that facilitate natural and self-regulated control in students.
This type of control is different from the one that we are more accustomed
to, the one that all too often censors and minimizes the potential strengths of
alternative learners.

The control elicited by educational drama is a more productive and powerful one because it respects the individual experiences and natural thought
processes of the student. When student impulses are respected and channeled toward productivity, they are extremely more compliant than when
impulses are being challenged and deconstructed for the purposes of "controlling" the class. This is especially true for children identified as having behavior problems. Educational drama allows us to manage and implement

tools that elicit true classroom control in a way that conventional approaches cannot. The experience is about prompting the students to become better equipped to meet their own emotional and intellectual needs, in accordance with the boundaries of the classroom, rather than enforcing compliance to meet the needs of the dysfunctional curriculum.

It is also understandable that teachers would feel uncomfortable or inadequate with using the forms and techniques of educational drama. As in any situation, breaking with convention isn't easy at first. Such an approach may be a very challenging one for some teachers to implement. I have no doubt, though, that any interested professional will be able to readily accommodate the concepts and assimilate their own dynamic and creative approach.

The following briefly lists forms and activities of educational drama, along with techniques derived from the more recent field of personal growth oriented *drama therapy* that will be presented in detail throughout parts II and III:

- *Sociometry and Warm-Up Games*—Students respond with movement, language, and personal perspective to specific, child-centered criteria that evoke and integrate thought and feeling, while providing a tool for measuring and understanding group response (Moreno, 1978).
- *Improvisation*—Students creatively and spontaneously apply existing knowledge to new situations or unfamiliar concepts, the foundation for acquiring new knowledge and skills.
- *Role-Play*—Students act as another, or portray themselves in another time frame or setting, through language, movement, and assumed identity, individually or in groups, within a prescribed boundary of shared meanings and contexts, to gain perspective and understanding. Costumes and props can be used to support role-play but are not essential.
- *Scene Study*—Students use role and improvisation to create small scenes around a shared context or topic to generate new ideas and knowledge.
- *Puppets and Masks*—Students project and express aspects of emotion, thought, and identity onto an object that can represent the self while maintaining the safe distance of existing as another (Landy, 1994, pp. 149–158).
- *Director's Hand*—A form of *world technique* (Landy, 1994, p. 185) in which students manipulate various figures representing a contained social setting to create and direct stories with, in order to gain understanding and develop skills.
- *Director's Chair*—Derived from Playback Theater (Fox, 1999), students direct reenactments of reality-based scenes from their lives in order to

empower emotionally intelligent expressive language that can address challenges experienced in the situation.

- *Character Development*—Students create and enact characters with specific identities and character traits relevant to the topic or concept being studied.

- *Set Building*—Students use materials such as sheets, fabrics, boxes, tables, chairs, and other available objects to re-create settings relevant to the topic or concept being studied.

- *Thematic Ensemble Enactment*—The whole class participates in a dramatic enactment using role, costume, set pieces, props, and multiple scenes around a specific context, topic, or theme, incorporating elements of spectacle and ensemble (Chasen, 2005) to engage and integrate subjective emotional experience with objective information, concepts, and skills of the academic curriculum.

Educational drama, as it connects students with the curriculum, specifically mirrors and facilitates critical learning processes and activates a wide range of individual learning strategies, creates a joyous and transcendent learning environment that breaks with convention and empowers, rather than negates, the natural course of integrated development. While the notion of employing the tools of educational drama may seem daunting to someone who has no previous experience with the modality, any teacher who is interested in transcending the limitations of the conventional classroom, and transforming the learning experience of their students, will be able to confidently and effectively implement the approach.

It is, in its purest and most ancient sense, a tangible structure through which conflicts may be played out and understood while potential resolutions are explored, a template for generating and guiding dynamics and procedures described in classic models of human development. It is a powerful tool that activates and instructs fundamental processes, and it cannot be ignored if we are serious about implementing more effective approaches to classroom instruction.

Summary

Integrating emotion-based information through educational drama activities to engage concepts and materials across the academic curriculum empowers developmental processing. It creates an ideal frequency that can more efficiently stream through the existing neurological wiring that facilitates optimum learning, restoring a crucial component to an otherwise fragmented dynamic.

These processes naturally occur in students as whole, integrated operations. When we compartmentalize the curriculum and train students to respond in a manner that is disconnected from personal, meaningful emotion-based experience, we are likely contorting students' natural processes and causing thought patterns to become equally disconnected, fragmented, and compartmentalized. An integrated curriculum restores a "whole" cognitive process by connecting students with materials and concepts through personal, emotion-based experiences that are uniquely meaningful rather than mass-produced.

One student commented that, in school, children are treated like "white paper bags, and nobody looks inside." Another boy named Robbie said, "If I had my wish, I would turn the school into a place for kids!" The irony of that statement speaks for itself. Fragmenting and compartmentalizing these naturally interlinked processes strongly hinder the reciprocal dynamic of intellectual and social progress. It's time to get to the root of educational dysfunction and take on the hard job of putting these pieces back together.

Parts II and III pursue this goal by providing specific models for language arts and social studies instruction that integrate the skills of emotional intelligence in the elementary classroom. While lessons and parts of lessons may be facilitated as separate components, the intent, as indicated in the spirit of this approach, is to facilitate the program as a whole, in the order presented to maximize opportunities for conceptual development and skill building. The work is presented in lesson plan formats and followed up by narratives of the process in action and anecdotal examples of student responses to the program.

The text is structured to provide teachers, who wish to reach beyond the intellectual and social limitations of traditional instruction, with language prompts and strategies, along with a detailed methodical approach, for implementing the activities of the programs. Our hope is that you will be confidently inspired to take on this awesome task of transcending decades of ineffective classroom conventions and fundamentally restructuring how we facilitate the materials and concepts of the academic curriculum so that our students may truly be empowered.

PART II

The Literacy Express
An Integrated Approach to English Language Arts Instruction

CHAPTER 5

Constructs of the Approach

The English Language Arts curriculum for the primary grades uses five words that describe a range of emotions - *mad, sad, scared, frustrated,* and *happy* - as a foundation for teaching reading, writing, and emotionally intelligent expression.

Educational drama provides students with techniques for constructing and expressing understanding around emotional experience. By prompting them to play as "another" or portray themselves in a fictional time frame or setting, drama gives permission, in a sense, for students to access and express a greater range of individual emotional experience without fear of reprisal for content that might otherwise be deemed inappropriate or unacceptable in the setting. The students are not held responsible or judged for enactment that occurs within the boundaries of the drama, as long as safe, appropriate, and respectful standards for general classroom behavior are upheld during the enactments.

Moreover, the tools of educational drama, including role, costumes, set materials, puppets, props, and dialogue, comprise a set of coded symbols that represent shared meanings projected onto them by the students. This process parallels the manner in which shared symbolic codes, words, and letters generate meaning in the development of language and literacy.

The content of the dramas, structured to reflect meaningful emotional experience and language generated by the students, is used to develop texts for reading and writing instruction. The resulting texts are facilitated through a balanced literacy approach of shared and independent reading and writing activities. These texts then serve to further enhance emotional intelligence and word study skills.

Balanced literacy, "a compromise between whole language and phonics" (Fountas & Pinnell, 1999, pp. 188–189) is comprised of a number of teaching strategies. *The District Two Balanced Literacy Program 1999: A Handbook for Teachers* of New York City identifies "read aloud, shared reading and writing, guided reading and writing, and independent reading and writing" as "key components" of a balanced literacy program.

Reading aloud to students provides "a crucial opportunity to model a range of reading strategies including fluent, well-paced oral reading" (p. 21). During shared reading, as the students "become more familiar with the text" that the teacher is reading with them, "they are expected to participate and engage in the reading process" (p. 24). In guided reading, the teacher works with a small group to "talk, read and think their way purposefully through a text" (p. 30). Independent reading "allows readers to spend sustained time with books within the context of a reading community" (p. 35). In the writing process, students are given the opportunity "to have writing modeled for them, to share in the writing process, to be guided in their own writing, and to write independently" (p. 40). "Word study" is described in the *Handbook* as "an essential strategy that readers and writers use to make meaning from a passage of text or to construct meaning in their writing" (p. 45).

Educational drama, a dynamic learning modality that engages emotional expression and language learning, unifies development in these areas to move participants between developmental processes and polarized sources of information discussed in part I. The activities of educational drama link emotional intelligence, in which emotions are identified, expressed, and processed accurately and effectively (Salovey & Sluyter, 1997), with literacy, in which purposeful, meaningful, and whole language experiences are engaged in real-life contexts to facilitate understanding and ability with the abstract signs of written language (Clay, 1991; Dorn, French, & Jones, 1998; Newman, 1985; Weaver, 1988).

By providing a format that integrates these developmental processes, students become motivated to gain expertise with the shared meaningful symbols and codes of literacy since they function as tools to further empower ownership, understanding, and management of individual emotional experience. Each related domain mutually informs skills and inspires operation and further exploration in the other, generating a synergetic approach to development that is whole, rather than fragmented, while creating a dynamic learning environment that is potentially transformative for our students.

The Program

In the pilot program, weeks one through nine began with a *Center* activities and routines period that lasted approximately forty-five minutes. The lesson and main activity period then ran for another forty-five minutes. Weeks ten through fifteen focused on composing and editing autobiographical final projects for the entire ninety-minute period. The lessons and activities outlined in part II can easily be facilitated in shorter or longer time frames over an extended or protracted number of weeks to address scheduling and classroom management needs. There are a few minor differences in some of the lessons between the lesson plan and the narratives that follow, due to adjustments that were made after the pilot study.

While the pilot study was conducted with ten students, later incarnations of the program have run with twelve to fifteen. Ideally, classes can be split in half, allowing each half to participate in the *Literacy Express* program at simultaneous or different times, depending on availability of space and staff. The program may take place in a multipurpose room or in the regular classroom. The regular classroom teacher may conduct the lessons with half the class in another space, while a para-professional supervises independent reading time with the rest of the class, or a trained professional such as a Literacy Coach or Reading Specialist may facilitate the program. Many of the lessons and activities are easily managed with the whole class participating as well. Extra supplies and materials, and the need to revision and restructure how the students move through the classroom, will be discussed as each lesson is subsequently outlined and described in detail.

During the first half of the fifteen-week program, it was often up to the students to decide which emotion and experience they wanted to portray, and which dramatic form to portray it with. Fantasy and fictional circumstances were mostly used to facilitate the basic language of emotionally intelligent expression. During the second half of the program, as we approximated more autobiographical, real-life experiences, the curriculum focused the students on specific emotions, but each child still had control over what individual experience to portray and how he or she wanted to portray it. The students explored their personal responses to these experiences with emotion through oral and written language.

The following summarizes important concepts that emerged during our study:

1. The students developed and applied skills of emotional intelligence during the program and, as reported by parents and teachers, in other aspects of their lives. The skills, including identifying emotions in physical feelings and thoughts, expressing emotions accurately, understanding meanings of emotion in the context of relationships, expressing needs related to emotions, directing anger effectively, managing mood and frustrations, expressing empathy and using emotional awareness to direct attention to topics of importance, were evident in the oral and written responses to program activities. Parents, who initially reported emotion-related behaviors and responses in their children characterized by physical aggression and acting-out, blaming and control of others, passivity, general immaturity, withdrawal, anxiety, and self-deprecation, noted significant improvements in the emotional intelligence of their children.

2. The composition process was enhanced as the students learned to articulate clear and full emotionally intelligent thoughts through participation in the dramas, which were then able to be translated into meaningful written text. In the initial assessment, all of the students struggled with

their writing samples, which were described as disconnected and at times incoherent, with random or loosely connected thoughts, represented by a few words, random strings of letters, or illustrations. The post-assessment writing samples showed a significant growth in the students' ability to compose full sentences with fluent thoughts.

3. Word problem solving skills were enhanced because of the connection to purposeful and meaningful text. The students consistently and enthusiastically participated in identification and formation of letters and words during shared reading and interactive writing activities and then transferred these skills to their independent writing. The students, in a figurative as well as literal sense, were more present during the mechanical processes of word problem solving since the codes and symbols were a direct reflection of their personal experiences. We often heard them stretching and articulating words during independent writing in their efforts to accurately represent the composition of their own thoughts and feelings elicited in the dramas.

4. A reciprocal relationship emerged between emotional expression and the written word, in which each served as an organizer, container, and vehicle for further exploration and skill building within the other. A greater range of emotionally intelligent expression experienced in the dramatic enactment functioned, for some students, as a tool to help process the development of reading and writing skills. The objective forms of reading and writing helped other students to access and articulate emotional expression in the dramas, and in their lives, in a more accurate and effective manner. This reciprocal relationship, integrated through educational drama and mutually conducive to a more whole and empowering approach to development, naturally motivated the students to move between the two in order to satisfy the desire to further explore and understand each of the modalities, which served to represent and clarify their personal experiences (Chasen, 2003).

Sign-In

As the students enter the room or begin the *Literacy Express* period, their first task is to identify and document their present emotional state. A large piece of poster sheet with approximately fifteen rows of lines drawn across it (corresponding to the number of students in the group) with three pieces of Velcro glued across each row is tacked onto the wall.

The first part of the each row contains one piece of Velcro, sectioned off by a vertical column that runs from the top to the bottom of the sheet. The top of the column can be labeled *Names*. The students find their names, written on a sentence strip backed with Velcro and stored in a basket beneath poster sheet, and place their names on the first part, the left side, of the row in the column. The students write their own names on the sentence strips the first day of the program, which are then used for the remainder of the program.

The next part of each row after the column has the words *Today I feel* already printed on it to begin a sentence. Two more pieces of Velcro are glued on each line after this phrase. Each student finishes the sentence in his or her row by choosing a sentence strip, from another basket alongside the names, with the word *mad, sad, scared, frustrated,* or *happy* printed on it, and placing it on the next piece of Velcro. Finally, the students choose icons of corresponding facial expressions, either in a separate basket or mixed in with the feeling words basket, and place it on the third piece of Velcro.

There is no formal review of how the students sign in, unless initiated by the students themselves. This allows them to simply state "where they are at" without any other commentary or unwanted attention. It is merely an exercise in identifying and documenting their present states of emotion.

Center Activities

After the students sign in, they participate in activity *Centers* for approximately twenty minutes. The *Centers* consist of a variety of reading and writing exercises integrated with emotional intelligence skills through creative activities to promote familiarity with the five emotion words, expressing and composing language, and word problem solving skills.

The students may be assigned specific centers or approach them on their own, according to teacher preference and/or assessment as to which ones may be more beneficial and appropriate for a particular student. In the pilot study and subsequent programs, we made sure each child participated in each center at least once. Some students were more purposefully drawn to a specific activity and we were respectful of that as well.

Big Books, Poems, and Songs—Students reread familiar texts and books made by the class to reinforce development of new knowledge and skills and promote fluency, phrasing, and self-reflection.

Family Play House/Play School—Students create stories and scenes with toy figurines and then write titles and/or phrases on large unlined paper describing what has occurred in their stories. Invented spelling and fragmented phrasing are acceptable as correct mechanics are secondary in this activity to the more important notion of connecting creative ideas with written language. A box decorated as a school or family home will suffice if no doll-house type structure is available.

Make the Face—Students match the appropriate emotion word, printed on an index card with Velcro backing, to an expressive felt face that the student creates by manipulating the adjustable mouth, eyebrows, tears, and other features to create different emotional expressions on a felt board. Two or three students can take turns making the felt faces and choosing the descriptive emotion words.

Read the Face—Students match emotion words written on index cards with photographs or illustrations of children's expressive faces glued onto a poster board sheet.

Fill in the Feeling—Students fill in incomplete sentences written on sentence strips with the five emotion words and a variety of phrases, also written on sentence strips, which describe different scenarios in which different feelings can occur. For example, a sentence strip may read: *I feel* _____ *when* _____. The blank spaces contain a piece of magnetic tape. The student may choose the word *mad* written on another sentence strip backed with magnetic tape, for example, and *my toy breaks* on another to place in the blank spaces and make a complete and coherent sentence. Emotion words and phrases describing various scenarios are kept in different baskets or small containers. These can be added to as the students become familiar with the experiences of their classmates through other activities of the program.

I Have Feelings. How About You? —Students read along at a listening center with sections of an original text by Marianne Franzese Chasen describing experience with the five emotions (see Appendix) recorded on cassette tape. Students then write responses on paper formatted with the questions *What does mad* (for example) *feel like in your body? What kinds of things make you feel (mad)? How do the (mad)*

Sample of Feeling Faces Center Activity

feelings come out of you? based on which of the five sections, representing the five emotions, they are reading.

Feeling Faces —Students draw expressive eyes, nose, and mouth within an outline of a child's head and face and write their own response to *I feel_____when_____* formatted on the bottom of the paper.

Puppet Show Titles—Students write titles, characters, and plot phrases on chart or large paper describing elements of puppet shows they create. As with the *Family Play House/Play School* activity, correct mechanics are secondary to creative connection with written language. Any makeshift playing area, such as a bed sheet pulled between two chairs, is fine if a puppet stage is not available.

Check-In

After the *Center* period, students are gathered together, each with a set of five expressive face masks made from paper plates and popsicle sticks, representing each of the five emotions. These faces can be drawn by teachers, students, or copied from existing illustrations and then glued onto the plates. The students use the sticks, taped to the plates, to hold the face up. They label each face with the emotion word it represents on the back.

At each *Check-In*, the teacher rhythmically chants *"Where is* (student's name)*? Where is* (student's name)*? There (s)he is. There (s)he is. How are you today* (name)*?"* The chant is adjusted to be appropriate for the age group of the class. The student holds up the face that matches his or feeling for that moment or day and responds with the word that matches the emotion. The teacher responds with *"I see you!"* and moves onto the next student.

For this activity, the desired response from the students is just one of the emotion words, without any other description or explanation. As with the *Sign-In* activity, any commentary or intellectually based question of *"Why...?"* from the teacher regarding the feeling, or the desire to transform or replace what is perceived as a negative feeling with a more positive feeling, is counterproductive at this point. Becoming comfortable in simply identifying and verbalizing the emotion is what will potentially facilitate intellectual awareness and transformation. Often, students will want to add on a "why," and that is fine, as long as it is kept short and time allows for it. Once students are warmed up to this type of expression, they sometimes want to provide a more extended narration, which may cut into other planned activities.

Another benefit of this exercise is that it grounds the students in appropriately expressing how they are feeling, and helps to avoid more disruptive, nonverbal means of expression that get in the way of learning and classroom management. The teacher's response of *"I see you"* is meant to convey the notion that any self-aware, verbal expression of feeling is acceptable and worthy of being seen and heard on its own merits, without necessarily needing any other explanation or intervention.

After all the students respond, masks are collected and another chant is begun that follows the familiar song *"If You're Angry and You Know It..."* While this activity may work well with a kindergarten class, it may not be age appropriate for second graders. The teacher chants the verse inserting one feeling word at a time, starting with *mad*. The chant *"If you're mad and you know it..."* is completed, the first week, with the phrase *"...make a sound,"* and the students respond, as a group, with an angry sound. The verse is sung again substituting *"scared"* for *mad*, and so on, until all five emotions are covered.

The students respond with different expressive modes each week. The week after *"...make a sound,"* for instance, we can ask the students to *"...make the face,"* the next week *"...use your bodies,"* then *"...find the words"* and finally, *"...say the I"* as the program moves into its final phase. The activity progresses, over the weeks, from more primal modes of expression, toward a more objective verbal response, and ultimately to a more subjective and self-aware language-based response as the program nears its completion.

Power Messages

After *Check-In*, each student is provided with an individual wipe-off board and dry erase marker to compose a *power message*. A power message is described to the students as any statement that identifies their emotional state and begins with the word *"I."* We explain how this type of ownership empowers them, because the emotion then becomes their own source of energy that no one else can control or mess with when it's portrayed through this type of self-aware language. We use this important connection to text as a springboard for instructing and modeling mechanics, word study skills, and the construction of meaningful text.

The students each construct their own message on their boards using any response they may have expressed during *Sign-In* or *Check-In*, or any other experience they might want to write about. Each student shares, if they want, his or her power message. One student is then chosen, ideally by the group, to come up to the easel and construct his or her message on the chart paper through an interactive writing exercise with the whole class. The teacher and student discuss the correct formation of the letters, spelling and structure of each word before writing, one word at a time, as the student composes the message on the chart tablet. The other students participate in the discussion and write the message on their wipe-off boards as it's being constructed on the chart paper. Any mistakes on the chart paper are corrected with correct

tape. The student illustrates his or her power message next week during *Centers*. The power messages composed on the chart tablet are made into a class big book, with new pages added each week, that becomes familiar text for rereading and *Center* activities. Big books also allow the class to read along with the teacher together as a group.

Sample of a page from the Power Messages class book

The Main Activity Period

The main activity period runs approximately thirty to forty-five minutes. Each lesson moves students toward a deeper understanding of and greater competence with the skills of emotional intelligence through educational drama activities, while providing opportunities to master word problem solving strategies using meaning, structural, and visual cues.

Meaningful emotionally intelligent language resulting from participation in the dramas is analyzed with regard to how words and letters look (visual), how they sound (phonological), and the relationship between how they look and how they sound (graphophonic) (p. 46).

Word study skills are demonstrated using materials such as highlighting tape, wikki sticks, and magnetic tape to frame and mask relevant words and letters. A word wall lists high frequency sight words that the students are able to automatically identify in familiar and new texts as a result of the lessons.

CHAPTER 6

The Mechanics of Meaningful Text

This chapter describes the first two lessons of the *Literacy Express* program. We engage the students to read, write, listen, and speak by offering an opportunity to gain information and understanding about themselves and each other and to respond by presenting a unique perspective on who they are. We integrate letter-sound relationships, structural and contextual cues, shared reading, read aloud and independent writing through improvisation to position the mechanics of print and language as accurate and powerful representations of the students' personal identities and experiences. Some of the activities prompt the students to move around the room, introducing them to new ways to use the classroom space and connect to printed text.

LESSON 1: *Power Names*

Purpose
- To provide students with meaningful contexts that engage and integrate subjective emotional perspectives with strategies for constructing objective meaning through print such as prior knowledge about a subject, structural and contextual cues, and letter-sound relationships.

Concept
- Empower students to apply existing knowledge of their names and interests to word study skills and create a class big book through shared reading and writing.
- Empower students to link subjective feelings and oral expression with objective symbols of written language using face masks and signs printed with the five emotion words *mad, sad, scared, frustrated,* and *happy.*

Goal
- Each student will appropriately structure their names from mixed-up magnetic letters, describe and document a personal interest through shared writing, illustrate their page for the class big book, express personal feelings in response to various criteria, print the appropriate emotion word on their set of corresponding face masks, and respond to the shared reading.

Procedure for *Power Names*
1. Students are gathered together in front of an easel with a magnetic board and sorted trays of magnetic letters. Each student is provided with a wipe-off board and dry erase marker. There are no *Sign-In, Center, Check-In,* or *Power Messages* activities on the first day.

2. The teacher places a mix of magnetic letters of one student's name on the magnetic board from a plastic bag that contains the letters of his or her name. The letters of the student's name are placed on the board in a random, mixed-up order. A bag is prepared for each student.

3. Students take turns recognizing their names and coming up to the board to form their names correctly using the magnetic letters. Word study prompts include letter and sound recognition, counting letters in each name, and verbal description of letter formation.

4. The teacher writes the name on a chart tablet next to the board and asks the other students to write it on their wipe-off boards.

5. The teacher asks the student at the magnetic board about an interest they have, something they like to do or something they are good at. The teacher writes *is a* on the chart after the student's name and writes the student's response.

6. The students model the writing on their wipe-off boards.

7. When all students have recognized and formed their name at the magnetic board, the teacher gives each student their corresponding page from the chart tablet to illustrate with markers or crayons. The pages are later bound to form a class big book with familiar text for rereading and *Center* activities.

8. Students are directed toward independent reading baskets, which contain books with the five feeling words and familiar text such as *I* and *am* as they finish their illustrations. When everyone has completed their illustrations, the students are brought back to the circle.

Procedure for *Choose It/Move It*

1. The teacher introduces the five emotion words—*mad, sad, scared, frustrated,* and *happy*—by printing each word on a separate piece of paper with an accompanying identifying facial icon, and then, after reading each paper with the students, tacking the papers on different walls on different sides of the room.

2. The teacher asks the class to stand up and different activities and topics such as *"going to the doctor...eating pizza...playing in your backyard...getting dressed...brushing your teeth...having a playdate...going to school...bedtime... babies...roller coasters"* that may evoke an emotional response in students are called out by the teacher.

3. After each phrase is called, the students respond by walking to the emotion word that best represents their feelings about the circumstance. Teachers can determine how many phrases are called. Ten or so is a reasonable amount. Students are encouraged to move toward and identify specific emotions, as making the choice is sometimes a difficult process. The teacher can ask the students to suggest topics as well. The students come back to the circle when the activity is complete.

Procedure for *Un-Mask/Label the Feelings*

1. The students are then each given a set of five face masks described in *Check-In*.

2.   The teacher tapes a copy of the mask onto the emotion word sign it represents on the wall from the previous activity for reference.

3.   The students label the back of each mask with their names and the appropriate emotion word, and then color the front of the mask, the facial features, as they wish.

4.   The teacher models the use of the sign-in board and each *Center* activity, described previously in *Sign-In* and C*enter* activities.

5.   The teacher can read the big book *My Name Is Johari* by Anne Sibley O'Brien (1992) to facilitate the shared reading experience to promote response to literature, personal connection to text, reflection and self-awareness. *Yoko Writes Her Name* by Rosemary Wells (2008) or any other text dealing with feelings around an individual's name may also be used.

6.   The students are given journals, simple notebooks, and a copy of the home activity sheet to be completed with parents for the next class.

Evaluation

Did each student recognize the letters in their names? Did each student form their name in correct sequential order with the magnetic letters? Were students able to identify and connect to the five feeling words in a meaningful way? Were they able to make personal connections to the feeling words? Were they able to express feelings through self-identified oral language? Did they make self-to-text connections during the read aloud?

Materials

- Easel
- Magnetic board and letters
- Individual wipe-off boards and markers
- Chart tablet
- Marker and crayons
- Masks with expressive faces drawn or copied from faces in a book, mounted on paper plates and held up with popsicle sticks
- Big Book *My Name Is Johari* or other text named above.

Home Activity

Sit with your child and take turns writing something that makes you mad, sad, scared, frustrated, and happy. For example, you may write I feel mad when the car breaks, *and your child may then write* I feel mad when I can't play. *Go through all of the feelings listed above in this manner. Try to follow the same pattern of writing for each emotion, such as* I feel…when…*Model the writing of your idea for your child, and then help him or her to express his or her own ideas on paper. Encourage your child to articulate the words slowly and record the appropriate letters that correspond to the sounds being made. See whether you can find any matches of things that make both of you mad, sad, scared, frustrated, and happy and list those as well.*

Rosalie and I prepare the room for our first meeting with a mix of eagerness and first-day anxiety. We set up the word wall for an alphabetical sight word list, easel for shared and interactive reading and writing exercises, magnetic board and letters for spelling names, chart tablet to create a class book, *Center* activities for demonstration, and a big book to read aloud.

As the students enter the room, I ask them to "look around" and tell us "what do you see?" I want them to initiate a sense of ownership and connection to the space. We begin the *Power Names* activity by gathering the group in front of the magnetic board positioned next to the easel and chart tablet. We take out the baggies we had prepared, each containing the magnetic letters of a student's name. We tell them that we are going to pick a bag, put the scrambled letters on the board, and see who can recognize the letters in their name. After they come up to the board and unscramble their letters, they will tell us something about themselves that we will write on a page of the chart tablet. We give each of them a dry erase board and marker to follow along. Quinn, a boy who tends to withdraw, whine, and act out behaviorally at home and in school, immediately says he wants to go last.

We put the first set of letters on the board. Alex raises his hand and says "That's me." Alex's parents had informed us how his previous year's kindergarten teacher "ripped up his work" when she felt it was not acceptable. Alex became very frustrated with this response and often directed his frustration at himself, and as the year progressed, became increasingly distraught with academic tasks, studied less, and began ripping up his own work. He comes up to the magnetic board and places the letters of his name in order. As the students come up one by one and unscramble their names, we engage them in letter identification, letter-sound correspondence, counting the number of letters and clapping the rhythms from each name we come up with. We ask the class to clap the syllables in Alex's name. Alex says he is *a gameboy player*. We lead the students in making a *g* with its "circle, stick, and hook" as we write on the top of a page in the chart tablet. When we finish, we turn the page for the next student.

Paul, a first-grade boy who is described as distracted and unfocused with short-term memory problems, comes next. He arranges his letters and says that he is *a baseball player*. We write it on the chart tablet and ask, "What do you hear in *baseball?*"

We put the next set of mixed-up letters on the board. Cordell, identified as an immature first grader who has difficulty with motor skills, reading, and writing, recognizes them. He comes up to the board and correctly arranges the letters in his name. The students count with us the number of letters in his name. Someone makes a connection and says, "That's how many letters I have in my name!" Cordell says he is a "good reader." We write on the chart and describe the formation of *d* with "a stick and a circle." Cordell makes the connection of "just like in my name!"

David, a first grader, comes next. David entered the room earlier with a great degree of anxiety, looking around in a worried manner. He went in only after some gentle reassurance from Rosalie, his mother, and myself. David's mother expressed great concern that David is not reading.

He recognizes and correctly arranges the letters in his name on the magnetic board and says that he *is a bike rider*. We write his words on a page of the chart tablet.

While each student takes his or her turn arranging the letters in their names, the rest of the group follows along, writing their classmates' names on their individual wipe-off boards, and then erasing as the next student comes up to the magnetic board. Quinn and David don't want to erase though, and they resist my attempts at getting them to do so to create more room on their boards. I notice that David has a number of completed words written on his board, and I defer, for now, to their mosaics of letters and words. Alex's letters fill the whole board and look, at times, like scribble.

Aaron, a learning disabled and behaviorally challenged second-grade boy, is vacillating at this point from writing nothing on his board to writing complete sentences.

After each student takes a turn at the magnetic board and chart tablet, we rip out their pages and ask them to draw a picture that shows the idea we wrote about on top. The students are enthusiastic and successful with illustrating their pages of the *Power Names* class big book, laughing as they draw libraries, video games, baseball players, and bicycles. We ask them to reread their page and write their name on the bottom when they are done. We direct them to the independent book baskets when they are finished. There are three book baskets. Each basket has a different level of difficulty, from three words per page with repetitive text, to full paragraphs. Each book reflects the theme of the group, beginning with *I like*, *I am*, or *I can*, and discusses the five feeling words.

After everyone is finished, we begin the *Choose It/Move It* activity. There are five pieces of paper taped to the walls in different areas of the classroom, each containing one of the five emotion words. I tell the students that I am going to describe something that might make them feel mad, sad, scared, frustrated, or happy. They then have to go to the sign that shows how they feel about the situation. I call out "Going to the doctor" and most move toward *Mad*, *Sad*, and *Scared*, although Aaron chose *Happy* "because you get a lollipop." Alex chooses *Mad* for "Pizza" and says, "I hate pizza!" Makenna chooses *Mad* for "playing in your backyard" and says "I get mad playing in my backyard because my sister pushes me off the swings." I invite the students to name some criteria. Cordell calls out "Parties!" and goes to *Happy*. Alex goes to *Mad*, saying, "I don't like parties." Makenna chooses *Scared* for "Parties." I am impressed that they are able to make unconventional and unique choices regarding their emotions in response to particular events. I am relieved that these somewhat atypical students are in an environment where their unique choices won't be "corrected" or herded toward a more standard response.

We gather the students together for a shared reading of the big book *My Name Is Johari*, about a girl who is teased because of her name. We read the story and ask, "Why does she look so sad?" Makenna, a second-grade girl with learning disabilities, answers, "Because they laughed and hurt her feelings." We ask, "What was different about her feelings from the beginning to the end of the story?" David says, "She was happy." Rosalie asks, "Why do you think she was happy, David?" He doesn't answer. We praise him for his initial observation. All responses are affirmed and supported. I hand out the notebooks we provided for them with the first homework stapled in and tell the students it's time to go.

The tasks facilitated and materials used in this lesson reflect each student's unique experience and point of view. The forms and symbols of the letters, words, and illustrations become symbolic extensions of who the children are, forging an initial and intimate connection between meaningful personal expression and the mechanics of reading and writing. This dynamic relationship is then documented in the form of a big book to be used for further reflection, insight, and skill building.

LESSON 2: *I Can*

Purpose

- To provide students with meaningful contexts in which personal perspectives are accessed and expressed to integrate emotionally intelligent communication with objective symbols of oral and written language.

Concept

- Empower students to identify and express personal accomplishments prompted by shared reading of a poem and big book, improvisation, read aloud and writing activities, in order to integrate objective representation through word study skills, phonics and context cues, high frequency sight word acquisition of *I* and *can* and independent writing.

Goal

- Each student will respond to the shared reading, improvise and identify an enjoyable activity they experience success with and independently construct meaningful text to communicate their perspective.

Procedure

1. After *Sign-In, Center,* and *Power Messages* activities, students are gathered to-gether for a shared reading of the poem "I Can" by Jill Eggleton from the text *Now I Am Five* (1988) written on large chart paper to facilitate word study skills, intro-duce the high frequency words *I, can, it,* and *is* for the word wall, and warm the students up to the improvisation activity, which will ask them to enact things they are able to do.

2. *All by Myself* by Mercer Mayer (1983a) is read aloud to promote personal connec-tion to text and prompt further creative inspiration around the theme of self-accomplishment. *I Like Myself* by Karen Beaumont (2004) or any text dealing with a similar theme and repetitive text may be used as well.

3. The teacher begins *Do and Tell* by using miscellaneous, ideally nondescript objects as props to improvise activities that indicate personal abilities and accomplishments, such as tying shoes, riding a bicycle, fishing, or getting dressed.

4. The students guess the activity the teacher is improvising.

5. When the students guess correctly, the teacher goes to the chart tablet and writes, for example, *I can ride a bicycle,* as the sentence is orally spoken.

6. The students are then invited to explore the props and objects for improvisation. Each student takes a turn showing his or her creative output to the rest of the class, which guesses what the object or activity is.

7. After all the students share their improvisations, the teacher refers back to the sen-tence originally written on the chart tablet as a model and provides the students with a large lined paper with a space for illustrations, pens, and crayons to inde-pendently write and illustrate their thoughts and actions. The students use pens so they can't erase and can learn to feel comfortable making and correcting mistakes. The teacher models how to cross out mistakes or unneeded information using the pens on the original example.

8. The teacher walks around the room, conferencing with the students as they write their pieces.

9. Students select from the independent reading baskets when they finish.

10. The students are gathered for a shared reading of the big book *The Monsters' Party* by Joy Cowley (1983), which includes the now-familiar words *I* and *can* to describe the abilities of a group of small monsters. The teacher indicates the title, author, il-lustrator, left-to-right directionality and return sweep, and other early concepts about print. Students are asked to make predictions based on this information. Af-ter a read through, the teacher asks comprehension and personal-connection-to-text questions that the students respond to by coming up to the easel and indicat-ing the corresponding passages in the text. Again, any similar text dealing with per-sonal accomplishment will suffice.

11. The students take turns sharing their independent writing pieces, which the teacher edits as the students share, responding positively to every attempt at constructing

meaning, even if the student made a line to indicate a particular word or phrase. The teacher later binds the pages into a class big book.

12. Students take out their journals and note down next week's homework assignment.

Evaluation

Did the students spontaneously respond to the theme of the shared reading and read aloud texts? Did each student conceptualize and demonstrate an activity or accomplishment through the improvisation activity? Were the students inspired to transfer the experience to independent writing and composition skills? Did students demonstrate word study skills and strategies such as articulation and letter-sound correspondence?

Materials

- Chart tablet with the poem "I Can" from the text *Now I Am Five* printed on it
- Any miscellaneous, nonspecific objects for improvisation
- Large, lined paper with space for illustrations
- Pens, markers, and crayons
- Big book *The Monsters' Party*, *All by Myself*, or other text mentioned above

Home Activities

Sit with your child and take turns writing sentences that reflect positive aspects of your family life. Begin the sentences with the words We can. *For example, you may write* We can solve problems, *and your child may write* We can play games. *Write your idea as a model for your child, and then help him or her to express his or her own ideas on paper. We focused on the word* can *in our lesson today, so your child should be familiar writing it. For the other words in the sentence, encourage your child to articulate the words slowly and record the appropriate letters that correspond to the sounds being made. After writing a sentence or two each in this manner, you can simply list ideas and words that describe things that your family can do without writing the whole sentence, such as* go on trips, eat ice cream, watch TV *together.*

The students enter the room, sign in on the chart, and settle into a *Center* activity. I overhear Alex's mother, with a mixture of disbelief and relief, mentioning to another mother in the hallway that Alex approached the homework activity positively with a proclamation of "They don't care if I make a mistake" as he "happily wrote a page for the first time in a long time!"

I take a quick look at last week's assignments as the students hand in their journals. Their sentences include statements like *I get mad at Jennifer. I feel sad when Mom is sick. I'm scared of bees. I feel mad when Robert bothers me in class. I feel sad when Mommy goes out without me. I feel mad when Mom takes activities away.* Paul's mother wrote the first part of the sentence, *I feel mad when* and then Paul finished with *my dad screams.* Alex's mother's own responses included *I feel mad when I have to say something more than once before everyone listens.* Cordell's mother wrote *I feel frustrated when my children do not listen.*

During *Sign-In*, Alex chooses *sad*. The rest choose *happy*. All of the students become engaged in the *Center* activities around the room. At the *I Have Feelings. How about You?* listen and respond center, Makenna chooses the *Mad* section, puts on the headphones, and reads along with the text. On her response sheet, she left *What does mad feel like in your body?* blank, and wrote *when my sister hits me* in response to *What kind of things make you feel mad?* and *I hit my sister* in response to *How do the mad feelings come out of you?*

The two books at the *Big Books, Poems, and Songs* center are last week's *Power Names* book created by the class and *My Name Is Johari*. Cordell reads these and then watches Aaron's performance at *Puppet Show Titles*. Aaron's title, an invented spelling rendition of *The dragon who gets mad at friends* is taped to the stage as the two puppets battle it out. Aaron's title demonstrates an objective and emotionally intelligent understanding of the dragon's experience expressed through the objective written form. The dragon is mad. The dramatic activity allows Aaron to feel relatively deeply in an acceptable and safe context, construct an experience around those feelings in an attempt to sort through and manage them, and then represent the experience through written language, which allows him to manage it further as he moves between subjective and objective processes. At *Make the Face*, David is excited as he makes a face that mixes sad and angry features. He announces, "I know that one! Frustrated!" I end the *Center* period after a two-minute 'warning' that we would be moving to another activity and ask the students to gather together on the rug for *Check-In*.

We ask them to look at the five faces on popsicle sticks they made the previous week and find the one that best matches their own face and feelings for that day.

The students respond with a range of emotions by holding up their choice of face and verbally expressing how they feel in that moment or day. We offer no commentary or judgment other than the acknowledgment of a simple "I see you" after each student presents.

We move into the *Power Messages* activity. Continuing with the theme of empowered language, I explain, "When we can say 'I am mad' or sad or scared or frustrated to the moms, dads, teachers, friends, brothers, sisters, and other kids, it gives us a lot of power because it makes us in charge of it!" Rosalie refers to the word wall where we have placed these words. She indicates an alphabet chart hanging above the word wall and has the students join her in a rhythmic chant, naming each letter of the alphabet twice and then the accompanying icon while pointing to the upper case and then the lower case letter. She then says, "So what do you hear when we say 'happy'?" She points to the picture of the horse: "It's like 'horse.' What letter is that?" The students respond, "H!"

We go through the five emotion words *mad, sad, scared, frustrated,* and *happy* in this manner, referring to the alphabet chart and then writing each word on the blackboard. We want to connect the written words to their own personal and meaningful contexts in which emotions are intelligently identified and expressed. We want the students to have automatic recognition of the five emotion words and establish them as high frequency sight words.

I go to the blackboard and say, "Boys and girls, these are our power words. Here's another important power word." I write *I* on the board in front of the feeling words. "Who knows what this word is? It's a letter *and* a word…" They respond, "I!" I then ask a very difficult question. "When we say 'I,' what are we talking about?" Someone says, "Igloo!" I say, "Igloo starts with I, yes, but what about the word 'I'?" Aaron says, "I will!" I say, "Good Aaron! That's a way to use the word 'I.'" I think of a way to make the concept more concrete and say, "If we say 'floor,' what would we point to, to show what that is?" They all point to the floor. "What would we point to if we said 'wall'?" They point to the wall. "What would we point to if we said 'I'?" They point to themselves. "Yes! When you say 'I' it means you! 'I' is a very powerful word!" Rosalie then says, "I have another power word, 'am.'" She writes *am* after the *I* on the board. I say, "Oh! 'Am' starts to tell us who and what we are!"

We hand out the wipe-off boards and dry erase markers and ask the students to write their own power message using the power and feeling words demonstrated on the blackboard. It was our intention to have all of them write their messages, share them, and then choose one to compose together in the *Power Messages* book we will create, but we see how time consuming this process is. We also see that they need work in composing their thoughts with correctly structured written language, so we decide to let them share their power messages verbally next time, then choose one message to compose together on the wipe-off boards and in the *Power Messages* big book as an interactive writing experience.

This time, each student writes their own messages on their boards. Paul writes *I am frustrated when my friend pushes me.* He writes *I am frustrated* clearly, and then *w m f p m*, making the letter connection with the first sound of each word. David writes *I am happy* clearly and then writes *pl*. He later shares that he is happy when he goes to the park. Makenna copies the blackboard and writes *I am happy I am sad I am scared I am frustrated I am mad.* She shares that she feels sad when her brother and sister grab things from her. Cordell shares, "I am mad when my brother Tommy punches me." When copied from modeled text and print around the room, they write clearly and neatly. When they compose on their own, their letters are poorly formed and often incoherent.

We collect the dry erase boards and read aloud *The Monsters' Party* to introduce the text *I can* and connect the students to identifying their own abilities and accomplishments. Rosalie asks, "Who remembers something that the monsters can do?" Cordell says, "Fly!" Rosalie says, "Good Cordell! Can you show me where it says that?" She turns to the page as Cordell comes up to the easel. He points to the word *fly*. "Yes!" Rosalie reaches for the magnetic board and says, "I'm going to show you another important word that we are going to put up on our word wall." She makes the word *can* on the board with magnetic letters and has them read the word with her. She then mixes the letters up again and says, "Aaron, can you make that word again?" Aaron comes up and forms it. She hands Alex a wipe-off board and says, "Alex can you write it on the board?" and "Cordell can you come up to the book and put this piece of [highlight] tape over the word?" They are all successful.

I say to the class, "Another way to be powerful is knowing what you can do. I'm going to show you something I can do and you see if you can guess what it is." I take out a few foam tubes and piece them together. Any type of general objects, shapes, and materials can be used for this type of improvisation.

"I'm going to pretend with these things to show you what I can do." I begin my improvisation. They guess correctly. "Vacuum!" "Yes!" I respond, "I can vacuum!" I pause and ask, "Is this a real vacuum? (indicating my props)." They say, "No!" I say, "Right! But I can pretend that these things are something else, like a vacuum. Now everybody think of something that you can do but don't tell us. Come get some pieces that you can pretend with that will show what you can do and we'll guess." They work for a minute or so with the materials and appear to be ready. I call them, one by one, to the center of the room where they demonstrate the activities they come up with, digging, hitting a ball, playing cars, while the others guess. Rosalie models the next step of the activity, connecting the process to independent writing, by writing an *I can* statement and illustrating their ideas on lined paper. She draws a toothbrush, asks the students to identify it, and writes *I can brush my teeth* on the paper. We hand out the lined paper and ask them to write what they can do, using an idea from the activity or anything else they can do, and make an illustration for it. We gather as a group and the students share their work.

We read the poem "I Can" from the text *Now I Am Five* that was meant to be read with *The Monsters' Party*. We didn't read it earlier because of time and pace considerations. We also didn't get to *All by Myself*, which begins each sentence with the text *I can*. Upon reflection, we decide that the charted poem would serve a better purpose read in the beginning of the lesson, along with *All by Myself*, to more clearly model concrete and realistic *I can* responses. *The Monsters' Party* would then be a fun read aloud for the end of the session. Rosalie reads through the poem again, leaving out words and asking the students to fill them in. I give them their journals with the next homework stapled in and tell them in an excited tone that next week we will be playing and making our big jungle story. They respond excitedly.

The sociometry motivates the children to make personal connections to text by adding movement and student-centered response to the process. They begin to associate the space of the classroom with their unique emotional perspectives, encouraged by verbal affirmation and reflected with printed text. The improvisation initiates a creative activity that symbolizes and reinforces a positive sense of who the students are within two interactive forms, dramatic and written.

CHAPTER 7

Constructing the Language of Self-Expression

The next group of lessons engages the students in reading, writing, listening, and speaking from a deeper understanding and empowered expression of their own unique and perhaps more vulnerable perspectives within the safe boundaries of dramatic enactment. They are encouraged to collect data, facts and ideas, and discover relationships by analyzing literary elements such as plot, setting, theme, and basic story structure using various sources of literature. Self-expression, social interaction, and different viewpoints are explored through read aloud, shared reading, independent writing, word mechanics, and study skills and interactive writing to create original pieces of literature prompted by thematic ensemble enactment and puppetry.

As the students gain experience and success with exploring, accessing, and expressing a greater range of meaningful emotional information, they become increasingly motivated to connect with the abstract symbols of language used to represent that meaningful information and participate more readily in the mechanics of decoding and constructing meaningful print. This initiates a reciprocal, interactive relationship in which each expressive form, verbal and written, works to inform and empower expression in the other.

LESSON 3: *Jungle Book of Feelings*

Purpose
- To provide students with access to a greater range of authentic emotional expression in order to motivate and integrate purposeful intelligent expression through oral and written forms.

Concept
- Empower students to express emotion by creating a story through shared reading and thematic ensemble enactment and document the experience with a class big book created through interactive writing, to represent and integrate subjective information with objective symbols of written language.

Goal
- Each student will create a character with an emotional perspective, participate in the enactment and then represent that perspective through written language by contributing a page in the big book.

Procedure for facilitating *thematic ensemble enactment*

1. Students are gathered for the shared reading of the big book *My Five Senses: A Lion's Tale* by Judy Nayer (1994) in which a lion walks through a jungle, describes its experience by beginning each line of text with *I feel,* and identifies aspects of a jungle such as trees, lakes, and vines. *Tiger's Story* by Harriet Blackford (2007) or any other text that lists aspects of a jungle may be used as well. Word study skills indicate patterns of letters and words, illustrations, clusters, and other familiar cueing sources of information. Comprehension questions such as "What is in the lion's jungle?" and "What does he feel?" help to set the stage for the drama.

2. The teacher makes an animal noise to begin a drama warm-up game and asks the students to guess what it is.

3. The teacher then makes the noise of the same animal, adding an emotional affect to the noise and asking the students to identify "What kind of (monkey) am I now?"

4. The students identify the animal and the emotion and take turns making and guessing emotional animal noises.

5. The teacher refers back to the shared reading and asks the students what they would need to include if they were to make a jungle.

6. The teacher provides the students with sheets and fabrics that help to create set pieces from classroom furniture. Chairs, couches, tables, desks, and bookshelves are moved, covered, and decorated to create mountains, caves, trees, waterfalls, flowers, and animal homes.

7. The teacher provides the students with fabrics to wrap around themselves and tuck into belts and waistbands to create fur, tails, and other animal costume pieces that the students choose to use.

8. Once the space is transformed and the students begin to assume animal roles, they are gathered together and asked, "What could happen in the jungle that would make the animals feel so mad?" The students respond with their ideas and the teacher asks them, on the count of three, to pretend that those mad things have happened in the jungle and to respond with the angriest animal sounds, in a chosen animal role until "Freeze!" is called and the students need to freeze their sound and movement. Each of the five feelings is warmed up in this manner. The teacher does not proceed unless the class complies with each freeze.

9. The teacher explains and demonstrates that, as the drama is enacted, any emotion in role that might be aggressive needs to be expressed as a "stage fight," in which *no actual physical contact can be made.* The teacher makes it clear that any breach of this boundary that is not corrected will result in an end to the activity for the individual or the group.

10. The teacher then turns out the lights, making sure there is enough natural light to ensure safety and narrates that "Night has fallen, and all the animals are finding their homes." As the students in role settle into the "homes" they have created, the

teacher calls for silence and stillness so that direction may be given and the new day may start. The teacher does not proceed until there is absolute silence. Sound effects may be used to reproduce the sounds of crickets and owls in the night, which can be found in a toy lantern, to enhance listening at this time.

11. As the students in role silently "sleep" in their "homes," the teacher continues to quietly narrate that when day dawns, the animals will make the sounds that will show what kind of animals they are. "Will there be mad animals in this jungle? Happy? What will happen to them during the day when the sun comes up? What will they need to do? Find food? Build their houses?" The teacher can also suggest some of the ideas that came up in the warm-up. "Will there be a storm? A fire? A hunter? Will the babies die? We'll see when the sun comes up…"

12. The teacher turns the lights on and allows the drama to ensue.

13. The teacher maintains the role of narrator and observer. Sometimes it is beneficial for the teacher to move into a role within the drama to facilitate dramatic action or provide direction if the emotional expression becomes too aggressive or too passive. Examples of these interventions are given in the passage following this lesson outline.

14. Sometimes the teacher may need to break role and the drama altogether if the expression becomes too aggressive or, as with any other classroom activity, safety is compromised. If the drama needs to be stopped and boundaries need to be reclarified, the students can then resume the drama when the teacher feels it is appropriate. Even the most aggressive students usually respond to direction by the teacher in role within the dramatic action. Often times, the teacher as narrator or in role can direct the other animals to attempt a communal response to the aggressive animals' needs. For example, calling out "Maybe the dinosaur is hungry!" or "Maybe the tiger needs a home!" can prompt the aggressor to find a dramatic motivation for his threatening, potentially destructive expression. Other students in role, usually without any prompting, almost always spontaneously scurry to find food or shelter for the disgruntled animal. This is a very productive intervention.

15. The teacher uses judgment to determine how long the drama should continue. Transitions from day to night and back to day again using classroom lights assist in cooling down and controlling the action as needed and providing time frames to develop the story.

16. The teacher can prompt and direct the ensemble to respond to a disaster, such as a flood or fire, food shortages, storms or illness among the players, in order to cooperatively bond the group together. The players themselves often initiate these plot lines.

17. The teacher can end the drama by a final transition to nightfall, during which the transition from the dramatic encounter back to regular classroom set-up can be narrated by reviewing events that occurred in the jungle and praising the students for their acting abilities and the cool stories they created. It is helpful, during this pe-

riod, to demonstrate authentic enthusiasm for what occurred in the drama and ex-press excitement at hearing the students tell about the events after the room is cleaned up.

Procedure for writing the class big book based on the enactment

1. The teacher gathers the students together and encourages each to orally retell a part of the story as preparation to create a class big book.
2. After each student tells his or her part of what happened in the story, they come up to the chart tablet or blank big book and write one or two sentences with the teacher about the experience in an interactive writing exercise. Correcting tape is used for any mistakes. If students developed part of the drama as partners, as is of-ten the case, they can come up to the page together and take turns composing the words in their part of the story. Each student or team of students writes on one page.
3. When all of the students have written in the book, the teacher reads the completed story to the group and takes suggestions for a title, attempting to incorporate as many of the students' ideas as possible and ultimately putting the title to a vote if needed.
4. The teacher leads a discussion in which students reflect on their experience in the drama and make meaningful, personal connections to their own lives that are emo-tionally intelligent and self-aware.
5. The teacher gives each student a piece of paper to illustrate their part of the story, which the teacher later pastes onto each corresponding page.
6. As the students finish their illustrations, they read books in the independent reading baskets and insert the homework sheet in their journals.
7. The teacher writes the title on the cover of the big book and decorates as desired to prepare the text for the next lesson.

Evaluation

Were the students able to function appropriately within the boundaries of the drama? Did each student experience and express emotion through the role of an animal? Was each student able to transfer the dramatic experience to oral retelling and interactive writing using word study and mechanics skills? Were they able to reflect on the drama and jungle big book and make meaningful, emotionally self-aware connections to their own lives?

Materials

- Big book *My Five Senses: A Lion's Tale* by Judy Nayer or text mentioned above
- Scarves, sheets and fabrics for costumes and set building
- Chart tablet or blank big book
- Crayons and markers

Home Activities

Sit with your child and take turns writing about how the different feelings mad, sad, scared, frustrated, and happy come out for each member of the family. You and your child may write Mad, *for example, and underneath write,* I yell a lot. Dad leaves the room. The baby throws her bottle. I cry. *Do this for each of the feeling words, for each member of the family. It seems as though you are helping your children to edit their writing for these assignments. That is fine and helpful, as long as you are being positive about what they are initially able to compose as well.*

The students enter the room and sign in. Most choose *happy*. Paul signs in with *mad*. Makenna signs in with *sad*. I collect their homework and staple in the next week's assignment as I quickly scan their responses to the previous week's assignment. Aaron, who often feuds with his mother, wrote, *We can love together. We can play together. We can pray together. We can drive together.*

At the *Family Play House* center, withdrawn Quinn and anxious David are having a great time. The two of them are laughing as they place the figurine characters in silly situations around the house. I join the spirit of their play and laughingly say to David, "The baby is in the mailbox??? Let's write it on the paper!" He takes the baby and hangs it off the balcony by its hair, laughing. I laugh along and encourage, "What are you going to write? The baby is in the mailbox? She's hanging by her hair?" He continues to laugh.

I go over to some of the other centers for a few minutes and am thrilled upon return to find that David has written *BiDdol* on the paper. I assume that the *B* stands for baby and the *dol* could be doll. It could also be a string of random letters. I excitedly say, "This is great David! What did you write? What does this say?" Even though my tone is completely positive and playful, David's beaming smile immediately falls, his eyes drop to the ground, and his shoulders constrict into a shameful shrug. His ownership of the integrated event, in which his joyful play was represented and documented by written language, is hijacked by what I suppose is his notion that the representative letters were not good enough. I want it to be good enough for him. I tell him, "It's really OK if the letters and words that you write aren't perfect. We just want you to find some way to write down and tell your funny stories." He starts smiling again and goes back to playing his stories.

I gather the students together for *Check-In* and hand out their faces. I tell them, "We want to know how you are today. When we know things about how we are, it helps us to be more powerful." I ask them to say, "I am" along with their feelings as their names are called and they hold up their faces. We collect the masks and prepare to interactively write a power message.

I set up a blank big book on the easel and tell the students that every week we will choose one friend and write his or her power message together. I use the blackboard to review the power words. I write *I* and ask them what the word is. They respond, "I." I write *am* and they read the word in unison.

I explain that we will look at five ways that we might be and write *mad* on the board. Alex reads, "mad." I say "Good Alex. David, what could we put in front of this *ad* to write *sad*?" Rosalie refers to the alphabet chart and says, "like in snake." David says "s." We say "Great David! Paul, what do you hear next in sccccccared?" I exaggerate and articulate the *c* sound in a way that conveniently affects a scared feeling. Paul says, "c." I add *frustrated* and *happy* on the board and ask the students to choose one of the words to use in their power message.

It is raining, so I model and say, "I am sad because it is raining." I add, "Or, 'I am happy because it is raining'" not wanting to judge the fact that it is raining. I will never forget an observation I did on a student in a religion-sponsored preschool where the teachers proclaimed during circle time that Jesus must be so sad and upset because it was raining out that day. David raises his hand and says, "I am sad because we can't go out." We praise his response and are relieved that he is volunteering, rather than shutting down from his experience during *Center* activities.

Cordell says, "I am mad because mommy yells at me." Aaron says, "I am mad because mommy hits me." This of course brings up an important issue when doing this type of work. As teachers, we are all required to report child abuse to the authorities. Presently, in New York, hitting a child is legal, so Aaron's response is not something that needs to be reported, but it does cue us to remain vigilant about his situation. I call on Paul. He says he doesn't know. I prompt him by saying, "I am…" He says, "I am mad because it's raining today," relying on what was modeled. All responses are praised.

We consider which message to compose for the first page of our *Power Message* book. There is a general murmur of agreement as we call Cordell up to the easel. Rosalie says the message to the class, *I am mad because mommy yells at me,* and asks the students to repeat it. She asks them to count how many words there are in the message. They count out eight words. We hand out the wipe-off boards and markers. She guides Cordell to begin writing the message with a marker in the big book. He almost writes on the inside of the cover page. She directs him to the top left corner of the first page and he writes *I*. Without prompting, he writes *am* and Rosalie says, "Good! That was a quick and easy word for you!" Rosalie articulates and stretches out each word of the message with them. She describes how to form letters, "d is a stick and a circle, n is a stick and a tunnel."

While all of the students start out engaged and focused on writing the message along with Cordell, some of them begin to lose focus in forming the letters and words on their boards halfway through the message. Surprisingly, Aaron is very focused and intent on writing the message. He calls out the next word of the message, "my!" I attribute Aaron's attention to the personal meaning the message has for him and the intrigue of bringing a mildly taboo subject out into an acceptable social context.

Cordell indicates a mistake he made in the book on the easel. Rosalie says, "Yes! You noticed that you need a space there! Excellent! We can fix that with this special tape." She uses correction tape to keep Cordell's message on track and ready for publication. Paul is on task as long as I work with him. I model the word and write it on his board and he copies it. He initiates some of the words on his own. Aaron continues to eagerly and appropriately call out ideas to help compose the message. Rosalie says, "What do you hear in 'yells'"? Aaron says, "Y like in yo-yo!" using the alphabet chart icon identification strategy that Rosalie previously modeled. We reread the power message together and collect the wipe-off boards. We tell Cordell that he can illustrate his message during next week's *Center* time.

In preparation for the jungle story, we read a big book, *My Five Senses: A Lion's Tale* by Judy Nayer, which describes elements of a jungle. After I read the big book aloud, I ask the students to identify natural sceneries in a jungle such as lakes, trees, rainstorms, grass, and flowers. I indicate some materials, sheets, and large swatches of colored fabrics, which we will be using to create our jungle.

I ask the students to guess what kind of animal I am and vocalize the sounds of a monkey. They say, "Monkey!" I tell them, "That was an easy one. This time I'm going to make it a little tricky." I ask them to tell me what kind of monkey I am. I vocalize again with a mad affect. They guess, "Mad monkey!" I say, "Right!" and then have them guess the other four feelings expressed through my monkey sounds. I ask the students to choose an animal and take turns vocalizing and then guessing what their classmates are pretending to be. Makenna roars like a happy lion. Quinn chirps like a happy bird. Cordell barks like a mad dog. Paul growls like a mad lion. Aaron barks like a mad dog.

I ask the students to stand in the center of the room and tell me what could happen in the jungle that might make the animals so mad. Aaron answers, "If the keepers started taking the animals away." I ask them to imagine that scenario and make the maddest animal noises when I say, "Go!" and continue until I call, "Freeze." We do the same for each emotion, eliciting hypothetical situations from the students and then vocalizing an emotional response to warm up the thematic ensemble enactment.

I explain that we are going to create a story, starting at the nighttime, which will come when I turn out the lights. I say that some of the story, like in any story, might have mad, sad, or frustrated parts, and demonstrate with Rosalie how mad and frustrated parts of the story and conflicts between animals must happen through "stage fighting" without any physical contact. We begin to build the jungle with simple bed sheets and colored fabrics. We make mountains, rivers, caves, lakes, trees, grass, and flowers. Tables and chairs are moved around and covered to make homes for the animals. Scarves and fabrics are tucked into belts and waistbands to create fur, tails, and other necessary costume details.

I tell the students that when nighttime comes, they have to find their shelter and remain silent until the day comes again. I turn the lights out and announce that its nighttime. The room is not dark, as light is coming in from behind the closed blinds on the windows, but the effect of the low lights and moving around and covering up a few tables and chairs succeeds in transforming the space. The students, in their animal roles, scurry into their hiding places. I narrate, with the lights out and all the animals silently secured in their homes, "We will see, when the morning comes, what kind of animals live in this jungle. Will we see mad animals? Happy? Scared? Frustrated? What will the animals need to do when the sun comes up? Find food? Water? Build their homes?" I turn the lights on and the jungle springs to life. Paul comes out of his cave stretching and yawning in role. The animals are sniffing around, looking for food and water.

Someone yells, "There's a hunter in the jungle!" Someone else yells, "There's two hunters in the jungle!" Makenna comes out of her lair and challenges the hunters, Alex and David, clawing at them and smacking at their "guns." In an aside, I quietly remind her not to make real physical contact. A minute later, she makes another run at the hunters. Other animals excitedly watch the encounter or stake out their part of the jungle. After a few minutes, I turn out the lights and call for nighttime in the jungle. The inhabitants scurry to the hiding places they have created. I wonder out loud what will happen in the jungle the next day. I tell them that this will be the last day in the jungle before the story ends.

For obvious reasons, having characters that use weapons against others in the drama is not ideal, even though the role is contained and the goal for the emotional intelligence skill is to work toward transformation of the aggressive impulse through verbal expression. Censoring a student's need for this type of expression will only serve to repress it for reemergence at some later time. The teacher/director, as described in the next paragraph, can work with aggression expressed through role, without compromising the authenticity of the role, by directing the dramatic action. It is also reasonable, though, to have a policy in which the use of weapons against others in the ensemble is prohibited. As described in the lesson plan for *Jungle Book of Feelings*, students usually inform the dramatic action with natural disasters such as floods, fire, illness, food shortages, and loss of children and parents, allowing the group to work together as an ensemble toward resolution. The teacher *should not* artificially impose a happy resolution. Mad and sad endings are fine.

The lights come on and the animals emerge again. The hunters start shooting at Makenna the lioness, but she is not affected by their shooting. I narrate, in a curious affect, "The hunters' guns aren't hurting the animals. The animals must be stronger than the guns!" Aaron the dog occasionally looks out from within his mountain cave and makes some type of shriek. Paul the lion says he has water for the animals. He sees the hunters approaching and runs toward his cave with a scared affect. All of a sudden, Paul lets out a deep, primal, moaning scream and yells that he is shot. As Cordell's animal moves to investigate and help, he is also wounded, convulsing on the ground. I immediately ask whether there are any doctors in the jungle.

Makenna rushes to the scene declaring herself a "helping doctor." She attempts to treat Paul and Cordell by gently brushing their bodies with scarves exclaiming, "Here's some medicine!" Aaron comes out of his mountain cave, surveys the scene, and slinks back in. Paul is still howling. Cordell is still convulsing. Quinn is out of sight. The hunters continue to explore the jungle. They come across Aaron's cave and attempt to flush him out. He roars his resistance. They don't pursue it. Paul cries out that he is on fire. Makenna is still trying to help him heal. I tell them they have two minutes to find an ending for their story. Each student creates a happy, mad, sad, scared, or frustrated ending for his or her character. I shut the lights and call for nighttime.

I start to derole the students, as they quietly "sleep" in their shelters, reviewing events that occurred in the jungle and praising them for their acting abilities and the cool stories they created. I tell them that when the lights come back on, they will turn back into boys and girls and help to clean up, so we will have time to sit together and hear their stories. Although the drama was intense and may sound as if it were out of control, it was actually contained and manageable. The initial game when they had to "freeze" after making their animal emotion sounds and the use of the switched-off lights for nighttime, provide effective tools for control. As we clean up, Alex hands a blue scarf to Paul and says, "Here's some water to cool you down."

I gather the class together and excitedly ask them to tell me the story. "What happened? Who were you in the story?" They are eager to respond. Each student tells about his or her part in the story. We put a blank big book on the easel and tell them that we are going to make our story into a book, with each of them contributing a page. Since this will be a "published" class book, we use interactive writing to compose accurate text with them as we go along, like when we compose power messages.

Each student comes up to the easel, one at a time, and writes on a page in the book about what happened to him or her during the drama. Cordell says, "The hunters couldn't kill the animals! They were too strong!" He goes up to the book and writes, with Rosalie's help, *The hunters couldn't because the animals were too strong.* Paul says, "I got shot!" He goes up and writes *One animal got shot,* on the next page. There is an excited but focused buzz among the students as they relate their experiences. Quinn, who remained in hiding during the enactment, writes, *The animals got together and kicked the hunters out of the jungle,* for the last page. We vote on *The Magic Jungle* for a title.

Sample of a page from the class big book composed through interactive writing after the thematic ensemble enactment.

The thematic ensemble enactment of *The Magic Jungle* allowed the students to shriek, moan, yell, claw, and convulse, expressing deep and primal levels of emotion within acceptable and contained boundaries of role, costume, setting, and props. The deep connection translated to the oral retelling and then to the interactive writing about the experience. Just as the materials of costume, setting, and props became the signs and abstract forms that symbolized meaning in the drama, now the letters—such as *j, u, n, g, l,* and *e,* and all the subsequent letters and words printed in the big book—become the materials and signs that symbolize and document the deep and meaningful emotion experienced in the jungle in written form.

We hand out paper and markers and ask the students to illustrate their story, which we later glue onto the big book pages they wrote. The students give us their illustrations and are dismissed with their journals and home-work assignments.

Unfortunately, there wasn't time during this initial pilot program to fa-cilitate an important part of the lesson, in which the students participate in a reflective discussion around what they experienced and expressed in the drama, in order to make self-aware, emotionally intelligent connections to their real lives. Examples of questions that could be asked during such a dis-cussion include "Quinn what did your animal feel when he was snarling? How does your (student-identified emotion) come out in your real life?" and "Paul that was some noise you were making! What was it like when you got shot? How does your (student-identified emotion) come out in your real life?"

The thematic ensemble enactment sends an important message to the students early in the program that the experience will often entail some un-conventional procedures that, within the safe boundaries of dramatic enact-ment, engage primal emotional expression and completely transform the classroom space. This spectacle of this activity raises student interest and in-vestment in the program and initiates our efforts to deconstruct many of the emotional conventions that have fragmented their ability to intelligently ex-press themselves.

LESSON 4: *Problem Stories*

Purpose
- To provide students with meaningful contexts for reading and writing that make reference to literary elements of plot, characters, ideas, and text structure to inte-grate and communicate intelligent expression of emotion through oral and written language.

Concept
- Empower students to organize and express personally relevant emotionally intelli-gent language through read aloud, *Director's Hand*, and independent writing activi-ties, to promote personal connections to text, comprehension skills, and an understanding of literary structures as meaningful containers that combine cogni-tive and emotional elements.

Goal
- Each student will demonstrate an understanding of dramatic plot and conflict, characterized as problems that occur in stories, respond to the read aloud, and cre-ate a problem story with characters and a beginning, middle, and an end that com-bine personally meaningful cognitive and emotional elements through independent writing in order to reinforce emotionally intelligent expression.

Procedure

1. The teacher gathers the students and introduces the concepts of *plot* and *problem* by discussing popular children's shows or movies and aspects of dramatic conflict and theme in each of them.
2. The students are asked to think of other shows and identify problems in them.
3. Emotional connections to problems are demonstrated by placing the five emotion words printed on paper on the walls around the room.
4. During *Name It/Move It*, the teacher shows the students popular toy *characters* from shows, one at a time, and asks the students to go to the word that represents the type of problem the character had in the show. There are no right or wrong answers. All choices are affirmed. One student may perceive Cinderella as having a sad problem, while another may identify her as having a mad or scared problem, for example. The students can share their perspectives as the activity unfolds.
5. The students are gathered again for a read aloud of *Leo the Late Bloomer* by Robert Kraus (1971), in which Leo, the shy lion cub, experiences a number of anxieties and resulting problems. *The Kissing Hand* by Audrey Penn (2006), *Three Cheers for Tacky* by Helen Lester (1994), or any other text that demonstrates a simple problem for the main character may be used.
6. After the story is read, the teacher asks the students what kind of problem they thought the different characters, Leo, his father, his friends, had in the beginning, middle, and end of the story. The students respond by moving to the feeling word that represents their ideas. Some of the ideas are shared.
7. The students are then provided with materials such as toy figurines, action figures, and dollhouses or decorated boxes to establish setting, to create individual stories using the *Director's Hand* technique. The students choose to create mad, sad, scared, frustrated, or happy stories. All stories need to have a beginning, middle, and an end.
8. After an announced period of time, the teacher walks around, with the lights out and a type of portable spotlight or flashlight if possible and goes to the story sites to hear each student recite the title and the type of problem story that he or she has created.
9. The teacher then provides the students with lined paper that has an area for illustration and asks the students to independently write and illustrate their problem stories with a beginning, middle, and an end. Students are encouraged to not worry about mistakes, as this activity seeks to connect ideas with written language rather than prepare a published work.
10. The teacher walks around the space, conferencing with individuals as needed.
11. The teacher collects the papers, gathers the students at the easel, and invites them to read their stories and show their illustrations. Other students are encouraged to make personal connections to any of the problems presented in the stories.
12. Students insert homework sheets into their journals.

Evaluation

Did students understand and identify the concept of problem as a structural component of the stories discussed? Were they able to distinguish and identify different aspects of emotion in the different problems and shows discussed? Were they able to identify the problems and emotional content in the beginning, middle, and end of the read aloud? Were they able to create a problem story based in emotion and transfer it to their independent writing? Were they able to structure their writing with a beginning, middle, and an end and apply word study skills and mechanics such as stretching and slowly articulating to their composition?

Materials

- Popular children's toy movie characters, collected from fast food restaurants
- Signs with the five emotion words printed on them
- *Leo the Late Bloomer* by Robert Kraus or other text mentioned above for read aloud
- Materials for things such as dolls, people figurines, action figures, dollhouses, and boxes to create stories
- Lined paper with a space for illustration

Home Activities

Sit with your child and take turns listing different types of problems that your family faces during various times and circumstances, such as in the morning, on vacation, with siblings, at mealtimes, bedtime, and so on. Also, make a list of a mad, sad, scared, frustrated, and happy problem that occurs in your family. You can make a guessing game out of it, in which you write your list first and then see whether your child's ideas match any of the things you wrote down. Then your child can write his or her ideas down as well. Encourage your child to express his or her opinion of what the problems are without being negative or judgmental toward his or her ideas.

During the week, I decorate *The Magic Jungle* class big book, gluing the students' illustrations on the page of text that they wrote. I also use jungle animal stickers throughout the book and green felt and golden tinsel for grass and a sun to decorate the front cover. I am very happy with how the book comes out. I look through it again and again. It occurs to me, as I look through, that it follows the same theoretical strand we are conceptualizing with regard to the students. I want to keep reviewing the text because of a sense of personal connection and ownership; it reflects an important aspect of who I am at this point in my life.

All the students sign in *happy* except for Alex, who signs in *mad*. I ask him what feels mad for him today, and he replies, "I was scared of those bullies last year." I assume that he is referring to the situation that his mother told me about during our initial assessment interview. A bully on his bus led a group of children in teasing Alex, causing him to have to go to the principal's office with the other children, which upset him tremendously. As I do a quick scan of the homework the students are handing in, I notice that Alex wrote *I feel scared when I had to go to the principal's office.*

The class settles into *Center* activities. There is a calm, connected feel to the activity in the room. I notice that the students are more comfortable with initiating and investing purposeful emotional expression into the literacy activities. They are dialoguing, interacting, sharing points of view, and collaborating for meaningful application of written language and word problem solving skills.

The students clean up and I gather them for *Power Message*. I say, "You've got to see this awesome book we made last week!" I read the title, *The Magic Jungle*, and begin to read the book. Cordell starts punching the air in excitement as I begin. When his page is read, he proudly proclaims, "That's mine! I made that one!" I start asking, each time I turn the page, "Who made this one?" They enthusiastically identify their illustrations on their pages of text. They are excited to see their adventures and experiences documented in the form of a book.

I finish the book and we move through *Check-In* and into *Power Messages*. Makenna responds with "I am happy because it is a great day!" Cordell says, "I am happy because I don't get beat up anymore." We say, "That makes us so happy too!" Paul says, "I am happy because I am going pumpkin picking." Alex says, "I am happy." Wanting to keep a balance and not have the students herded into automatic knee jerk "happy" responses, I ask them, "Do the power messages always have to be happy?" They say "no" and I reiterate that it is also very powerful when we say that we are mad, sad, frustrated, and scared. I'm conscious of my struggle to present a balanced picture, wanting to give them the OK to access their full range, while at the same time not wanting to talk them out of their happy feelings.

We vote on which power message we should write. Rosalie has them recite the alphabet chart before we write the message. The students chant the rhythmic "Aa apple Bb…" and so on. She also adds on a reference to a chart with "*th thumb, sh shoe, ch check* and *wh wheel.*" Makenna comes up to the easel and Rosalie asks her to say her message. We repeat it two times. We count the words in the message. We hand out the wipe-off boards and dry erase markers. Everybody writes the first word, *I*, on his or her boards while Makenna writes it in the *Power Message* big book. Everybody is focused and engaged. They write *am*.

Rosalie asks, "What do we hear in 'happy,' like in horse?" referring to the alphabet chart. The class responds, "h!" She says, "Then *a*, like in apple." She demonstrates its formation "…a circle and a stick." Rosalie says, "What's at the end of happy?" Paul says, "y!" I notice that Paul, who is usually playing catch up when it comes to writing, had *happy* all written out perfectly, even before it was completed in the book on the easel. This is what we are looking for. We want the students to build a bank of high frequency sight words that include the five emotion words, and have automatic access to them for literacy and emotional intelligence purposes.

Someone spells *it* and Rosalie models how to use the word to get to *is*. We write the word *a*, saying, "that's an easy one." Rosalie asks, "What do you hear in *great*?" Aaron says, "*gr*." For *day*, David says, "Like in my name!" We are thrilled with how well everybody is doing. These are all children who have been identified as having difficulty in one way or another, especially with attentiveness and writing. We finish the message and start to collect the boards. To save time, Rosalie erases. As she tries to collect his board Cordell makes a frustrated, agitated sound. I say, "Are you mad Cordell? Can you tell us with a power message?" Cordell says, "I'm mad because I wanted to erase." We praise his use of the language and let him erase his board.

I gather the students and say, "Guess what? There is one thing that is in every single story you've ever heard or read, seen on tape or in the movies. What do you think it is?" They respond, "Words? Title? Pictures?" I affirm all of their answers as correct and say, "Also, every story has some kind of problem built into it! Sometimes it's a mad, or scared, or sad, or frustrated or happy problem, but the problem is always part of the story. Who can think of a story?" Makenna says, "The three little pigs!" I say, "Yes! Any problems in that story?" Someone says, "The wolf wanted to eat them!" I say, "Yes! What kind of problem was that?" Cordell says, "Scared!" Aaron chimes in with, "Mad that the house fell down!"

I refer to the five emotion word signs that I put on the different sides of the room, tacked to the wall. The students read the familiar words. I say, "Great! I'm going to show you a character. You tell me who it is and then go to the sign that describes the type of problem the character had." I hold up a small plastic Snow White figurine. Some of them go to *Scared* and say, "The witch tried to hurt her!" Some go to *Mad* and say, "She ate a poison apple!" At *Sad* they say, "She went to sleep!" and at *Happy*, "She woke up!" I hold up a few other characters from popular shows collected from fast food children's meals, and have the students respond similarly. They identify and assign different emotions from various perspectives to the common situations.

We sit the class down and read aloud *Leo the Late Bloomer* to continue the theme of introducing the concept of problem (conflict) as a literary element. At the end of the story, before the last page, we ask, "What do you think his first words were?" The students respond, "I love you...I bloomed...I'm happy...I talked for the first time." We praise all the responses and read the last page, which is *I made it!* I ask whether there was a problem in the story. Paul says, "Yes, he couldn't do nothing." I say, "Right! That happened in the beginning." Cordell says, "At the end he got better." I say, "Yes! There was a beginning, middle, and an end! Boys and girls, think about the kind of problem there was in the beginning of the story, and go to the sign that tells what kind of problem you noticed." Alex goes to *Mad* and says, "He didn't do nothing." I ask what kind of problems there were in the middle of the story. Cordell goes to *Sad* and says, "He couldn't do anything the others were doing." I ask what kind of problem there was in the end. Makenna goes to *Happy* and says, "He could read and write."

I tell the students that they are going to make their own problem stories with a beginning, middle, and an end. Their stories can have mad problems, sad problems, frustrated problems, scared problems, or happy problems. We approach the activity with the *Director's Hand* technique, in which students are provided with toy human or human-like figurines to create individual stories. Dollhouses, toy buildings and structures, or boxes can be used to represent houses, schools, or any setting the student chooses to direct his or her story in.

The students collect their materials and find a space in the room. We walk around the room, prompting, "You need to think about what happens in the beginning, middle, and end of your story" and "Does your story have a mad, sad, scared, frustrated, or happy problem?" I tell them that it is time to find an ending for their stories. Two minutes later we hand out pieces of large lined paper with a space on top for illustrations. We tell the students to write the stories that they just played, starting with the beginning, then the middle, and the end. I say, "I wonder what kind of problems the stories will have?"

We walk around, individually conferencing with them as they write. We help them to stretch out words and coordinate the formation of the letters. Cordell asks for the correcting tape we used for the *Power Messages* book and our class big books because he made a capital letter for a word that didn't need one. I explain that the mistake is ok. "For this writing, our ideas are more important than making the letters and words the exact right way." All are engaged and focused on the independent writing activity. Alex writes one sentence and says that he is finished. I tell him that he wrote the beginning; he needs a middle and an end. We put out markers for the illustrations.

At this point I stick my head out the door and call the parents' attention to the *Power Messages*, *Power Names*, and *The Magic Jungle* books we have created that I put on a table in the hallway. The parents who have already looked through them while waiting for their children respond with comments like "Great work!" and "Wonderful!"

We gather the students at the easel and tell them we will take turns reading the stories they wrote. Makenna reads hers first. "The mad castle. There are horses fighting the castle. The horses killed the castle." Makenna says her story has a "sad and frustrated problem." Alex goes next. He reads, "I'm mad when I watch TV. When the TV is off I feel happy to play. I feel happy." The problem is "happy and mad." Paul reads next: "The witch knocked down the man on the castle. The guards came and knocked down the witch." The problem in Paul's story was a "mad" one. Aaron read next: "The man fell off the building. He got hurt. He died." It was a "mad" story. Cordell says his story is "mad" and reads, "The man didn't battle the dragon. His friend helped him. They killed the dragon. They were happy."

We praise their work, hand out journals, and dismiss the class. The relatively positive, on-task response that we are consistently observing from the students, who have otherwise been identified by parents and teachers as troubled, distracted, oppositional, and consistently off task, affirms that our approach is engaging their learning processes in a deep and meaningful way. The children are seeing, hearing, and experiencing themselves in the abstract forms and signs of the language, inspiring them to attend to the objective and mechanical process of problem solving words in order to obtain optimum reflection.

LESSON 5: *The Puppet Express*

Purpose
- To provide students with meaningful contexts through which they can articulate, construct, present, and integrate—through oral and written expression—unique subjective experiences with the objective language of emotional intelligence.

Concept
- Empower students to construct meaningful text using mechanics and word study skills as a means for purposefully communicating individual emotional experience accessed through read aloud, puppetry, and independent writing activities to promote personal connection to text and emotionally intelligent self-awareness, expression, and reflection.

Goal
- Each student will use a puppet to represent an emotional perspective prompted by the read aloud and communicate a personal emotional perspective through independent writing and oral presentation.

Procedure
1. Students are gathered for a read aloud of an original text titled *I Have Feelings. How about You?* (see Appendix) that follows a pattern describing physical aspects

of how the five emotions feel in the body, events that trigger the emotions, and self-aware language through which the emotions can be expressed.

2. The teacher provides students with individual wipe-off boards.

3. *Explore the Range* begins when the teacher presents five puppets to the students that portray different emotions through facial expression. These can be purchased or made with paper bags or socks, using felt, construction paper, or any convenient material to create corresponding facial expressions.

4. The teacher holds the puppets up, one at a time, and asks the students what the puppet might be feeling, and to write the emotion on their wipe-off boards. The students are then asked to construct a statement on their boards, beginning with the self-identifying high frequency word "I" that the puppet might say based on the emotion.

5. The students share responses.

6. After each emotion has been addressed in this manner using the puppets and the wipe-off boards, the teacher collects the boards.

7. The students are asked to go to a puppet area or basket containing a pile of puppets, and pick a puppet they think has something mad to say.

8. When the teacher says "Go!" the students walk around the room with their puppets and "Practice saying mad words" until the teacher calls "Freeze!" The students do this, as a group, at the same time, for half a minute or so.

9. The teacher then tells the students to find a puppet that has something sad to say, and the same exercise is undertaken. Each of the remaining emotions is warmed up in this manner.

10. For *Meet the Puppets*, the teacher asks the students to choose one puppet they want to use to make a show. As the students make their choice, the teacher asks them to silently think about and decide whether their puppet is a boy or girl, how old their puppet is, who's in the puppet's family, where the puppet lives, whether their puppet is mad, sad, scared, frustrated, or happy, and what kind of story the puppet wants to tell.

11. The students leave their puppets by the playing area when they are ready (if a puppet stage is not available, a sheet over a table, desk, or chair works fine) and sit in an audience area of the room. If possible, the lights are turned off and a spotlight, flashlight, or track lamp is focused on the playing area.

12. The students come up to the stage, one at a time, and present their puppet shows. An interview format is helpful with the teacher asking the puppet the questions that were addressed to the students in step 10. The teacher can ask, after the puppet identifies the emotion, about feelings and events connected to the emotion. The student finishes the presentation by having the puppet tell its story and then answering any questions from the audience.

13. After all of the students have had a turn presenting the puppets, the teacher directs the students to five large sheets of chart paper on the walls on different sides of the

room. Each sheet is headed with one of the five feeling words surrounded by the phrase *I feel* (one of the feeling words) *when…*

14. The students are divided into pairs or small groups, and each group is assigned one of the sheets.
15. The students are asked to list personal responses on the sheet.
16. After a few minutes, the groups rotate and move to a new sheet. Each of the groups responds to each of the five sheets.
17. The students are gathered together to read and reflect on the lists that have been circulated around the room. Each student takes a turn choosing one of their responses to read to the class. The teacher guides student responses to begin with the word *I*.
18. Other students are encouraged to listen to their classmates and make connections with their own lives.
19. Students insert homework sheets into their journals.

Evaluation

Did students respond and make personal connections to the read aloud? Did each student present a "puppet show" and express an emotional quality through their puppet? Did each student construct meaningful text with the objective symbols of written language to communicate and reflect personal, subjective emotional content on the chart paper? Did the students present their responses orally with self-aware language of emotional intelligence?

Materials

- Read aloud *I Have Feelings. How about You?*
- Puppets with faces that reflect emotion
- Individual wipe-off boards
- Assortment of puppets
- Puppet stage or playing area
- Large chart paper
- Markers

Home Activity

Sit with your child and take turns writing a dialogue that conveys and explores a feeling about a situation. For example, your child may start by writing I feel *mad when you yell, or,* I *get frustrated doing my homework.* You then take the book and write a response, such as* I *hate it yelling too, or,* I *wish homework time was easier for us. Then pass the book back to your child so that he or she may respond to what you wrote. Encourage your child to verbally express the ideas first, then search for the letters and words that will compose his or her statement on the paper. Try to begin each sentence with* I, *and take at least five turns each, passing the book between you as you respond to each other and write your dialogue.*

Cordell starts us off and signs in with *mad,* Alex signs in with *frustrated,* and all others sign in with *happy.* Quinn's mother speaks with Rosalie in the waiting area. She reports that Quinn is getting in trouble in school every day and getting into big power struggles with his teacher. He is shutting down from doing any work, and his teacher is responding angrily to his oppositional behavior. The mother says that she found this out because of a previous week's homework activity from our program when Quinn wrote that his teacher is slamming his books, grabbing his pencils away, and speaking to him with quite a negative tone.

I look through his journal. He writes *I feel happy when I take a shower, when I play soccer. I get mad when someone yells at me. I feel scared when I get in trouble. I feel sad when someone hits on my book.* In his journal, his mother writes, in a note to us, that she asks Quinn who does that to his books. He answers, "My teacher." She asks why. He responds, "Because I'm not paying attention." Quinn's mother writes that she is hearing about this for the first time through the exercise of the assignment, and she is thankful for getting the information for him. Quinn was able, by reflecting and writing about purposeful and meaningful emotional experiences, to express something that he may not have expressed verbally.

During *Center* time, Makenna goes to the puppets. Cordell goes to *Feeling Faces.* Quinn and David work together on *Fill in the Feeling* while Paul rereads familiar class materials at *Big Books, Poems, and Songs.* Rosalie notices that the students' "learning behaviors" are much more responsive and sustained to the tasks at hand. They are not as distracted during activities, with less looking away, lying down, scribbling, or bothering others. While I attribute this, in some degree, to the natural course of development that helps any group to settle in, I am also gratified by the fact that these students, who have demonstrated ongoing problems with learning, attention, behavior, and emotional expression in their schools and homes, are responding so positively and successfully to the program.

During *Check-In,* David holds up all his faces and says he feels "Happy, scared and frustrated, mad and angry and everything!" Aaron says he is "Happy." Alex says he feels "Happy and frustrated." Makenna says, "I feel sad, scared, frustrated, mad and happy." Quinn says he is "Happy." Paul says he is "Sad." Cordell says he is "Mad!" I answer, "I see you" to each.

We collect the masks and gather for *Power Message.* We read the messages from the previous weeks. I say, "What's always the first word of our messages?" The class responds, "I!" I ask David whether he can go to the word wall and find the word *I.* He is successful. I ask what the second word is. They respond, "am!" I ask Quinn to find it on the wall. He does. I ask them to "Think about your power message for the day. When you know what it is, raise your hand and we can hear it." We hear the messages, "I am mad when my brother hits me!" "I am happy because I have a loose tooth." "I am mad when my friends make my room a mess." We choose Quinn, the happy boy with the loose tooth, for today's *Power Message*.

The class chants the alphabet charts with Rosalie. We hand out the wipe-off boards and ask Quinn to say his message. He does. We say it together. We count the words. We ask what the first word is. They respond, "I!" Rosalie asks what is special about the *I* since it is at the beginning of the sentence. Makenna says, "Capital!" We stretch out the message, "Good...straight stick and a circle...right...great job!" Everyone is focused on and participating in writing the message on their boards, identifying and forming letters and words and keeping pace with the writing in the book on the easel as we compose together. When we finish, I tell them to cap their markers and turn around to me while remaining on the cushions.

I read the original text *I Have Feelings, How about You?* to the class. Aaron answers, "I do!" after I read the title. As I read the words, which speak about events and physical reactions related to the five feelings, Cordell quietly mimes the different ideas being read. As I turn the pages, the students recognize the words and say, "Sad!" for example, when I reach that page. Makenna points to the *Sad* sign on the wall. Paul howls when a passage in the text mentions howling. They respond to the text making personal connections and recalling high frequency words.

I finish the book and refer to the puppets in my lap. Each puppet has a specific emotional expression that matches the five emotion words we have been working on. After we identify the different emotions, I tell the students, "I am going to put a puppet on my hand and you write the words on your board that you think the puppet will say." I put the scared puppet on my hand. Cordell says, "I am scared!" I say, "Write it, Cordell!" We go through the rest of the puppets.

I say, "Let's practice for the big puppet show!" I direct them to go to the puppet area and choose a puppet that they think has something mad to say. I tell them that when I say, "Go!" they will all take a puppet around the room and practice saying mad words. We warm up sad, then scared, then frustrated, then happy language using the puppets in this manner. After we go through the five feelings, I ask them to choose a puppet that they want to make a show with. I ask them to walk around with their puppet and silently think about a name for the puppet, its age, whether it's happy, sad, scared, frustrated, or happy and a story that the puppet might want to tell about its life.

The students lay their puppets down against the wall and sit in the audience section against another wall. I take out the puppet stage, which can be two chairs with a sheet across, turn off the lights, and position the floor lamp as a spot light. Quinn, while asking to go first, moves to the other side of the room. I make a general announcement that only children who are sitting in the audience area will have a turn in the stage. He moves over with the others. I call Cordell up first. In the role of the puppet, Cordell says he's mad because he always gets "blown up." Alex's puppet says, "I'm scared of the bully on my bus. He said mean words to me." Rosalie asks, "Is the bully still there?" He says, "The bully is not on the bus anymore."

David is next. His puppet peeks out of the stage. I ask him his name. He quietly says, "Nobody." I ask him how old he is. He says, "I don't know how old I am." I ask him whether he's mad, sad, scared, frustrated, or happy. He says, "I'm happy." I ask, "What happens that makes you feel happy?" He says, "I don't know." Makenna takes two puppets into the stage and announces, "Messy Hair is scared." I ask why Messy Hair is scared. The puppet says, "My mom pokes my hair to find my eyeballs." Paul asks, "Why do you have messy hair?" She says, "Because I don't brush it."

Quinn, who has been sitting with the group, asks whether he can go next. He has two dragons. They are twin six-year-old boys who want to be left alone. They are happy because they fight. Makenna asks, "Do you blow fire at each other?" Quinn answers, "No." Aaron asks, "Do you go to school?" He says "No." Rosalie asks, "Did you ever go to school?" Quinn says, "Yes. They were mean. The teachers yelled at me." Someone else asks, "Do you have any friends?" Quinn's puppet answers, "No, I don't."

After each student takes a turn, I indicate five large chart sheets tacked onto the walls, each with a heading of either *I feel mad when...*, *I feel sad when...*, *I feel scared when...*, *I feel frustrated when...*, or *I feel happy when...*I pair them into four "teams" and start each team on a sheet. I tell them to respond to the sheet and write their answers below the headings. I want them to take the experience of oral expression through the puppets and transfer it to independently written expression of emotional experience in their own lives.

I work with David at the *frustrated* sheet. He tells me he gets frustrated "when Connor yells." We work to get the letters by stretching out his words like we do in the interactive writing of power messages. Hopefully, we can transfer some of those skills to this independent writing activity. He shows little to no letter-sound correspondence. I take him to the alphabet chart for each sound that we hear in his statement. It is helpful. I say, "'yells'...what do you hear in 'yells'?" David asks, "t?" I say, "yells, /y/, /y/, yo-yo." We go to the chart. "Look for the yo-yo." He asks, "v?" I say, "Close." He asks, "y?" I say, "Good!" I continue to stretch *yells* with David. He gets the *l* and the *s*. All of a sudden, it seems to start clicking for him.

I take David to the *sad* sheet and say, "Which one is this?" He says, "Scared." I say, "Close! You saw the *s*. Look at the picture…now check it with the *ad* after the *s*. He says, "sad." I say, "Good! When do you feel sad?" He says. "When my tire breaks." As we stretch it out, he is independently able to come up with *Tir brks*. This is a terrific breakthrough for David. Up until now, he has only been able to write random strings of letters, with very little if any letter-sound correspondence. This is the first time in any of our activities that he has been able to independently compose meaningful text. I tell the group to finish up the last idea they are writing. After half a minute, I bring everyone to the middle of the room.

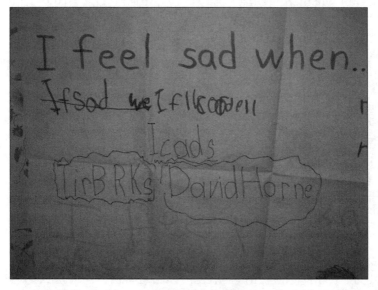

David independently constructs meaningful text on the chart paper.

I tell the students to raise their hands when they are ready to show us and read one of the things they wrote. Alex goes to the *scared* sheet and reads, "I feel scared when my smoke alarm goes off." I say, "Great! Who wants to show us one…Aaron?" Aaron goes to *frustrated*. "I feel frustrated when my sister hits me." Quinn is next. He goes to *scared* and reads, "I feel scared when I see scary movies." Makenna reads, "I feel sad when mom does not eat an apple." Paul goes to *scared* and reads, "I feel scared when my brother hits me." David tentatively goes to *sad* and reads, "I feel sad when my tire breaks." We praise David and all of the students. I tell all what a great job they did, hand out their journals, and dismiss them.

Rosalie comments that the students are much freer with their writing and are taking more risks in composing their thoughts." I notice that their ideas are more personal, authentic, and connected.

We identify a reciprocal relationship we see emerging between the expressive forms. Quinn's reluctance, reported by his mother in the initial interview, to verbalize emotions and use expressive language, was offset by his ability to communicate about the unpleasant experience with his teacher through written language, which then facilitated verbal communication between him and his mother, prompting an important intervention at school on his behalf.

David, on the other hand, used his relative comfort with verbalizing emotion to finally express meaningful emotional experience through the abstract forms and signs of letters and words. Supported by the dynamic of the dramatic enactment and verbal expression, David was able, perhaps for the first time, to represent his experience effectively through meaningful written language. The lesson, integrated through the drama, kept him focused on his authentic and meaningful experience, rather than pressuring him into producing "correctly" written language, and he was able to employ the abstract forms and signs to communicate that experience.

Our general observations about the students' positive response to learning seem to be a result of our emphasis on their personal experiences as the vehicle that carries them from form to form. Our reverence for their meaningful experience and points of view, engaged and enacted by the dramatic forms of expression, and then reflected by the abstract forms and signs of language, seems to be holding and engaging the students' attention, as they experience themselves more fully in the integrated activities of the program.

LESSON 6: *Puppet City Tales*

Purpose
- To provide students with a meaningful context that incorporates literary elements—interpretation and presentation of information gathered from literature to promote emotionally intelligent expression and social problem solving strategies—and inspires use of text mechanics and word study skills to clarify communication of subjective experience.

Concept
- Empower students to intelligently express emotion and implement problem solving strategies by creating a story through puppets and thematic ensemble enactment, based on information interpreted from a read aloud, and document the experience in a class big book composed through independent and shared writing.

Goal
- Each student will respond to the read aloud by analyzing, organizing, and writing relevant information on chart paper, participate in the enactment, respond to their

experience with independent writing and contribute a page to the class big book through interactive writing.

Procedure

1. Students are gathered together for a read aloud of *Franklin's Neighborhood* by Sharon Jennings (1999), which focuses on different centers of the community, which is later used as a reference source for set building ideas in the enactment. *Miss Bindergarten Takes a Field Trip with Kindergarten* by Joseph Slate (2001) or any similar text that identifies different areas of a neighborhood or town will also suffice.

2. After reading the book, the teacher refers to three large chart sheets on the wall, one headed with *Play*, one with *Family*, and one with *Learning*.

3. For *Write It/Build It*, the teacher divides the students into three groups and assigns each group to a chart paper.

4. Each group recalls, researches and lists community centers and structures from the book that connect to the theme on their heading.

5. The teacher asks the groups to rotate to another chart, read what the other group listed, and add any other ideas that the group comes up with. The group rotates one more time to cover each chart.

6. The teacher instructs the students to regroup by moving to the chart sheet that describes parts of the community they would like to create.

7. The teacher provides the students with sheets, fabrics, and boxes and instructs them to create a part of a town for the puppets to live in. This is accomplished, as with the thematic ensemble enactment of Lesson 3, with tables, chairs, desks, and sheets.

8. When the town is complete, the teacher tells the students to choose the puppets they want to live and work in the part of the town they created.

9. The teacher turns the lights out and narrates that night has fallen. The puppets find their homes and settle in silently. The teacher continues to narrate that when the lights come on, the day will begin, and "We will see if the puppets that live in this city are mad, sad, scared, frustrated, or happy. What will they do during the day? Go to work? School? The park? A restaurant?" The story does not continue until the class is able to be silent and receive direction during the "nighttime" period.

10. The teacher turns the lights on and the drama ensues. The teacher structures the drama like *The Magic Jungle* drama of Lesson 3, using the lights to indicate night and day, and role and narration, to help manage and facilitate the dramatic action. Dramatic conflict and problems that spontaneously occur serve to initiate self-aware emotional expression through the role of puppet.

11. The teacher may proceed with the drama as long as it seems appropriate, facilitating two, three, or four "days." Narrative prompts during the different nighttimes can include "What job does your puppet have? What does your puppet need? How can your puppet get what it needs in the town? What kinds of places are in this

town? Who else is like your puppet in the town? What kinds of places does your puppet want to visit in the town? What kind of problem comes up for your puppet in the town? How might your puppet try to resolve the problem? Is there anybody who can help him or her?"

12. The teacher lets the students know which "day" will be the last one for developing the story, allowing the students to create an ending.

13. The teacher turns out the lights for the final narrative, which serves to transition the students out of role by reviewing events that occurred in the story, praising the students for their acting abilities and expressing authentic interest in hearing the stories after the room is cleaned up.

14. The teacher provides each student with a formatted paper for independent writing response that asks *What part of the town did you build? What happened in your part of the town? Were the things that happened in your part of the town mad, sad, scared, frustrated, or happy? Why? Was your puppet mad, sad, scared, frustrated, or happy in the story? Why?*

15. The teacher models responding to a large version written on chart paper placed on the easel. The students respond on their papers and then gather together and share their responses.

16. The teacher engages the students in a discussion on who the characters were in the story, what the plot and problem was, and what happened in the beginning, middle, and end. These elements can be organized and listed on chart paper.

17. The students take turns sharing their writing. As each student shares his or her independent writing, the teacher uses the text to make, with the class, a big book about the experience through shared writing.

18. The students create illustrations with paper and crayons, which the teacher pastes into the big book on their corresponding pages.

19. Students reflect on the conflicts and problems that occurred in the drama and composed in the big book, and make personal connections with their own lives using self-aware language of intelligent emotional expression.

20. The students insert the homework activity sheets into their journals.

Evaluation

Were students able to recall community centers from the read aloud and record the information onto the chart paper? Were they able to address conflict and problems in the drama using self-aware language of emotional expression through role? Did each student transfer the experience of the drama onto the independent writing and shared writing of the big book? Did students use mechanics and word study skills and strategies to clarify communication? Were they able to reflect on the experience and make personal connections to their own lives?

Materials

- *Franklin's Neighborhood* by Sharon Jennings or other text mentioned above for read aloud and reference

- Large chart paper
- Colored sheets, fabrics, and boxes for building materials
- Puppets, prepared formatted response sheets, chart tablet for big book

Home Activity

Sit with your child and write a list of rules for communication, such as using power messages (I am…), no yelling, name-calling, or hitting, and so on, that everyone in the family can agree to. Make a poster of your family's ideas and display it in your home. Encourage your child to express his or her ideas and write them down on the poster. You can also illustrate and decorate the poster. Have a cooperative contest to see how long everybody in the family, parents included, can stick to the rules. Plan a family event like a pizza party to celebrate any success.

Paul signs in with *mad*. Cordell, Makenna, and Quinn sign in with *happy*. Alex signs in with *sad* and Aaron, who comes about forty-five minutes late, signs in with *happy*. Quinn asks whether he can go to *Feeling Faces*. We say, "Sure," even though we had other plans for him. He fills in *happy* when *I come here.* That's nice to see.

Alex's homework dialogue apparently captured an issue that the family was dealing with at the time. It reads: *I feel mad when you left me in the toy room by myself. I feel frustrated when you growl and answer "whatever" when I try to find out what is bothering you. I feel frustrated when you didn't let me come upstairs. I feel upset when you don't hear or understand what I am saying. If you remember daddy and I kept asking you to come upstairs but you refused. I feel happy when we did our one big happy family hug and went to the mall to eat. I am glad you finally decided to come upstairs so we can find out what's wrong and then be able to talk about it. Then we were all relieved and happy so we could enjoy the rest of the day.*

Makenna's was written by her and her mother: *I feel mad when mom yells. I don't like to yell at you. I don't like when mom wakes me up. I feel frustrated when you don't follow directions. I feel sad when you don't kiss me. I kiss you all the time even when I am angry at something you have done or not done. I feel happy when you hug me. I am happy you are happy when I hug you, because I love to hug you. I feel happy when you cuddle with me. I like to cuddle with you.*

I like the homework dialogues. I wonder whether the parents perceive any shift in family dynamics from this type of communication. Makenna's mother, before class starts, asks, "How is she doing?" to which I reply, "Great! She's involved, focused, responsive, participates in all the reading and writing activities…" Her mother says there has been a "big improvement" in Makenna's attitude and abilities with regard to reading and writing.

We move through *Center* activities, *Check-In*, and *Power Messages*. I gather the class and prepare them for the next activity by reading aloud

Franklin's Neighborhood. I tell them to listen as I read for the different places that Franklin goes in his neighborhood because we are going to build a city for the puppets and make our own story in it.

After the story, I place three large chart sheets on the wall. One is headed with *Play*, another with *Learning*, and another with *Family*. I explain that we are going to break into three groups of three. Each team will be assigned a sheet to work on. Using the book as a reference when needed, the team will list all of the places they remember from the story that fit under their heading. As the groups start to list the places in Franklin's neighborhood, I hear someone say, "We need the book!" They start using the text as a guide and resource to check their ideas. The students are writing their lists in an engaged and focused manner.

I gather the students at the center of the room, read, and praise their ideas and ask them to go to the sign that describes the part of the town that they want to build for our puppet story. I take out our set building materials, sheets, colored scarves and fabrics and give them three minutes to build, encouraging them with, "Come on, we've got to start moving those puppets in soon!" Makenna volunteers, "I made a house for the puppies!" We ask the rest of the students what they made. Paul says, "A fire station." Alex says, "I don't know yet," and Aaron says, "A fire hydrant." Their ideas reflect the text from the read aloud.

I ask them to pick a puppet to move into the city and decide whether their puppet is mad, sad, scared, frustrated, or happy. After they make their choices, I announce that it will soon be nighttime, and the puppets will need to move into their homes so we can start the story. I turn off the light and call, "Nighttime!" Cordell anxiously calls out, "My puppet doesn't have a home yet!" I tell him that might be a part of his story. I narrate, "When we turn on the lights, the show will begin and we'll see which puppets are mad, sad, scared, frustrated, and happy…" What will the puppets need to do?" I turn on the lights and say, "First day!"

Within the first minute or so, Makenna cries out, "There's a fire in my house!" Paul says, "There's a fire on the playground!" Puppets are running around, looking for help, responding to the crisis. Cordell's puppet puts the fire out at Makenna's house. After a few minutes I turn out the lights and call, "Nighttime!" Everybody settles. I reflect what I saw happen on the first day in the city and call for "Next day!" as I turn the lights on. Paul announces, "The fire station broke down!"

Paul, who becomes very animated in the drama, calls out, "Fire! I'm on fire!" Cordell rushes to Paul's aid and pours water, blue scarves, over him. I call for nighttime and narrate that the last day of the puppet story is coming. I turn the lights on and Paul yells, "Water, I need water!" Someone else yells,

"I'm dead!" Paul's theme of intense drama and pain occurs again, as it did during *The Magic Jungle*. The commotion ensues with fires springing up and Cordell and Aaron racing around to put them out. Paul continues to burn and Alex and Makenna rebuild their houses. Nighttime is called.

We begin to derole and prepare for clean up. I call the students together. They are wound up from the intensity of the drama. I hand out formatted response sheets that ask *What part of the town did you build? What happened in your part of the town? Were the things that happened in your part of the town mad, sad, scared, frustrated, or happy? Why? Was your puppet mad, sad, scared, frustrated, or happy in the story? Why?* for an independent writing activity that we will use to develop a class big book through shared writing. The students take turns reading their responses and composing sentences to write in the blank big book. We tell the class that we will do illustrations next week during *Centers*. I explain that next week the friends who weren't here will add to the book but we get to think of the title. I ask for suggestions. Cordell says, "The fire town!" Someone, maybe Paul, says, "Fire day!" Alex says, "There's a lot of fires in it?" Quinn seems to have an idea but backs off. I try to combine and suggest, "How about *Fire Day in the Town?*" They seem happy about it. I hand out the journals and we dismiss them.

CHAPTER 8

Power Words
Analysis and Evaluation

The next group of lessons engages the students in reading, writing, listening, and speaking from a variety of perspectives in order to organize and present, through oral and written language, meaningful information relevant to their individual experiences. Students are encouraged to analyze and evaluate main ideas and character traits from existing works of literature to enrich understanding of social interaction and build skills of emotionally intelligent expression unique to their points of view.

Specific language strategies and models are provided to facilitate personal empowerment and effective response to situations that cause challenging emotions such as anger and frustration. Shared reading and writing, read aloud, and shared and independent writing activities function as reflections of individual experiences and self-empowered responses developed within role-play and scene study activities.

LESSON 7: *If You're Angry and You Know It/Super Power versus Sour Power*

Purpose
- To provide students with a meaningful context that uses literature to prompt identification and intelligent expression of anger through the integration of subjective experience with objective symbols of oral and written language.

Concept
- Empower students to transform reactionary, destructive acts of anger (*sour power*) into productive, self-aware expressions of anger (*super power*) through analysis and presentation of information from literature, shared reading and writing, role-play, oral expression, and independent writing activities.

Goal
- Each student will respond to the shared reading, offer personal perspectives on the character's expression of anger, participate in the role-play, and reflect, through independent and shared writing, how they might transform their own angry displays into more empowered, productive expression.

Procedure
1. Students are gathered together for a shared reading of big book *Noisy Nora* by Rosemary Wells (1984), which tells the story of a girl mouse who acts out her anger and frustration in a destructive way. *Nobody Notices Minerva* by Wednesday Kirwan

(2007), *I Was So Mad* by Mercer Mayer (1983b) or any other text that portrays the main character as acting out inappropriately from anger may be used as well. High frequency words such as *her, had, has, to,* and *she* are taught and added to the word wall and punctuation is highlighted to promote fluency and phrasing. Comprehension questions focus on the actions that Nora takes to deal with her anger.

2. For *Chart the Power*, the teacher introduces the concepts of *sour power*, when anger comes out in a way that is hurtful, gets us into trouble, and doesn't get us what we need, and *super power*, in which anger comes out in a way that gets people to listen to us, can't get us in trouble, and is more likely to get us what we need. It is important to note that expressing anger the super power way does not mean being polite or apologetic. Apologies and polite responses, while welcome and appropriate, do not express anger. It means expressing anger in a manner that is loud, clear, and strong with self-aware rather than reactionary language.

3. The teacher places a two-column chart on the easel with one column headed *Sour* and the other *Super*.

4. The teacher asks the students to identify Nora's acts of sour power and lists them on the chart under the heading.

5. The students then construct and share alternative super power responses that Nora could have made and the teacher lists them in the second column under *Super*.

6. The students are then divided into groups of two, three, or four for *Sort It/Scene It*.

7. Each group is given a simple setting, written on a piece of paper, such as *on the playground, with mom or dad, at a friend's house, with a brother or sister,* or *in the lunchroom* with an accompanying icon.

8. The students are instructed to come up with two ways, a sour power and super power way, that show anger being expressed in that situation or setting.

9. Each group creates two scenes, one showing the sour power way of expressing anger and the other showing the super power way. The students are coached to take on roles of characters in the setting and come up with a line or two that can express the anger.

10. The teacher conferences with each group to facilitate the activity and make sure that the students have read the setting correctly and are on track with developing their two scenes.

11. Each group takes a turn presenting their two scenes. The other students guess which scene portrays the sour power response and which portrays the super power response.

12. After all the scenes are viewed, the students are provided with a sheet of paper that follows the two-column format on the easel. The first column is headed *It came out sour*. The next one is headed *I can make it super*. The teacher places a large copy of the format on the easel and models how to personally respond with situations from their own lives.

13. The students write their responses in the appropriate columns.

14. Students gather together and reflect on the activity, sharing their independent writing and personal connections to the text and scenes.
15. Students insert homework sheets into their journals.

Evaluation

Did students understand and demonstrate the difference between super and sour power? Were they able to come up with and write alternatives for Nora? Were they able to express anger in role and distinguish between the language of super and sour power in the scenes? Did each student make personal connections and transfer the information to their writing? Did each student share those connections through oral expression?

Materials

- Big book *Noisy Nora* by Rosemary Wells
- Chart paper
- Formatted paper for independent writing response

Home Activity

We have been reading and writing about different feelings, especially anger, that affect our behavior and the way we handle situations. The expressive language aspect of our program teaches that it is not necessarily "bad" to feel and express anger, as long as it comes out in a way that does not hurt, insult, or disrespect anyone else. A strong expression of anger can help us to solve problems, protect ourselves, and stand up for what's right. Most of us think that the "right way" to express anger is by "using nice words" or "saying sorry." This confusion can cause children to disconnect from their anger in a manner that creates even more aggressive reactions or social withdrawal. We are teaching that the expression of anger is best accomplished by using strong words that begin with "I" and speaking about our own experience in a way that authentically expresses the anger, helps to solve the problem, and doesn't get us into trouble. We refer to this concept as "Super Power." The opposite of super power, "Sour Power," is demonstrated by hitting and any physical aggression, name-calling, blaming, breaking things, shutting down, slamming doors, screaming, and throwing tantrums as a way of expressing anger.

Sit with your child and divide a sheet of paper into two columns, one headed with "Super Power" and the other headed with "Sour Power." Have each member of the family identify and list their own expressions of super and sour power in the columns. Since you are your child's most important teacher, the adults in the family bear the primary responsibility for setting the example and identifying your own sour and super expressions. You can also hang a similar two-column chart on the refrigerator with the headings "It came out sour" and "I made it super!" to help all family members, adults included, transform acts of sour power into super power during the week. A big "I..." on the refrigerator can help to remind everybody to communicate in this healthier, more empowered, and mature manner.

The students enter the room and sign in. Makenna signs in *mad*. Alex signs in *mad* and *sad* and Paul signs in *mad*. The rest of the students sign in *happy*. Aaron comes in late and signs in *happy*. They make their illustrations and move toward their favorite stations as they finish. Makenna comes up to me and whispers, "I got a shot and didn't cry" and goes to the *Family Play House*. As she sets up the different elements of her story, she soliloquizes, "The boys have to sleep in their own beds and the girls sleep on their side…"

We gather the students together for *Check-In* and *Power Messages*. I hand out the faces and say to the group, "I love to hear where you are at and how your day is and how anything is. It is always fair to say whatever is true for you. So if you are sad and mad, we want to hear about it loud and clear! If you are happy, we want to hear about it loud and clear!"

Cordell says, "Happy!" Aaron holds up the happy face and says nothing. I say "Happy?" He says, "No. Happy, happy, happy, happy!" I say "Oh! A lot of happy!" David says, "Happy." Makenna says, "Happy, sad, scared, frustrated, really sad." Alex says, "Sad and happy." Quinn says, "Scared and happy." Paul says, "Mad."

I acknowledge that I see them all and collect the faces. Makenna leans into me and says, "I'm getting an operation on my feet." I lean toward her and say, "Maybe that'll be part of your power message…" We reread the messages from the previous weeks in our *Power Message* book and hand out the wipe-off boards. I say, "Makenna, come on up!" She tells us her power message, "I am happy because I did not cry when I got a shot." The students are stretching out the words and using the charts. All are writing. Aaron writes in a circle. I let him be. He says, "It's tricky to write in a circle." I agree with him.

We prepare for the next activity with a shared reading of the big book *Noisy Nora* by Rosemary Wells to introduce the theme expressing anger. After the reading, we talk about how Nora's anger was expressed. Cordell recalls that she "knocked the lamp down." Aaron says, "She threw the kite!" Paul says, "She threw the marbles!" I say, "Yes! Nora was very powerful, but did her parents listen to her?" They say, "No!" I ask, "Did she get in trouble?" They say, "Yes!" I ask, "Did Nora get what she needed?" They say "No!" I tell them, "Nora had sour power! When our mad power comes out in a way that gets us into trouble, gets the grown-ups mad at us, and doesn't get us what we want, we call it sour power."

I present a page from a chart tablet with the heading *Nora has power!* across the top. Underneath that heading, the page is split into two columns, one side with *Sour* written on top and the other with *Super*. I ask, "What were some of the ways that Nora's mad power came out in a sour power way?" Alex says, "She knocked the chairs down" and I write his words under the *Sour* column. I ask, "How else did her mad come out in a sour power way?" Cordell says, "By knocking down marbles." I write his words in the *Sour* column. Aaron says, "Throwing the kite down the stairs." I ask for more examples. Cordell says, "She knocked over the lamp." I write all of their responses and ask, "Do you think Nora is going to get what she wants by doing these things?" They answer, "No!" I say, "I think she's going to get in more trouble and get more mad and not get what she wants!"

With perfect timing, one of the students asks, "What's this one?" indicating the other column on the page. I say, "Yes! This side says *Super*. Nora is mad and I want her mad to come out. I don't want it to stay stuck inside, but, I want Nora's mad to come out in a way that gets the grown-ups to listen to her so she can try to get what she wants without getting into trouble. Instead of knocking the chairs down (referring to the words on the chart), who can think of some super power words that she can say instead to get her mad out?" Aaron says, "I am mad!" Makenna says, "I want you to listen to me!" Cordell says, "Please can you play with me?" I say, "Yes Cordell, those are terrific and important words…what words could she use to say her mad?" I model, "I'm mad because…" Cordell, in an angrier tone, says, "Can you play with me?" He is still in the "orbit" of the other with regard to this concept. With one more attempt he comes up with "I'm mad because you won't play with me!" That is closer to what we are looking for. My goal is to enable the students to express anger independently through self-identified language, words that identify their state of being rather than what someone else is doing to them.

I divide the students into three teams. Each team gets a "secret" paper saying, *School, Family,* or *Friends.* I tell the teams that they are getting a paper with a word on it that names a place where they might get mad. I explain that each team needs to make two scenes; one showing a sour way mad can come out at that place and one showing a super way it can come out.

Cordell, David, and Paul get the *Friends* paper. They come up with and practice the idea of two friends playing while a third seeks to join them. Cordell says, "Hi guys can I play?" They ignore him. He says, "I hate you!" to illustrate sour power. Cordell suddenly realizes, with a thoughtful, reflective, and apologetic tone, "I do that. I say it that way to my friends sometimes."

We are ready to act the scenes to the rest of the class. The audience has to guess where the team is, which scene is super, and which one is sour. The *Friends* team goes first. They do their sour power scene. Someone says, "Sour power!" We do the second scene. Cordell says, "Can I play with you?" They ignore him as planned. He says, "I'm mad! Why can't I play with you?" Makenna calls out, "Sour! Because he was mad that they wouldn't play with him!" I ask, "Did he call them names or hurt them? Would he get in trouble from his words?" The class answers, "No." I say, "This is what I want us to understand boys and girls. It is OK to be mad if we use our strong super power words like Cordell did. He showed us a good and fair way to get his mad out." The rest of the teams take their turns.

I indicate the chart we made earlier using *Noisy Nora*. We reread the top of the chart: "Nora has power!" I hand out a similar two-columned formatted response sheet to each student for an independent writing exercise that reads, across the top, *I have power!* I tell them to think of a time when their mad power came out sour and list it in the *Sour* column. Then think of and write down how they can turn the mad sour power into super power mad words and write it in the *Super* column. I hand out the papers and pens.

Spontaneously, Cordell says, "When I think I'm going to punch my brother, I go like that (clenching gesture)." Aaron says, "I feel like I want to punch my friends." I say, "Any words you can say Cordell?" referring to his clench. Alex is writing *the is the is the is* on his paper. I say, "Alex, you have to think of some things to write other than *the* and *is* because you are a smart boy with a lot of good ideas!" As they are writing, I hear the students spontaneously saying purposeful and insightful things like "I got a good one!" and "I hit and raise my voice!" We are pressed for time and this process is much more hurried than I want it to be.

I ask, "Who can tell us some of the ways your mad comes out in a sour power way?" Paul reads from his sheet, "I scream and push." Makenna reads, "I yell." Alex reads, "I smack my mom." Cordell reads, "I jump on my brother." Aaron reads, "I hit and yell." They move on to write their super power words, and then we run out of time. It's time to go.

In looking at their papers afterward, I see that some of them got it; some I couldn't tell. Paul, who wrote *I hit, I push, I scream* under *Sour*, wrote what looks like *I'm mad* under *Super*. This is a lesson that needs to be learned over a lifetime.

I called all of the parents this week just to check in, see how the students are doing with the program, explain any homework, and answer any questions. Paul's mother says that Paul loves coming to the classes, but she is concerned about his progress. I explain how, although he is not reading, he is able to write with invented spelling to the point where I can read it as meaningful text. That was surprising and significant information for her. She says she would bring it to the meeting with the first-grade teacher, which was taking place this week, as the school is not aware of this ability.

LESSON 8: *Super Power Hero Cards*

Purpose

- To provide students with a meaningful context that uses literature to analyze and organize information that reflects the theme of personal empowerment, to promote effective response, through oral and written language, to personal situations that cause anger and hinder development of emotionally intelligent expressive language skills.

Concept

- Empower students to reflect and express, by connecting to the read aloud and participating in role-playing and shared and independent writing activities, emotionally intelligent, self-aware responses to personal challenges through oral and written language.

Goal

- Each student will respond to the read aloud by suggesting an empowered response for the main character, reflect on their own personal sense of empowerment, compose, through independent writing, empowered responses to personal challenges, and express the empowered responses orally.

Procedure

1. Students are gathered together for a read aloud of *Chrysanthemum* by Kevin Henkes (1991) that tells the story of a young girl, Chrysanthemum, who finds it difficult to stand up for herself, to introduce the theme of developing empowered language. *Wemberly Worried* by Kevin Henkes (2000), *Chester Raccoon and the Big Bad Bully* by Audrey Penn (2008), *Purplicious* by Elizabeth and Victoria Kann (2007), *Oliver Button Is a Sissy* by Tomie dePaola (1979), or any other text dealing with a theme where the main character is not able to stand up for himself or herself may be used.

2. After some general comprehension questions, the teacher recalls the previous week when the students thought of super power words for Nora and asks whether they can think of any super power words for Chrysanthemum to address her situation.

3. For *Power Words Express*, The teacher refers to a sheet of chart paper on the easel with the heading *Chrysanthemum's Super Power Words* written across the top. The words *I am, I know, I feel, I can,* and *I will* are written underneath with a space for response after each phrase.

4. The students construct empowered responses for Chrysanthemum beginning with those phrases while the teacher writes them on the chart.

5. The teacher then refers to three signs with identifying icons placed at different locations around the room that say *School, Family,* or *Friends.*

6. For *Choose It/Move It*, the teacher asks the students to go to the sign that identifies the place where they wish they had more power in their own lives. The students go to the signs of their choosing.

7.   Referring back to the text, the teacher says something to the effect of, "Victoria and Jo were the ones who showed sour power to Chrysanthemum. Who shows you sour power at school, at home, or with friends (turning to each group as they are identified)?"

8.   The teacher asks the students to draw a picture, after handing out paper and crayons, of a person who shows them sour power in the situation.

9.   The teacher walks around conferencing with the students.

10. The teacher collects the pictures and says, "You helped Chrysanthemum with super power words she could say to Victoria. We are going to write our own super power words to say to the people we just made pictures of!"

11. The teacher shows the students formatted response sheets with the heading *My super power words* followed by the words *I am, I know, I feel, I can,* and *I will* and hands them out with pens for the *Character Development* activity.

12. The students complete the sentences on their response sheets. When they finish, they can choose from a small assortment of simple costume pieces such as capes, hats, scarves, wands, and masks to create super power characters.

13. When the students are ready, the teacher sets aside a chair, places one of the students' pictures in the chair and, using a cheap karaoke type of voice enhancer or microphone, addresses the group in the role of emcee or host as if they were at a convention, for example, "I'd like to welcome you all to the super power hero convention...we've heard of your many powerful deeds and we're looking forward to hearing from you all! So let's introduce our first super power hero! Let's have a big hand for (whoever made the picture in the chair)!!!! (Name), can you tell us who is sitting in the chair? How does (person identified by student) show sour power to you?"

14. The teacher hands the microphone over to the student. It is important, if the purpose of this activity is truly to empower, not to censor the students' sour power subject, even if it's a parent, principal, teacher, or other child in the class, as long as the student is operating in a respectful and purposeful manner. It is an opportunity to accomplish exactly what the lesson intends, to guide the student toward authentic empowered satisfying language that is clear, strong, self-aware, and more likely to meet needs and solve problems. The teacher as emcee then asks the super power hero whether they can demonstrate some of their super power words by addressing the picture of the person in the chair and reading the words to them as if they were there. The student uses the microphone to express and direct the amplified words written on the response sheet toward the "person" in the chair.

15. The students reflect on the text and role-play experience and share related thoughts and comments about each other's empowered language.

16. Students insert homework sheets into their journals.

Evaluation

Did students demonstrate comprehension of the read aloud and construct language, oral and written, relating to the theme of the text? Did students transfer their understanding of the theme to personal experience and construct self-aware language that addressed a challenge in their own lives?

Materials

- *Chrysanthemum* by Kevin Henkes or other text named above.
- Chart paper
- Simple costume pieces such as masks, capes, hats, and fake glasses
- Formatted response sheets
- Voice-amplifying microphone or children's karaoke machine

Home Activity

Sit with your child and discuss the positive things that he or she knows about himself or herself, especially with regard to learning, and take turns writing sentences about what you know. Begin the sentences with I know, I am, I feel, I can, *and* I will. *For example, you may write* I know you are smart *and your child may write* I am good at saying the letters.

Everyone signs in *happy* except Cordell, who signs in *mad* and puts a sad face icon up. I take a quick look at the homework the students hand me. David does not, for the first time, hand it in. I see a note from his mother instead. Many of the parents didn't quite get the concept of *Super* and *Sour Power* and the intelligent way of expressing anger. Super power, not surprisingly, was interpreted as following directions, behaving, doing fun things, or apologizing.

Aaron and his mother got it. For Aaron's *Sour Power,* they wrote *I hit. I throw things. I slam doors. I scream. I kick my sister Jennifer.* Aaron's mom wrote *I spank. I may yell. I sometimes shut down and ignore the problem.* For *Super Power,* Aaron's ideas include *I can say I'm mad. I can hug my sister. I can hug my mom.* Mom's *Super Power* ideas include *I try to redirect thought. I try to speak softer. I try to think before I act. I can give a physical hold instead of spank. I can tell my child it is ok to be mad or angry. I can say sorry if I make a mistake. I know all situations are changeable.*

We put out only three *Center* activities on this day, the *I Have Feelings* listening center, *Feeling Faces,* and *Big Books, Songs,* and *Poems.* To that we add books we have used and books we have published as a class and the three baskets of independent reading books. David is reading with Rosalie. He knows very few sight words, only those with one or two letters. Alex is reading very well. It is a struggle for him to write. Is it the mechanics of letter, word and text formation, composition, expression of his thought process, or a combination? He is reading the *Power Names* book we made on the first day. Quinn walks by him, smiles, and says, "Did you read mine yet?" proudly referring to the page he wrote. Makenna listens and responds at the *I Have Feelings* listening center. For *What does mad feel like in your body?* She writes *yell.* For *What kind of things make you feel mad?* She writes *When my brother tackles my cat.* For *How do the mad feelings come out of you?* she writes *Yell.*

We skip *Check-In* and *Power Messages* today because I want to make sure that we have enough time for the main activity. I tell the class that we will be doing things a little differently today. I read *Chrysanthemum*, a girl who gets teased because of her name and finds it hard to respond, to introduce the theme of building empowered language. The students listen intently. I finish the book and Makenna says, "That's a happy ending!" I say, "That *was* a happy ending, but some not so happy things happened to Chrysanthemum in the story. What were some of the not very happy things that happened?" Cordell says, "They were laughing." I say, "Yes! Who?" He says, "Everybody." I say, "Yes! What were their names?" Makenna says "Victoria!" Quinn says, "Jo!" I ask whether Chrysanthemum said any words to them. Cordell says, "No." I ask, "What did she do?" He says, "Just stared." I recall last week when we thought of super power words for Nora. I ask the class whether we can think of any super power words for Chrysanthemum.

I use a sheet of chart paper with the heading *Chrysanthemum's Super Power Words.* The words *I am, I know, I feel,* and *I will* are written underneath with lines following each phrase. Other phrases that can be added include *I can, I* want, and any other appropriately affirming phrases that follow the pattern. I ask the students, "What could she say? Look at this one...'I am...'" Cordell calls out, "Mad! I am mad!" Rosalie writes it and we say, "Yes! Good one! What else?" Makenna says, "I know my name is perfect!" I write it on the chart and say, "Aahh...'I know'...Great! What else? Quinn?" Quinn says, "I feel happy." Rosalie writes Quinn's response and then adds on to the others, verbalizing as she writes, "I am mad that you are teasing me. I know my name is perfect. I feel happy about my name."

We prompt, "I will..." Rosalie says, "I will...tell the teacher?" I say, "I will...not listen?" Alex adds, "to your mean words." We write it. We praise their use of the words. I say, "Here's the hard question now. Chrysanthemum needed more super power in school. Where do you wish you could have more super power words to get your mad out in your life?" I refer to three signs tacked onto the wall, headed with *School, Family,* or *Friends,* with identifying icons next to the words. I say, "Do you wish you had more power at home in your family, at school, or with your friends?" and direct them to go to the sign that best suits their response.

I bring up Victoria again. I say, "Victoria and Jo were the ones who showed sour power to Chrysanthemum. Who shows you sour power at school (turning to school group), at home (turning to them), or with friends (turning to them)? Think of the person who shows you sour power and draw a picture of them." I hand out paper and markers. We walk around and conference with them to make sure they are getting this. They are. I collect the pictures and speak into the microphone in the small toy karaoke machine to pique interest and say, "You helped Chrysanthemum with mad super power words to say to Victoria. We are going to write our own super power words to say to the people we just made pictures of!"

I show them individual response sheets formatted to look like the chart we just did, with lines after the words *I am, I know, I feel,* and *I will.* I hand out the response sheets, boards to lean on, and pens. Everyone is writing and focused. Aaron gets a little distracted after filling out *I am.* I try to work with him and ask, "What do you know about you?" He shrugs. I say, "I know a lot of things about you. You are smart. You are a good boy. You are helpful. What good things do you know about yourself?" He says, "I am a good brother." I leave him to write that. They are all tuned in to their writing. As they begin to finish, I direct them to some costume pieces and props they can use to create a super power character role through which they may speak their super power words.

For some, the costumes turn out to be somewhat of a distraction. I say, "When you have your super hero power costumes, take your words on the sheets you wrote and come sit in the audience." I take the mike and say, "Ladies and gentlemen super heroes, we see that you have created some super power words to say to those who have shown you sour power! We are going to put the sour power person you drew in this chair (across the room). You will then come up to the microphone and say your super power words to the person!"

I place the pictures in the chair one at a time and the student who drew it comes up to the microphone to speak their super power words. After a few of the students take a turn, I choose David's picture next. I ask him, "Who is sitting in that chair?" He says in a barely audible voice, "Friends." I ask, "What are your friends doing with their sour power?" He says, "Throwing fits at my mom." I notice his sheet refers to hitting. I ask, "Are they hitting you also?" He nods. I say, "Let's tell those friends the super power words!" He reads, in a slow and quiet voice, with my prompting, "I am mad when you hit me. I know that I am strong. I feel mad (these three words come quickly and easily) when I get hit. I will tell you to stop." As I look over David's shoulder at his paper, I see that he has independently composed meaningful and purposeful text that I am able to follow.

Aaron, in a cowboy hat and camera, is next. I ask him who's in the chair. He says, "My family." I ask, "What do you want to say to your family?" He reads, "I am mad!" I prompt his next sentence on *I am:* "I am a ..." He says, "Good." I say, "Good what?" He says, "Brother." Rosalie wrote out the rest for him. I read, "I know I can..." He reads, "...hug you." I read, "I feel..." He says, "...happy when I hug you." I read, "I will..." He finishes, "...be nice to you."

Rosalie says, "Come on Quinn, you ready?" Quinn says, "I don't want to do it." Rosalie says, "Can I read it? I'll read it. This is to Ms...?" Quinn says his teacher's name. I say to the rest of the group: "Oohh it's a teacher. Quinn has super power words for a teacher!" Rosalie reads, "I am mad when you yell at me! I know I am smart! I feel happy when you are nice to me. I will do my work." Quinn smiles.

We have half a minute. I ask the students how the moms and dads did with writing about their sour power in this past week's homework. Makenna says, "Good. We made two columns." I recall that Makenna's mother did not include any of her adult sour power behaviors. I say in general to the group: "Sometimes grown-ups forget to tell about our own sour power, but it's important that we do! What are some sour power things that grown-ups do?" They say, "Yelling! Hitting!" We affirm their responses. It's time to go. I give them their journals.

The activity brought the fictional and real life, subject and object, and oral and written language, in close proximity of each other through the drama, integrating the intelligent language of emotional empowerment within a real-life context.

CHAPTER 9

Composing Personal Narratives

The final group of lessons of the *Literacy Express* engages the students in reading, writing, listening, and speaking to compose an autobiographical project that integrates information and concepts from the previous lessons. The students choose specific situations from their personal lives that evoke emotional response and use their ability with emotionally intelligent language to construct a book of self-aware observations and empowered responses to the specific situations they choose.

Shared reading, writing, and independent writing activities, along with sociometric warm-up, puppetry, *Director's Hand,* and *Director's Chair* activities, prompt development of the students' unique stories, which are then organized and edited by prewriting, drafting, revising, and proofreading exercises for accurate spelling, punctuation, sentence, and paragraph structure. The pieces are then illustrated, bound, and presented orally by the students to affirm an empowered sense of self and emotional intelligence documented and reflected by the symbols of printed text.

LESSON 9: *The Mad Page*

Purpose
- To provide meaningful contexts in which students construct informational texts about subjective emotional experiences that conform to basic objective writing conventions, including processes of prewriting, drafting, revising, and proofreading, to integrate and enhance competence with purposeful oral and written expression that demonstrates emotional self-awareness, empathy, and emotionally intelligent response.

Concept
- Empower students to intelligently express, articulate, and manage personal experiences with anger using shared reading and writing, *Director's Chair,* and independent writing activities, to compose a page of their autobiographical writing project.

Goal
- Each student will respond to the read aloud, participate in the *Director's Chair* activity, and engage the writing process to compose a page of the autobiographical writing project.

Procedure
1. Students are gathered together for a charted, shared reading of a section of *I Have Feelings. How about You?* (see Appendix) that explores intelligent identification and expression of anger.

2. Word study skills and reading strategies are taught, and the students answer comprehension questions by locating words and passages within the text.

3. After the shared reading, the words *More* and *Less* are placed on opposite sides of the room with corresponding expressive icons reflecting anger drawn on each for *Know It/Move It*.

4. The teacher asks the students to move to the word that best describes how mad they get in certain situations, such as *doing homework, eating dinner, taking a bath/shower, getting picked on, reading, looking in the mirror, losing a game, dealing with brothers, sisters, the playground, parents,* and *playdates*.

5. These are read one at a time, allowing the students time to move and respond with spontaneous verbal interaction. The students may suggest criteria as well.

6. The students are then asked to sit on one side of the room, creating an audience section to view a staging and playing area that is at least seven by ten feet. One chair is set apart from the audience area as the director's chair.

7. The students are told that they will each get a turn to direct a "reality TV show" about a time in their lives when they were mad and angry. On the director's chair are optional props of a television remote, a megaphone, and a toy scene indicator.

8. The teacher can provide a large sheet of banner paper, with a number of television screens drawn on it, for the students to write the title of their "show" inside one of the screens.

9. The teacher explains to the students that the director who is chosen to sit in the chair will first tell the story, which has to be from real-life experience, and then cast the roles of the story, including himself or herself, from the rest of the class, and then watch the scene from the chair.

10. The teacher serves as story coach to the director, helping to develop important elements of the scene, such as where the scene takes place, who was there when it occurred, and what lines the actors will need to say to each other. The students in the audience listen to the director's story, hoping to get cast as an actor in the "show." Not all students are cast in each show.

11. After telling the story, the director casts the roles, tells the actors where to stand, provides some lines and yells, "Action!" in the megaphone or holds up the remote and says, "Play!" to start the scene.

12. If the director feels as though the actors are not being accurate enough with their lines, he or she can call "Cut!" or "Pause!" to provide information to the actors that will make the scene closer to the real experience, and call "Action" once again. The teacher can explain to the class that the scenes won't be a perfect rendition of the experience they are enacting, but a close approximation of what happened.

13. After each scene, the teacher asks for a show of hands from the students in the audience who have experienced a similar feeling and situation.

14. The teacher asks for a quick sharing of one or two emotion words from the audience that describe the main character's experience in the scene, and what they think it would be like to personally experience it.

15. The teacher then asks the director to think of any super power words that could help address the situation.

16. The director redirects a part of the scene, directing one of the actors in the show, preferably the one playing his or her role, to use the power words in the scene. The director calls "Cut!" when the scene is completed.

17. When all of the students have directed a scene, the teacher explains that they are going to use their shows to start writing their own book, an autobiography about their lives.

18. They are each given a formatted response sheet that says *I am mad when___, I feel it in my___, The mad feeling comes out when I___,* and *I can say___.* There is a table on the bottom of the page with four rows of three boxes across the page labeled *1st try, 2nd try,* and *correct spelling* adapted from Diane Snowball and Faye Bolton's *Spelling K–8* (1999).

19. After the students write their responses, they find any words they think are not correct in their writing. They then attempt a more accurate spelling of those words by articulating and stretching them out and writing them again in the boxes provided. The teacher provides the correct spelling after their attempts.

20. The students then transfer their writing, including the formatted prompts to a sheet of lined paper with a space on top for illustration. This format will comprise, over the next five weeks, their final project in the form of a published book about their five feelings. The final draft can be copied and composed at a later lesson if time is a factor.

21. The students gather together and share one idea or sentence from their writing.

22. Students insert homework sheets into their journals.

Evaluation

Did the students respond to comprehension questions by locating words and passages in the text? Did they make personal connections to the text? Did each student orally construct an autobiographical story about the emotion and develop a scene directing the other students? Did they respond empathetically to others' stories? Did each student transfer ideas into the independent writing? Did they identify and attempt to correct words they thought were misspelled? Were they able to share their written ideas through oral language?

Material

- Original text of *I Have Feelings. How about You?*
- Director's style folding chair
- Props such as old television remote, plastic megaphone, and scene marker (available at party discount stores)
- Formatted response sheets

- Lined paper with space for illustrations

Home Activity

Sit with your child and have him or her recall, in as much detail as possible, a recent time that he or she felt mad. First discuss it and then ask your child to write down what the anger felt like in his or her body (were their fists clenched, face tightened, heart pounding...?), how the mad feeling came out (tears, yelling, throwing...?), and whether any super power mad words could have helped to deal with the problem. As always, modeling and writing about your own experience is a helpful tool to get your child involved.

David's mother brings him in early and asks whether the program is also geared for reading and writing instruction and not just for emotional disturbance, as she is concerned with his lack of progress. I tell her that the program is filled with reading and writing instruction, and David has made significant progress with being able to write meaningful text that I can read and make sense of. She responds with, "Oh his copying is great, we never had a problem with that. It's the writing on his own that's so hard for him." I say, "Oh no, I am talking about David going off after an activity and independently writing a response that I can read and make sense out of!" I tell her I could show her a number of samples of David's successful independent writing. She is shocked and does not seem to believe me. She says that it would be absolutely "phenomenal" if he was doing that and that he was showing no such progress or ability in his first-grade class.

She also says that although our class and the work activities are "much more challenging" than the work they are providing in his regular classroom, David is much more open to our homework activities and loves coming to our class. She also says that she had previously thought that David was emotionally well adjusted and able to express himself, but now, as a result of our homework activities, she feels that he is not as well adjusted as she thought and has learned the steps to help him with that.

At the end of the class, I show her David's independent writing activity he did that day. She says, "This is incredible!" I am amazed that his first-grade teacher is not aware that David can independently compose meaningful text. It reminds me of the surprise Paul's mother expressed when I told her the same thing about Paul's abilities and that his teacher was not aware either. Maybe it is because we are focusing more on writing meaningful text rather than reading as the primary approach to learning literacy skills. Rosalie confirms that our approach is not the norm.

The students all sign in *happy* except for Alex and Paul who sign in *mad*. The whole class is peacefully reading with focus. We have put away the stations except for the *Feeling Faces* and the *I Have Feelings* listening response center. Like last week, we set up three baskets of books and familiar texts and guide the students to the appropriate levels. One basket has books that have up to three words to a page with repetitive text that follows familiar themes such as *I am...* or *I like...* We also put our *Power Names* book in that area. Paul and David read those books. Books that have two or three sentences per page with familiar themes and the *Fire Day in the Town!* book that we made comprise the second reading area. Quinn, Aaron, and Cordell read there. Books that have paragraphs with familiar themes and our *Magic Jungle* book comprise the third area. Alex and Makenna read from there.

David says to Rosalie, "Can I look at this?" referring to the *Power Names* book. Rosalie says, "Of course!" She reads the other books with him as well. He masters the simple repetitive text and smiles at Aaron while proudly saying, "We read all these books!" Cordell colors a feeling face and writes I feel *mad* when *I get scratched*. He says, "Can I take this home?" I say "Sure" thinking that he needs to show it to somebody, likely his mother who I suspect is having a hard time, especially after seeing their homework responses, feeling comfortable with allowing Cordell and her other children to express anger. Makenna makes a face and writes I feel *happy* when *mom is good to me* and asks whether she can take hers home and whether she can have one for her sister.

I make an announcement saying, "Boys and girls! We are going to be making our Director Chair TV shows today!" They cheer. I say, "Let's do our faces and our power messages!" Paul says, "Where's my Paulie?" as I hand out the faces. I call on Paul. He says, "Mad!" I say, "I see you." David is next. He says, "All of them." I ask whether he can name them. He says, "Happy, sad, frustrated, mad, scared." Alex, Makenna, and Quinn all say, "Happy." Cordell is playing, hiding behind me. I say, "You're trying to trick me! How are you Cordell? Which one are you?" He says, "None."

We transition to *Power Messages*. I ask to hear from them. Makenna says, "I am happy because on Monday I have half a day and today I'm going to call my friend and she might come over!" David is holding his hand up. He says, "I am sad because I have no one to play with and I'm happy because I'll ask my mom and she'll say 'yes.'" Nice increase in range of expression for David.

We do a shared reading of *I Have Feelings. How about You?* printed on large chart paper. David points to the chart page and reads the first word "I!" Rosalie says, "I noticed you recognized the first word 'I' David!" David says, "Mr. Lee read us that story!" Rosalie says, "That's right! You remember!" Paul reads along as Rosalie does a read through. The text reads *No!* and Paul says, "No!" loud and strong. Rosalie says, "Paul you knew how to say it loud because what mark did you see?" Someone, maybe Paul, says "Exclamation!" Rosalie says, "Good!" Rosalie does another read through, letting the students fill in the last word, which she covers with correction tape, of the rhyming pattern.

I have two signs on opposite walls. One says *More* and across the room the sign says *Less*. I tell the students that I am going to say something, and if it makes them more angry, then they should go to the *more* sign, and if it makes them less angry, then they should go the *less* sign. We agree that if what I say doesn't make the students angry at all, then they can go to the middle. I make a very angry and mildly angry face icon to match the *More* and *Less* words on the signs.

I call out a series of words describing objects or events and the students choose which sign to go to. The first word I call is "homework." Alex goes to *More* and volunteers, "I hate it because my teacher erases my work and my mother erases my work!" For *Dinner* and *Bath or Shower*, Alex stays at *More* while most everyone else goes to the middle or *Less*. For *Getting picked on or teased*, everyone goes to *More*. For *Reading*, Alex is the only one at *More*. For *Writing*, Alex is the only one at *More*. He says, "I hate writing because my mom always erases!" I repeat his statement empathetically. He adds, "And so does my teacher!" I say, "And that makes you hate writing…I get it."

We start our Director's Chair Mad Story TV Shows. We have moved from objective and emotionally distanced engagement of the language using techniques such as puppets and fantasy in the earlier weeks. We are now moving into a more personal use of purposeful emotional expression through presentation of realistic scenes from the students' real lives. I indicate the "director's chair," a wooden folding chair with a fabric seat and back, and show them a megaphone and remote control props. I explain that when it's their turn, they will sit in the chair, tell a story about what makes them mad in their real life, cast the different roles in the show with the other students in the room, who will assemble in an arranged area of the room, and call "Action!" into the megaphone to start the show. I tell them they can also use the television remote and push *play* to start the action. I model an abbreviated version of a story from my past involving a shaming teacher who made me feel mad.

Cordell says, "Let me go first!" but Rosalie picks Quinn to go. I reinforce the need to listen to his story so they can act in the show if they get cast. Quinn sits in the chair and tells the story of getting yelled at by his teacher for not doing his work. He chooses Paul to play him and Makenna to play the teacher. They come up to the "stage" area and I quickly reiterate approximate lines that each of them might say. Quinn calls "Action!" and the scene starts. Paul and Makenna successfully reenact Quinn's story. After the scene is over, I ask the students in the audience to think of a word that could describe what it might be like for Quinn in this situation. Paul says, "Scary,

scary aahhh!" Alex says, "Like screaming in my ear, like shouting." Aaron says, "Mad." I then ask director Quinn to "redirect the scene by giving Paul power words to say." He tells Paul to say *I feel mad* and they redo the scene using the power words.

Cordell is next. The story takes place at recess with his friends. They keep throwing him on the ground. I ask whether they are mad or joking when they do it. Cordell says, "Joking." I empathize with him, "But it's not very funny!" He casts Paul as himself and Aaron, David, and Quinn as the three friends. Paul is practicing falling down as Cordell sets up the story. Cordell calls, "Action!" and they play the scene. I ask for empathetic words to describe what it must be like for Cordell. Many of the students yell, "Mad! Mad!" Makenna adds, "Frustrating!" For super power redirection, Cordell tells Paul to say, "Get off me or I'm telling the teacher and the principal!" We emphasize the "I" part of his statement and redo the scene.

David is next. He tells us about being home with his friends who don't listen when he tells them to stop. He chooses Quinn to play him, and Aaron, Cordell, and Alex to play the friends. He says that he tries to get them to go outside. I prompt Quinn to say the lines "I'm going to tell my dad" as per David's direction. I ask what's it like when your friends don't listen and David says, "Mad." We acknowledge that his super power response is already built in to the scene.

Now that they have composed their pieces through the drama, we start the process of composing it on paper. In the formatted response sheets, the students write responses to *I am mad when_____ I feel it in my_____ The mad feeling comes out when I_____ I can say_____*. There is a table on the bottom of the page with four rows of three boxes across the page labeled *1st try, 2nd try,* and *correct spelling* adapted from Diane Snowball and Faye Bolton's *Spelling K–8*. After writing their responses, they find any words they think are not correct in their writing. They then attempt a more accurate spelling of those words by articulating and stretching them out and writing them again in the boxes provided. We write the correct spelling after their two attempts. They then transfer their writing including the formatted prompts to a sheet of lined paper with a space on top for illustration. This format will comprise, over the next five weeks, their final project in the form of a published book about their five feelings.

We put up a model of the response sheet on the easel. I indicate *I feel it in my* and describe what it means. Makenna says, "Heart" when I ask where they might feel it. For *The mad feeling comes out when I*, Cordell says, "I raise my hands and scrunch them." We are ready to write. All are busy and focused. Rosalie and I walk around and conference with the students. Half of them write about the scene they just did. The others write about another mad issue from their lives that I suppose they became warmed up to. Quinn writes about his teacher yelling and feels it in his hands. He is successful with writing self-aware expressive language. David writes *stop* after *I can say*, which is more about controlling the other rather than being empowered with a self-aware statement, such as *I can say I don't like this*, but I am excited that he is writing independently and coherently.

The spelling attempt grid on the response sheet was successful. Everybody except Alex reworked some of the words. The deeper experience evoked by the drama was apparent in the students' writing. Their desire, need, and interest in communicating who they are during the writing activity was more fully engaged, I believe, because of the authentic engagement of the whole person experienced through the dramas. The students could have sat and talked about their experiences, but their active re-creations, initiated through a symbolic, dynamic, and concrete process of bringing personal experience to a social context of shared meaning, evoked a greater presence of personal response evident in the details of their writing.

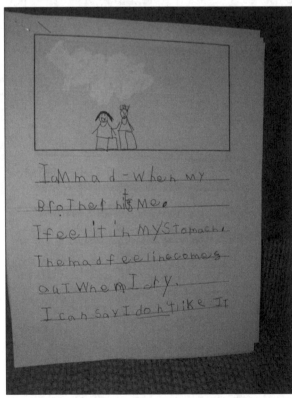

Sample of the mad page from a student's autobiographical final project

As I dismiss the group, David pulls his mom in to the room and glows as he points to the basket of books he read earlier. He says, "Look mom I read all those books!" I show her his response sheet for the day. She is incredulous and thrilled that he was able to do this. Rosalie talks to Quinn's mother. She is surprised that he chose the scene about his teacher and that it affects him so much and that he is willing and able to show it to the whole class. Quinn's ability to be more present and expressive in his dramas reflects, I believe, his increasing ability to express himself more clearly through verbalization and writing, illustrating a link between the expressive forms that facilitates access from one to the other, empowering increased understanding and management.

Aaron's mother, like David's before her, notes that doing the homework for our program, while more challenging, is easier to accomplish with her child compared to his regular classroom homework. Our assignments reflect who the children are and what their experiences are like. Alex's mother tells Rosalie: "All week he looks forward to coming and reading in your group. He asks, 'How many more days until Mr. Lee and Ms. Rosalie?'"

Paul and David's ability to independently construct meaningful text is significant. The fact that these skills are not showing up for them in school, according to their mothers who heard it from the boys' teachers, suggests that the more meaningful connections to reading and writing and the connections between the expressive forms are not being accessed in their regular classrooms.

These responses to our program, the apparent development of literacy skills, increasing ability to verbalize emotional expression, and others such as requests by students to take home copies of the *feeling faces* activity sheets continue to indicate that the interaction of the expressive forms are working together through dramatic enactment to empower abilities and skills in the areas of emotional intelligence and literacy.

LESSON 10: *The Sad Page*

Purpose
- To provide meaningful contexts in which students construct informational texts about subjective emotional experiences that conform to basic objective writing conventions, including processes of prewriting, drafting, revising, and proofreading, to integrate and enhance competence with purposeful oral and written expression that demonstrates emotional self-awareness, empathy, and emotionally intelligent response.

Concept
- Empower students to intelligently express, articulate, and manage personal experiences with sadness using shared reading and writing, a choice of dramatic enactment techniques and independent writing activities, to compose a page of their autobiographical writing project.

Goal
- Each student will respond to the read aloud, participate in some form of dramatic enactment, and engage the writing process to compose a page of the autobiographical writing project.

Procedure

1. Students are gathered together for a charted, shared reading of a section of *I Have Feelings. How about You?* (see Appendix) that explores intelligent identification and expression of sadness. Word study skills and reading strategies are taught, and the students answer comprehension questions by locating words and passages within the text.

2. After the shared reading, the words *More* and *Less* are placed on opposite sides of the room with corresponding expressive icons reflecting sadness drawn on each. The teacher asks the students to move to the word that best describes how sad they feel in certain situations, such as *going to school, bedtime, getting yelled at, getting left with a babysitter, being ignored, a brother or sister getting more than you, watching a sad movie, not getting picked for the team,* and *being left out,* that are read one at a time, allowing the students time to move and respond with spontaneous verbal interaction. The students may suggest criteria as well.

3. The teacher can provide a large sheet of banner paper, with a number of television screens drawn on it, for the students to write the title of their "show" inside one of the screens.

4. Along with *Director's Chair* stories described in the previous lesson, the students are also given the option to present their stories using any of the modalities, *Puppet Express, Director's Hand,* song, costumed role-play, or improvisation, previously used in other lessons. Students can assist in dramatizing others' stories as well as presenting their own. After each scene, the teacher asks for a show of hands from the students in the audience who have experienced a similar feeling and situation.

5. The teacher asks for a quick sharing of one or two emotion words from the audience that describe the main character's experience in the scene, and what they think it would be like to personally experience it.

6. The teacher asks the students to think of any super power words that could help address the situation.

7. When all of the students have portrayed a scene, the teacher explains that they are going to continue writing their autobiography.

8. They are each given a formatted response sheet that says *I am sad when___, I feel it in my___, The sad feeling comes out when I___,* and *I can say___.* There is a table on the bottom of the page with four rows of three boxes across the page labeled *1st try, 2nd try,* and *correct spelling.*

9. After the students write their responses, they find any words they think are not correct in their writing. They then attempt a more accurate spelling of those words by articulating and stretching them out and writing them again in the boxes provided. The teacher provides the correct spelling after their attempts.

10. The students then transfer their writing, including the formatted prompts to a sheet of lined paper with a space on top for illustration. The final draft can be copied and composed at a later lesson if time is a factor.

11. The students gather together and share one idea or sentence from their writing.

12. Students insert homework sheets into their journals.

Evaluation

Did the students respond to comprehension questions by locating words and passages in the text? Did they make personal connections to the text? Did each student construct an autobiographical story about the emotion and develop a dramatic enactment represent-ing its content? Did they respond empathetically to others' stories? Did each student transfer ideas into the independent writing? Did they identify and attempt to correct words they thought were misspelled? Were they able to share their written ideas through oral language?

Materials

- Original text of *I Have Feelings. How about You?*
- Props for the *Director's Chair*
- Puppets and puppet stage or playing area
- Colored scarves and costume pieces
- Materials for *Director's Hand*
- Formatted response sheets
- Chart paper
- Blank response sheets
- Pens, markers, and crayons

Home Activity

Sit with your child and have him or her recall, in as much detail as possible, a recent time when he or she felt sad. First discuss it and then ask your child to write down what the sadness felt like in his or her body (were their eyes filled with tears...faces buried in pil-lows...shoulders slumped down...?), how the sad feeling came out (crying, whining, silence...?), and if any super power sad words could have helped to deal with the prob-lem. As always, modeling and writing about your own experience is a helpful tool to get your child involved.

Alex signs in *mad* while Paul signs in *sad*. Everybody else signs in *happy*. I scan the homework. Alex and his parents wrote *I was so mad one time that my muscles were tightened and I was yelling. I feel like my blood is boiling, muscles tighten up, and I raise my voice. I felt so mad at mommy when she made me do my writing 100 times. I felt like throwing a bottle of syrup. I was yelling and scream-ing, "I am so mad! I hate to do this!" I was crying.* Paul wrote *When my brother hits me I feel mad. I squeeze my teeth together and make a fist. I yell and tell him I am mad and to stop.*

We begin by having the students write their final drafts from last week's formatted and edited responses to the mad stories. During the week, I circled in green and corrected any misspelled words that they were not able to get to. All the students are focused on their writing. There is hardly a sound in the room. I conference with David and Paul as they start to rewrite their work. I tell them, "What a great job you guys did! Look at these words! You were exactly right on some and so close on these others. You had a lot of the right letters! Some of them just need a few more letters!" I want to focus on what is right. We stretch and articulate and write more accurately.

Alex is telling Rosalie that he throws things when he gets mad, and that he keeps it in otherwise. They work to find something he can say to get it out effectively. Alex works hard and is successful with his writing and his expression. Then he starts to randomly cross words out on his final copy. We say, "You don't need to cross anything out! You did a great job!!" It was almost as if it were an automatic reflex for him. Makenna makes *Feeling Faces* after she is through with her mad page. Many of the students have come to use this activity almost as a comforting ritual. Makenna writes I feel *happy* when *I am good* on the paper. She also asked to take a blank one home for her brother.

We read through the *Power Message* book together. We start handing out wipe-off boards and dry erase markers. We acknowledge that Aaron, David, and Alex need to write in the book. I say, "Aaron, anything mad happen this week?" He says, "No." I excitedly say, "For real?" Then I say, "Alex, come on! We need help!" Alex comes up and says, "I am mad because I did not get the computer fan." We say the message together. We count the words in the message. We clap and chant the letters in the words. We stretch and listen for sounds. David and some of the others start writing in a circle. I say, "Let's not play the writing in a circle game." Rosalie says, "Right, because when we're writing books we read side to side and move to the next line."

A few of the students are a little "off" with their writing and keeping up as we compose the message in the book and on the boards, maybe because there was a week off for Thanksgiving. Aaron is again a helpful presence, cleaning up, cooperating, much different than what his mother reports about his relentlessly destructive behavior in school and at home.

Rosalie reads the charted *I Have Feelings. How about You? Sad* section. At the end of the passage it asks *How about you?* Cordell spontaneously volunteers, "I hate it when my brother calls me a jerk when he takes my scooter. I feel like hitting him." He makes a personal connection to a passage in the text, which reads *when my brother calls me a baby and a jerk.*

We do the *More/Less* criteria for sadness, during which the students move between the signs as objects and events are named. For *Bedtime*, Makenna goes to *Less* and says, "I got to stay up and watch 'Frosty!'" They make their choices for *Getting yelled at* and *Having a babysitter*. We measure

Brothers and sisters getting more than me and *Getting blamed for things.* For *Leaving me out,* David moves to *Less* and says, "They leave me out all day."

For this lesson, I offer the students the puppet stage, costume pieces, the toy figures and house, or the director's chair to construct scenes and shows around the sad events that occurred in their lives for the next page in their books. They set out to prepare their stories. I help Aaron, Paul, and Cordell who choose the puppet stage. They are very inspired by the puppets but are able to focus on sad situations from their lives and plan their shows together.

Aaron starts with a sad story about when his sister goes to college. Cordell plays his sister. I ask him how the sad comes out. Aaron says it stays in. Paul is sad when his father goes to work in the morning. Aaron plays his father. I ask Paul how his sad comes out. Does he cry? Does he say "I'll miss you?" Paul says he cries. Cordell is sad when his father goes fishing and doesn't take him. He says, "I am going too!" and cries. I ask the audience whether any of them have an older brother or sister they miss. Makenna says she feels sad when her older cousin leaves after a visit.

I ask the audience, "Whose daddy goes to work and stays for a long time and you miss him? Some of us have daddies who don't even live at home. Some of us have daddies who live in other houses. Sometimes we're there, visiting at the daddy's house...Anybody know about that sad feeling?" Aaron's hand is raised. I say, "Aaron, what do you want to say?" He slowly says, "My mom and dad are getting a divorce." I say, "Aaron, what's it like for you? Mad? Sad? Scary? Frustrating?" Aaron says, "Scary."

Alex chooses *Director's Chair.* His sad story takes place in his toy room. He says, "My mom makes me do extra homework. Then I walk right out and then my mom's supposed to say, 'Come back here' and then I don't come back." He picks Paul to play him and Makenna to play his mom. He clarifies and directs as he sets the scene up between the two. "No, you do your homework in the playroom...You think you're done, you go and don't come back." Paul tries a primal scream of "No!" Alex corrects him with "You just be quiet, go like this (sighs) and don't come back." The scene enacts to his satisfaction. He redirects it with the power words "I want to be done!"

A somewhat reluctant David comes to the chair. I say, "What's something sad that happens to you David? It could be something that happened to somebody else, something you saw on TV..." David says, "When I fall." He picks Paul to play him. I ask, "How does the sad come out? Do you cry? Stay quiet?" He says, "I stay quiet." We direct Paul to trip and hold in his sad. David calls "Action." Paul trips, cries, and smiles. I call "Cut!" I say, "Paul, listen to the direction, you can do it! I know you are a really good actor so try to do it without smiling. David trips but he holds in his sad." David calls "Action" and Paul does a truly accurate and moving job. I say, "Wow! Great job!"

We hand out the response sheets that follow the same format as the previous week, substituting *sad* for *mad*. Everyone is focused on composing and writing and attempting new words. Quinn writes about his sister pushing him. David writes about tripping. Paul writes about his dad going to work. Alex writes about his mom yelling at him. Makenna writes about going to her room and feeling it in her foot. Aaron writes about his sister going to college and Cordell writes about his father going fishing without him. They are identifying the words they feel are misspelled and stretching and articulating for more accuracy. We write in the correct spelling when their attempts are not entirely successful.

As we dismiss, David says to Rosalie, "Remember last week when I was so smart? Do you remember that whole bunch of books I read? Do you think I can read those books again?" Rosalie says, "Sure!" David says, "OK, then tell my mother to pick me up at 2:00." We are delighted and respectfully laugh at his enthusiasm. Rosalie gives the books to his mother to take home for the week.

We are excited about how focused the students are in their writing and impressed with how aware and in depth their descriptions are with regard to how they feel their feelings.

The experiences and feelings that are being expressed through the concrete forms of the dramas are showing up in the composition of their work. Authentic feeling around experience, rather than the objective content of the experience itself, is the driving force that is linking the verbal, dramatic, and written forms of expression, empowering the students' progress with emotional intelligence and literacy skills.

LESSON 11: *The Scared Page*

Purpose
- To provide meaningful contexts in which students construct informational texts about subjective emotional experiences that conform to basic objective writing conventions, including processes of prewriting, drafting, revising, and proofreading, to integrate and enhance competence with purposeful oral and written expression that demonstrates emotional self-awareness, empathy, and emotionally intelligent response.

Concept
- Empower students to intelligently express, articulate, and manage personal experiences with fear and anxiety using shared reading and writing, a choice of dramatic

enactment techniques and independent writing activities, to compose a page of their autobiographical writing project.

Goal

- Each student will respond to the read aloud, participate in some form of dramatic enactment, and engage the writing process to compose a page of the autobiographical writing project.

Procedure

1. Students are gathered together for a charted, shared reading of a section of *I Have Feelings. How about You?* (see Appendix) that explores intelligent identification and expression of feeling scared. Word study skills and reading strategies are taught, and the students answer comprehension questions by locating words and passages within the text.

2. After the shared reading, the words *More* and *Less* are placed on opposite sides of the room with corresponding expressive icons reflecting a scared feeling drawn on each. The teacher asks the students to move to the word that best describes how scared they feel in certain situations, such as *the first day of school, the dark, watching scary movies, getting yelled at, dogs, meeting new friends, getting picked on, roller coasters, swimming in the deep end, getting hit,* and *trying new things,* that are read one at a time, allowing the students time to move and respond with spontaneous verbal interaction. The students may suggest criteria as well.

3. The teacher can provide a large sheet of banner paper, with a number of television screens drawn on it, for the students to write the title of their "show" inside one of the screens.

4. Along with *Director's Chair* stories described in the previous lesson, the students are also given the option to present their stories using any of the modalities, *Puppet Express, Director's Hand,* song, costumed role-play, or improvisation, previously used in other lessons. Students can assist in dramatizing others' stories as well as presenting their own. After each scene, the teacher asks for a show of hands from the students in the audience who have experienced a similar feeling and situation.

5. The teacher asks for a quick sharing of one or two emotion words from the audience that describe the main character's experience in the scene, and what they think it would be like to personally experience it.

6. The teacher asks the students to think of any super power words that could help address the situation.

7. When all of the students have portrayed a scene, the teacher explains that they are going to continue writing their autobiography about their lives.

8. They are each given a formatted response sheet that says *I am scared when___, I feel it in my___, The scared feeling comes out when I___,* and *I can say___.* There is a table on the bottom of the page with four rows of three boxes across the page labeled *1st try, 2nd try,* and *correct spelling.*

9. After the students write their responses, they find any words they think are not correct in their writing. They then attempt a more accurate spelling of those words by articulating and stretching them out and writing them again in the boxes provided. The teacher provides the correct spelling after their attempts.

10. The students then transfer their writing, including the formatted prompts to a sheet of lined paper with a space on top for illustration. The final draft can be copied and composed at a later lesson if time is a factor.

11. The students gather together and share one idea or sentence from their writing.

12. Students insert homework sheets into their journals.

Evaluation

Did the students respond to comprehension questions by locating words and passages in the text? Did they make personal connections to the text? Did each student construct an autobiographical story about the emotion and develop a dramatic enactment representing its content? Did they respond empathetically to others' stories? Did each student transfer ideas into the independent writing? Did they identify and attempt to correct words they thought were misspelled? Were they able to share their written ideas through oral language?

Materials

- Original text of *I Have Feelings. How about You?*
- Props for the *Director's Chair*
- Puppets and puppet stage or playing area
- Colored scarves and costume pieces
- Materials for *Director's Hand*
- Formatted response sheets
- Chart paper
- Blank response sheets
- Pens, markers, and crayons

Home Activity

Sit with your child and have him or her recall, in as much detail as possible, a recent time when he or she felt scared. First discuss it and then ask your child to write down what it felt like in his or her body (were their hearts racing...body trembling...hands in front of face...?), how the scared feeling came out (screaming, crying, laughing...?), and if any super power scared words could have helped to deal with the problem. As always, modeling and writing about your own experience is a helpful tool to get your child involved.

I met during the week with David's parents. Their initial thrill and surprise upon seeing his writing samples earlier in the week gave way to veiled disappointment, it seemed, regarding the books Rosalie sent home with them. They, mostly the mother, felt that he just memorized the books and wasn't "reading" them on a level that the school was expecting him to read. I pointed out that if they asked David to find words such as "I" and "am" in the text, he would be able to do so. They agreed. I also suggested that he could find the word "red" on a page of text, even if he was reading it mostly from memory. They agreed, saying he would find it by recognizing the "r." I reassured them that these skills are key to emergent reading and repeated exercises such as this would soon build into fluent reading with one-to-one matching. This is a first-grade boy, I thought to myself, who came into our program eight weeks ago recognizing a little more than half of the alphabet and no sight words. The fact that he now recognizes a number of words and can decipher and construct meaningful text is a big jump.

They were polite but did not seem convinced and mentioned some other interesting discrepancies. They said that David's teacher is concerned that David recognizes hardly any simple sight words such as *and* and is not writing. I told them that I can think of a number of times when David spontaneously recognized words, such as the time when the "am" fell out of the bag and he identified it, and I have seen firsthand how he has recently learned to independently compose meaningful text. I showed them the chart sheet when he broke through and moved from responding with random strings of letters to writing meaningful text. They said they appreciated my interest and asked me if they should have David write assignments for our class the way the school instructs him to write, "making sure the letters touch the top and bottom of the lines on the paper."

The fact that David's first-grade teacher has not identified any of his emerging abilities made more sense to me now after hearing that. I tell his parents (as I did in the orientation) that in our program we are connecting to meaning and content before mechanics, so they don't have to worry about the letters touching the lines for my assignments. It seems as though David loses his emergent skills when they are not supported by the integration of meaningful experience accessed through the other forms of expression.

I think what a terrible mistake it is, at least in David's case, to teach reading and writing the way he is learning it in his school. Focusing on the more specific and detailed parts of reading and writing mechanics before engaging personal meaning was not working for David. The fine-tuning of mechanics, making sure one's *e* is touching the top and bottom line, can always be addressed later on a foundation of meaningful connection. I don't think meaningful connection can easily be established on a foundation of mechanics, especially if such a foundation is fraught with doubt, frustration, and shame.

I also spoke with Aaron's mother during the week. She shared with me that in church, Aaron asked her for pen and paper and spent his time, rather than fidgeting and arguing with her, writing things like *I like movies. I like to eat,* on the paper. His mother said that he had never requested writing as a recreational activity. Any writing that Aaron has done has always been in the context of a power struggle, according to his mother. I recall that last week, Aaron said he hates reading and writing and that it is "dumb." What he and other students for that matter hate is the method of instruction, the dissociation from purposeful meaningful content, and the affect created by teacher and student around the activity of reading and writing. I don't sense any hate on Saturday mornings when we read and write, some frustration yes, but not hate.

Cordell and Aaron sign in *mad*. Paul signs in *sad*. Makenna and David sign in *happy*. We move right into writing final drafts for our sad stories from the previous week's formatted response sheets. I collect the homework. David did a lot of writing this week. For *Sad*, he wrote *Ian is a big fat liar. I hate Ian forever*. For *Mad, I feel mad when somebody hits me. I feel mad when my friends do not listen. I hold it in*. He also made a *Super/Sour Power* chart, writing *You are mean! I hate you! I am not talking to you!* For *Sour* and *I am happy. I am mad. I am sad. I am frustrated. I am scared* under *Super*.

Rosalie tries to encourage Cordell toward his writing work. He is resistant and whining, moving toward the *Feeling Faces*. I tell Rosalie to let him settle in and do a face first before he gets to his writing. It is incredibly quiet. Everyone except Cordell is completely focused on his or her writing. David rereads his piece to Rosalie. Rosalie mentions to me that he is reading with one-to-one matching, recognizing and identifying individual words. Later on, she mentions how David's mother gave her the books back with no enthusiasm or acknowledgment of David's abilities while he was standing right there. I share the conversation I had with his parents earlier in the week. Apparently, the conditions and environment we create in our program make it safe for David to read and write here.

Cordell comes to me with his feeling face colored in. It has a mad expression and no words. I ask what the face is showing. He says, "Mad." I ask him what's making him feel so mad. He shrugs and withdraws. I suggest, "When I have to write?" He nods. He is otherwise very shut down and will not write it. I write it as he spells the letters for me. He works with Rosalie to write his final draft for *sad*. She tries to elicit some response from him. He does go to the sign-in board and gets a card with *sad* written on it and brings it back to his paper. Rosalie works with him to find out what makes him sad. He whines, "I'm sleepy." We notice that he looks sad and sleepy and suggest, "I am sad when I'm sleepy?" He nods. They take turns writing his words.

We make the transition to *Power Messages*. I say, "Come on over and sit. I want to tell you something about power messages. Making a connection, Aaron says, "Oops, I forgot to sign in!" He does so. I say, "I know that writing can sometimes be really hard. Do you know why we want you to write?

We want you to write so you can have more..." Makenna says, "Learning!" I say, "Yes! What else?" I indicate the *Power Messages* book next to me on the easel. "What's this?" The students say, "Power Messages!" I say, indicating the word *Power*, "What does this say? Look at that first letter..." They say, "P!" I say, "Right! So what could that word be?" They say, "Power!" Paul sings, "Power power!" I say, "Yes. When you say and write 'I am mad' or 'I am sad' it gives you more power because..."

Cordell interrupts by moaning, "It's hard." I say, "I know it's hard, Cordell. It's hard for a lot of us, but, when you write what's going on inside of you, the grown-ups can hear you, listen to you, and understand what you are trying to tell them and then sometimes you can change it or fix it together. That's how it gives you more power. That's why we do our power messages. Some of our power messages are mad; some are sad, and some are happy and we want the grown-ups to listen to you. When you feel mad, we don't want the grown-ups to say 'Stop acting that way. Don't be mad. Be nice.' We want the grown-ups to say, 'Oh! I get why you're mad. Let's see if we can fix it or help it to get better...' So, to have more power, we have to let the grown-ups know. That's why we're writing the words and reading the words about being mad, sad, scared, frustrated, and happy, so you can get more practice and have more power. That's why we want you to write. Not just because we're forcing you and that's what you have to do. We want you to have more power."

Makenna says, "I am happy because I am going to the mall today!" I say, "David, how about you?" He says, "Happy." I say, "Can you think of a reason why?" He answers, "I'm going over a friend's house." I turn to Cordell and say, "How about your words, Cordell? What are your mad words today?" He slumps. I playfully say, "Oh no! Cordell's losing power!! No one's going to know about his mad!! We want to hear his mad words! 'I am mad because...' Can anybody guess?" David raises his hand. I say, "Yes! David?" He says, "Look over there" pointing to the sign-in board. I want to support his somewhat loose association. "Yes! Let's look! Today he wrote...do you know what the orange card says, David?" David says, "Mad!" I say, "Now who has a guess of what Cordell's mad words might be? Go ahead, Makenna." She says, "I am mad because I can't go to sleep late?" Cordell shakes his head no. Aaron says, "Mad because he didn't want to write?" Cordell shakes his head no.

Rosalie, referring to an incident that I hadn't seen, guessed, "Are you mad because you didn't go first on the sign-in chart?" Cordell nods. I say, "Is that it? Ms. Rosalie got it? Wow! Can you say the words 'I'm mad because I didn't get to sign in first on the sign-in board'?" Cordell says, "I don't want to say it." I say, "You know what though? If you can say it, guess what I can do for you? I can write down *save first spot on sign-in chart for Cordell next week.*"

Cordell says, "I'm mad because I didn't get to sign-in first." I say, "Do you want to be on top next week? You can because you told me and that helped me to understand you're mad. This is so important! If Cordell just held in his mad and curled up and didn't want to write and went 'uungh' when we spoke to him, he wouldn't get what he wants and the teachers and friends might even get mad at him because his mad was coming out on us in a sour power way. But Cordell said the words 'I am mad because I didn't get to sign in first,' and I can say, 'Oh! I get your mad! I understand it and now we can do something about it!' So, I'll write it down for next week. You get to sign in first." Cordell has a complete change in affect. He is smiling faintly and sitting up rather than withdrawing in a fetal or passive position. For the rest of the day, Cordell shows marked improvement in his attitude, cooperation, and willingness to read and write.

Aaron steps up to the easel to write his power message. He says, "I am mad because I can't go to the mall." Rosalie has them say the message together and count the words. We hand out wipe-off boards and markers. Before beginning to compose together in the *Power Messages* book, David holds up his board, beaming, having already written the words *I am* on it. We say, "Great David! We know *I am*…Hey! We know *mad* too!" They all write it automatically. Rosalie continues, "We've also had a lot of practice with *because*…How does it start? Right, *b, e*…then /c/, /c/, like in *cat*…Good! *c!* Now remember that /au/ sound?" David pops out with "au!" I am impressed with his memory and associations that are really starting to develop. "Great David!" We stretch the word out. The students say, "s!" as the next letter. Rosalie says, "And what's that silent letter at the end?" They call out, "e!" Rosalie says, "Look at that! You all remember how to spell *because!*"

We go through the rest of the message. Aaron takes the lead in spelling *can't* and the sight words *I, go, to* and *the*. We stretch out the word *mall*. The students are proud of their writing and spontaneously hold up their boards periodically to show their work. I say, "Let's cap the markers and put away the boards so we can get ready for our scared stories!" Rosalie reads through the charted portion of the *I Have Feelings* text that talks about feeling scared. The students read the last word of each line with her on the second read through.

We do the *More/Less* criteria for *Scared*, and the students move between the signs, sharing and commenting on their choices as they go. For *Reading* and *Writing*, David, Cordell, and Paul go to *More*. I address the group and say, "It is scary sometimes to try and get your letters and words right. I've also heard you guys say that you hate reading and writing and that it's dumb, but when I read what you write, and when I listen to your ideas after you read, I think your reading and writing is so smart!"

I tell them that we are going to show a story of when we felt scared using the puppet stage, dollhouse, or director's chair like last week. David, who was conferencing with Rosalie while the other students were preparing their shows, chooses the director chair. He gets in the chair and anxiously says, "Uuuuuuhhhhhhh" when I ask him to tell a scary incident that happened to him. Rosalie says, "I remember. You woke up in your house and mom wasn't there. Dad was at work and grandma was outside gardening." I say, "So you were scared because you were all alone in your house?" David nods. "Who can play you?" David points to Aaron, and we start the scene. I coach Aaron and narrate as he looks for his family and gets increasingly agitated until he sees his grandma outside. I ask the group whether anybody ever got lost or thought they were alone. Various responses included getting lost in a store or outside, leading to scared feelings that caused shaking and crying. They offered consoling power words such as "I know I'm safe and I can call 911" and David redirects the scene.

We go over the same formatted response sheet that looks at the feelings and provides opportunities to attempt new words. The students are very focused on their writing, conferencing their ideas, reflecting on where they felt the feeling in their bodies, figuring out super power words they could say, writing, circling the words that they think aren't right, stretching them out and trying again. After Paul finishes writing, he asks whether he can go look at a book. I say yes and saying an excited "Yes!" he eagerly goes to get the *Fire Town* book the class made weeks ago.

The students continue to become more comfortable and skilled with word problem solving and composition of thoughts when representing their experiences. As they focus on and engage in the communication of their experience with specific detail, description, and articulation accessed through the drama, they demonstrate a parallel investment and enthusiasm for the "fine-tuning" of their written expression through word problem solving.

LESSON 12: *The Frustrated Page*

Purpose

- To provide meaningful contexts in which students construct informational texts about subjective emotional experiences that conform to basic objective writing conventions, including processes of prewriting, drafting, revising, and proofreading, to integrate and enhance competence with purposeful oral and written expression that demonstrates emotional self-awareness, empathy, and emotionally intelligent response.

Concept

- Empower students to intelligently express, articulate, and manage personal experiences with frustration using shared reading and writing, a choice of dramatic enactment techniques and independent writing activities, to compose a page of their autobiographical writing project.

Goal

- Each student will respond to the read aloud, participate in some form of dramatic enactment, and engage the writing process to compose a page of the autobiographical writing project.

Procedure

1. Students are gathered together for a charted, shared reading of a section of *I Have Feelings. How about You?* (see Appendix) that explores intelligent identification and expression of feeling frustrated. Word study skills and reading strategies are taught, and the students answer comprehension questions by locating words and passages within the text.

2. After the shared reading, the words *More* and *Less* are placed on opposite sides of the room with corresponding expressive icons reflecting frustration drawn on each. The teacher asks the students to move to the word that best describes how frustrated they feel in certain situations, such as *getting a wrong answer, losing a game, making a mistake, not getting what you want, a brother or sister getting more than you, doing chores, not getting picked for the team,* and *being left out,* that are read one at a time, allowing the students time to move and respond with spontaneous verbal interaction. The students may suggest criteria as well.

3. The teacher can provide a large sheet of banner paper, with a number of television screens drawn on it, for the students to write the title of their "show" inside one of the screens.

4. Along with *Director's Chair* stories described in the previous lesson, the students are also given the option to present their stories using any of the modalities, *Puppet Express, Director's Hand,* song, costumed role-play, or improvisation, previously used in other lessons. Students can assist in dramatizing others' stories as well as presenting their own. After each scene, the teacher asks for a show of hands from the students in the audience who have experienced a similar feeling and situation.

5. The teacher asks for a quick sharing of one or two emotion words from the audience that describe the main character's experience in the scene and what they think it would be like to personally experience it.

6. The teacher asks the students to think of any super power words that could help address the situation.

7. When all of the students have portrayed a scene, the teacher explains that they are going to continue writing their autobiography about their lives.

8. They are each given a formatted response sheet that says *I am frustrated when___, I feel it in my___, The frustrated feeling comes out when I___,* and *I can say___.*

There is a table on the bottom of the page with four rows of three boxes across the page labeled *1st try, 2nd try,* and *correct spelling.*

9.   After the students write their responses, they find any words they think are not correct in their writing. They then attempt a more accurate spelling of those words by articulating and stretching them out and writing them again in the boxes provided. The teacher provides the correct spelling after their attempts.

10. The students then transfer their writing, including the formatted prompts to a sheet of lined paper with a space on top for illustration. The final draft can be copied and composed at a later lesson if time is a factor.

11. The students gather together and share one idea or sentence from their writing.

12. Students insert homework sheets into their journals.

Evaluation

Did the students respond to comprehension questions by locating words and passages in the text? Did they make personal connections to the text? Did each student construct an autobiographical story about the emotion and develop a dramatic enactment representing its content? Did they respond empathetically to others' stories? Did each student transfer ideas into the independent writing? Did they identify and attempt to correct words they thought were misspelled? Were they able to share their written ideas through oral language?

Materials

*   Original text of *I Have Feelings. How about You?*
*   Props for the *Director's Chair*
*   Puppets and puppet stage or playing area
*   Colored scarves and costume pieces
*   Materials for *Director's Hand*
*   Formatted response sheets
*   Chart paper
*   Blank response sheets
*   Pens, markers, and crayons

Home Activity

Sit with your child and have him or her recall, in as much detail as possible, a recent time when he or she felt frustrated. First discuss it and then ask your child to write down what it felt like in his or her body (were their fists clenched...feet stamping...tears on their faces...?), how the frustrated feeling came out (screaming, crying, whining...?), and if any super power frustrated words could have helped to deal with the problem. As always, modeling and writing about your own experience is a helpful tool to get your child involved.

Everyone is focused on writing their final drafts from last week's *Scared* response sheets. I spontaneously call out, "We are going to make the coolest books out of these!" I look at their homework as they hand me their books.

David walks over to the *Power Message* book and says, "Today I do this." I hear Makenna say, "Cordell, are you happy or sad?" Aaron comes in and signs in. I say, "Aaron, you're frustrated today?" He nods. I say, "Guess what stories we're doing today? Frustrated!" Everyone is doing his or her work. The room is quiet except for a low focused buzz of letters and words being stretched out as the students write.

I announce, "Let's get ready for power messages!" David says, "I need to do this today." I ask to hear everybody's power messages. Makenna says her power message first: "I am happy because I am going to Florida." Quinn is next with "I am happy because I'm going to New York City to see the big tree." We "oooh" and "aaah" and he says, "Wait, there's more...I'm going to see the Christmas show too!" I say, "How about your frustrated, Aaron?" He says, "I am frustrated because I can't go anywhere..." I repeat his message and say, "I am frustrated too for you!" He continues "...And I have to do homework!" There is a common buzzing about homework and frustration.

We call David up to the easel. He says his message. We count twelve words. We start forming the message. David writes *I am* automatically, like everybody else. Quinn spells *happy* as everybody writes it. David is doing great, spelling and writing, especially words like *to* and *my* with confidence and success. He actually spelled *to* with two *o*'s, but was not at all put off or upset when we pointed out the three different ways to spell *to*. He rereads his message with one-to-one matching.

We read the charted piece *Frustrated* from the text *I Have Feelings. How about You?* Rosalie says, "I am going to read it first, then you read it with me." I add, "Think about what you hear in the poem and see if the same stuff happens to you, in the things that happen and the feelings in your body."

She asks, after the first read through, "Who remembers how the frustrated feelings came out?" David and Paul recall passages from the poem describing frustrating events and how they felt on the person's body. Rosalie reads it again as the students read the last rhyming word of each line. At the end, when it asks, *How about you?* I pose the question directly to the students. Cordell says, "When my brother hits me." Paul says, "When my brother doesn't let me play with him."

We start the *More/Less* activity. Who can say where they feel frustration in their body?" Paul says, "My stomach." Aaron says, "My heart." I call out the criteria. For *Getting a wrong* answer, Quinn goes to the middle, everyone else is at *Less*. Paul and Aaron go to *More* for *Making a mistake*. For *Not getting what you want* and *When brothers or sisters get more than you*, everyone goes to *Less*. They are spontaneously differentiating between frustration, sadness, and anger as they choose. Paul goes to *More* for *Doing Chores*. He also goes to *More* for *Not getting picked for the team*, while David goes to *Less* for

Being left out, claiming "I'm happy when they leave me out." I ask them to come up with their own ideas. Quinn says, "Flipping backward off a swing" and goes to *More*. Paul says, "When my brother doesn't want me to play with him" and goes to *More*.

I ask the students to think about a story from their lives that is frustrating for them and pick the family house, puppet show, or director's chair to show it. Aaron goes to the puppet stage. I work with him and try to create interest in the writing response activity to come. I say, "Let's think of the super power words we can say when we're writing so mom can understand your frustrated words." Aaron pops a puppet out of the stage and says, in a low, throaty voice, "I hate these freaking chores!" Paul hears Quinn telling Rosalie about his director's chair story about when he flipped backward off of a net he was swinging on and Paul starts quietly auditioning for the role in front of Quinn.

Makenna enacts her story in the family house. She narrates, "My dad was walking inside and my brother and sister were in their beds. I took them out and I put them on the couch. Then they snuck away. Then my mom came in and they jumped on her." I ask, "Which part was frustrating for you, Makenna?" She answers, "When I couldn't concentrate on my homework." I say, "Ah. Makenna, can you have the Makenna doll say any super power frustrated words?" She takes the doll, goes up to the mother doll, and politely says, "Mom, I can't concentrate on my homework!" I say, "Can you say those words in a strong, frustrated voice?" looking for the balance between assertiveness and respect. She says, "My mom will say it's too mean and I'll get in trouble." I coach her toward a balanced response that's not too mean.

Quinn is up in the director's chair. He tells us how he was swinging on some golf netting in his backyard and he flipped off of it. I ask him how his frustration came out. He answered, "I cried." I say, "Mad or sad crying?" He says "Mad crying." I say, "Ok who will play you?" He chooses Paul, who is ecstatic. Quinn tells us that he needs to cast his sister who was also in the backyard and picks Makenna for the role. They play the scene and I ask the group whether anybody ever felt frustrated from getting hurt. I tell them that I get frustrated when I stub my toe into the furniture. There is a buzz of agreement and sharing about "my leg one time…" and other types of frustrating injuries.

David sits in the director's chair and tells us about his three friends who knocked on his door and came in anyway after he told them they couldn't come in. I say, "Wow! That is frustrating! How did your frustration come out?" David says, "I went 'Hhhmmmm!'" He chooses Paul to play him and Aaron, Quinn and Cordell to play the three friends. They play the scene. David says, "I have to play with them every day." I say to the audience, "Who gets frustrated with their friends?" Aaron raises his hand and says, "I had some stinky ones before." I ask, "Who can think of some super power words David can say?" The students offer various appropriate responses until Paul says, "Get out of here you rats!" I say, "Whoops! Calling them names would make it…" They answer, "Sour power!" He chooses a super power phrase and redirects the scene.

I go over the *frustrated* response sheet with them, reading "feel it in my…" Someone spontaneously calls out, "Heart!" I continue, "it comes out…" Someone else yells out, "Yell!" I continue, "I can say…" Someone else calls out, "I am mad!" We walk around and conference with the students as they write with enthusiasm and focus. Some of them indicate the words that they got "wrong." I reframe it by pointing out that they got three out of five letters in the word "right."

We notice how much freer and spontaneous the students are with identifying the feeling of the emotions in their bodies and composing the super power words. Rosalie notes that they are writing with less hesitation and are much more comfortable taking pen to paper. They are describing and articulating, in detail, personal feelings and experiences through dramatic and written forms. The transitions between these forms are guided by the spontaneous, emotionally intelligent responses that they are enthusiastically verbalizing with more and more consistency. As the students become freer and more comfortable with these transitions, the expressive forms begin to integrate as a "whole" system for learning.

LESSON 13: *The Happy Page*

Purpose
- To provide meaningful contexts in which students construct informational texts about subjective emotional experiences that conform to basic objective writing conventions, including processes of prewriting, drafting, revising, and proofreading, to integrate and enhance competence with purposeful oral and written expression that demonstrates emotional self-awareness, empathy, and emotionally intelligent response.

Concept
- Empower students to intelligently express, articulate, and manage personal experiences with happiness using shared reading and writing, a choice of dramatic enactment techniques and independent writing activities, to compose a page of their autobiographical writing project.

Goal

- Each student will respond to the read aloud, participate in some form of dramatic enactment, and engage the writing process to compose a page of the autobiographical writing project.

Procedure

1. Students are gathered together for a charted, shared reading of a section of *I Have Feelings. How about You?* (see Appendix) that explores intelligent identification and expression of feeling happy.

2. Word study skills and reading strategies are taught, and the students answer comprehension questions by locating words and passages within the text.

3. After the shared reading, the words *More* and *Less* are placed on opposite sides of the room with corresponding expressive icons reflecting happiness drawn on each. The teacher asks the students to move to the word that best describes how happy they feel in certain situations, such as *going on vacation, winning a game, getting good grades, hearing your parents say they are proud of you, getting along with your brother or sister, weekends, ice cream,* and *having a play date,* that are read one at a time, allowing the students time to move and respond with spontaneous verbal interaction. The students may suggest criteria as well.

4. The teacher can provide a large sheet of banner paper, with a number of television screens drawn on it, for the students to write the title of their "show" inside one of the screens.

5. Along with *Director's Chair* stories described in the previous lesson, the students are also given the option to present their stories using any of the modalities, *Puppet Express, Director's Hand,* song, costumed role-play, or improvisation, previously used in other lessons. Students can assist in dramatizing others' stories as well as presenting their own. After each scene, the teacher asks for a show of hands from the students in the audience who have experienced a similar feeling and situation.

6. The teacher asks for a quick sharing of one or two emotion words from the audience that describe the main character's experience in the scene and what they think it would be like to personally experience it.

7. The teacher asks the students to think of any super power words that could help address the situation.

8. When all of the students have portrayed a scene, the teacher explains that they are going to continue writing their autobiography about their lives.

9. They are each given a formatted response sheet that says *I am happy when___, I feel it in my___, The happy feeling comes out when I___,* and *I can say___.* There is a table on the bottom of the page with four rows of three boxes across the page labeled *1st try, 2nd try,* and *correct spelling.*

10. After the students write their responses, they find any words they think are not correct in their writing. They then attempt a more accurate spelling of those words

by articulating and stretching them out and writing them again in the boxes provided. The teacher provides the correct spelling after their attempts.

11. The students then transfer their writing, including the formatted prompts to a sheet of lined paper with a space on top for illustration. The final draft can be copied and composed at a later lesson if time is a factor.

12. The students gather together and share one idea or sentence from their writing.

13. Students insert homework sheets into their journals.

Evaluation

Did the students respond to comprehension questions by locating words and passages in the text? Did they make personal connections to the text? Did each student construct an autobiographical story about the emotion and develop a dramatic enactment representing its content? Did they respond empathetically to others' stories? Did each student transfer ideas into the independent writing? Did they identify and attempt to correct words they thought were misspelled? Were they able to share their written ideas through oral language?

Materials

- Original text of *I Have Feelings. How about You?*
- Props for the *Director's Chair*
- Puppets and puppet stage or playing area
- Colored scarves and costume pieces
- Materials for *Director's Hand*
- Formatted response sheets
- Chart paper
- Blank response sheets
- Pens, markers, and crayons

Home Activity

Sit with your child and have him or her recall, in as much detail as possible, a recent time when he or she felt happy. First discuss it and then ask your child to write down what it felt like in his or her body (were they jumping...tickly inside...smiling...?), how the happy feeling came out (laughing, talking, skipping...?), and if any super power happy words could have expressed the feeling. As always, modeling and writing about your own experience is a helpful tool to get your child involved.

It is December 22 and only four students, Alex, Quinn, Cordell, and Aaron, show up. Cordell, Alex, and Quinn sign in *happy*. Aaron signs in *mad*. While Quinn is finishing his *scared* piece, he tells us that he got really scared the other day when his father grabbed him in the theater. His homework reflects the event. He wrote *When my dad pulled me in the city, I was shaking. I did nothing. Later I told my dad I was sad.*

On the bottom of the page, Quinn's mom writes *Quinn was in the aisle of the theater as the show was letting out. His father grabbed him out of the aisle, away from the people leaving. Quinn uncharacteristically said nothing, no yelling, no tears, no anger at all. Later that night, he started a conversation with his dad about how that episode made him sad and upset.* This is another example of how the students are spontaneously using written language to identify and support verbal expression of complicated emotional situations. On another page, Quinn wrote *At school I wouldn't ask anyone for a pencil. I covered my face and acted up.* His mother continued for him. *I didn't use any super power words. I could have said, "Can I borrow a pencil." Then I would have finished my project.*

The boys work on their final drafts of last week's frustrated stories. They also work on unfinished drafts and illustrations from previous weeks. Cordell asks whether he can change how he wrote about the scared feeling in his body. I tell him, "Of course!" Cordell is on track with writing today. Aaron is writing, as long as I frequently coach him. Alex and Quinn are eagerly writing on their own. Quinn muses in a thoughtful and reflective way that he always gets "mixed-up with 'then' and 'than.'" Alex, who had originally wrote *nothing* on his *sad* page elaborates his sad story by explaining that his mother and father yell in Armenian, leaving him sad and worried that they are yelling about him. We praise his insight and he proceeds to write, in detail, about the experience, a detailed expansion of perspective from the *nothing* that he originally wrote on his paper. He writes the expanded version on his final draft.

I read the charted *Happy* from *I Have Feelings. How about You?* with the students. I ask them to read the last word of each line by looking at the first letters of the word and following the rhyme scheme. I ask them at the end of the read through: "What makes you happy?" Cordell says, "Fishing!" Alex says, "When my teeth pop out!" Quinn doesn't know and Aaron says, "Traveling."

We do the *More/Less* activity. First on my list is a good segue from Aaron. I call out "Vacation." Quinn, in the middle, says "On a long ride I get bored in the car." We acknowledge his thinking. Everyone, except Quinn, goes to *More* for *Getting good grades*. Same for *When your parents are proud of you.* He stays in the middle. Cordell goes to *Less* for *Getting along with your brother or sister.* The group splits on *Ice cream.* I ask for their suggestions. Quinn says, "Getting in trouble." They all go to *Less* except for Quinn, who says with a shy, sly smile on his face, "I like it a little." It's an interesting and potentially significant insight for him.

I tell the boys that it is time to make our happy stories using the director's chair, playhouse, or puppet stage to show a happy story from our lives. There is a general buzz as the boys share their happy stories and events from their lives and prepare their shows.

I ask Aaron whether he's ready. He says, "Yes," and sets up a scene in his kitchen. He chooses Alex to play his role and Rosalie to play his mom. He gives them their lines. He tells Alex to say, "Oh man, how come I have to do the dishes every day?" I say, "How are you when the dishes are done?" Aaron says, "Happy." I say, "Great, let's do the frustrated part and see it turn into happy." They play the scene. I ask, "How does the happy come out, Aaron?" He says, "I'm finished! I don't have to do nothing else! Now I can go watch TV!"

Quinn, who has an anxious and tentative approach to presenting his ideas to the group, is coaxed by Rosalie to direct a show of when he baked cookies with his mother for the holidays. He picks Alex to play his role and Rosalie to play his mom. He explains how he twirls two pieces of dough together to make a candy cane while Alex and Rosalie go through the motions.

The rest of the group plays their scenes and starts writing their response sheets. I work with Aaron, trying to help him identify how his happy feeling comes out. He says it doesn't come out. I try to explain and help him understand that I saw two ways that it came out in his story. It came out by walking to the TV after he was finished, and it came out with his words. He had a tough time and seemed distracted with regard to that particular concept of how the happy comes out of him. He finally wrote that the feeling comes out *when I'm done*, which finishes the statement but in a more objective, rather than subjective, self-aware way. The boys all finish their writing.

By facilitating a whole expressive system of learning, the students are more empowered to initiate and articulate emotionally intelligent expression through verbal and written forms.

LESSON 14: *I Am*

Purpose
- To provide students with a meaningful context in which they can expand and document a positive sense of self, and acknowledge and express positive aspects of others, through oral and written language.

Concept
- Empower students to identify and express, through dramatic and independent writing activities, an empowered sense of self represented by written language, and compose the *I am* page, the title page, and the final page of the autobiographical independent writing project.

Goal
- Each student will identify and express a positive aspect of self and others in the class and complete the *I am* page, title page, and final page of the autobiographical independent writing project.

Procedure

1. Students are gathered in front of a sheet of chart paper on the easel headed with the words *I am*.

2. For *Do and Tell*, the teacher writes a list on chart paper on the easel as the students identify the many roles that they have in their lives, such as *artist*, *brother* or *sister*, *athlete, son* or *daughter, swimmer, student, dancer, friend, joker, reader, writer, cousin,* and so on. This can be embellished with a simple game of charades, in which students can act out a role while the rest of the class guesses, culminating with the student proclaiming, "I am a (role)!" as the teacher writes it on the paper.

3. For *Spotlight Kid*, each student then takes a turn sitting in the "spotlight chair," any chair set apart from the group, possibly decorated in some special way, like with a strand of rope lights.

4. Students take turns saying positive things that they notice about the person in the chair to support development of ideas for the *I am* page. Three or four comments for each turn should suffice.

5. The teacher shows the students the *I am* response sheet, which lists the words *I am* followed by lines for written response.

6. The students rewrite their drafts onto a final copy and are ready for the final binding of their books. Another page may be added composed from a formatted response sheet with the prompts of *I am good because, I wish,* and *When I grow up*.

7. The students choose a front and back cover from a variety of construction paper colors.

8. The teacher conferences and reads through each book with the students, who then create and write a title and their names on the front cover.

9. The teacher binds the pages together, beginning with the *I am* page, then *mad, sad, scared, frustrated,* and *happy,* and staples them between the colored covers chosen by the student.

10. Each of the students practices reading their books from the author's chair in preparation for the following week's publishing party.

11. The students use the remainder of the time to partner up and read their books to each other to practice for the next week's publisher's party.

12. Students insert homework sheets into their journals.

Evaluation

Were the students able to identify an expanded sense of roles within the context of their own lives? Were they able to recognize and express positive qualities about themselves and other students in the program? Were they able to transfer this knowledge to their independent writing? Did they create and compose authentic meaningful language in their autobiographical writing projects?

Materials

- Completed pages from autobiographical writing projects
- Formatted response sheets

- Chart paper
- Blank response sheets
- Colored construction paper
- Pens, crayons, markers

Home Activity

Write a letter to your child acknowledging his or her improvements with regard to read-ing, writing, and using super power feeling words. Then have your child write a letter to himself or herself about the same topics. Ask your child to write about what he or she is good at, and what he or she wants to get better at, in reading, writing, and using super power feeling words.

Aaron and Alex sign in *mad*, and the rest of the students sign in *happy*. We are finishing the pages for our books and writing the final drafts from previous weeks. David, who came in half asleep, is working hard stretching out and writing words. He spells *laugh* as l-a-f. I tell him he is "so right to spell it that way, but it's a weird word which has letters that you don't hear." I spell it out for him.

We gather for *Power Messages*. Quinn says, "I am happy because I am going to Disney World in February!" Paul says, "I am happy because next summer I may go there too!" Aaron says, "Mad!" and he wants us to guess. We guess reasons regarding his mom, school, sister, being in group, but he says no to all. He finally tells us, with a smile, that he is mad because he couldn't go first on the sign-in chart, copying Cordell from a previous week. Alex says he is mad because he likes being mad. He says this with a smile on his face.

I focus the class on a large sheet of chart tablet paper with the words *I am* written on it as a heading. We brainstorm and list some of the things that we are, through shared writing. Quinn says, "I am happy." Alex says, "I like to fix computers with my dad." I say and write, "I am a computer fixer." Aaron says, "I like to go skiing. I am a skier." Paul says, "I am an artist." Aaron says, "I am a football player." Quinn says, "I am a basketball player." Paul says, "I am a soccer player." I wrote the responses.

Each student takes a turn in the "spotlight chair" and we say things that we notice about the person to support development of ideas for the *I am* page. Alex is first. He sits in the chair. Aaron says, "You are an artist." Quinn says, "You are a computer fixer." Rosalie says, "You are a great reader." I say, "You are funny." Paul says, "You're a good friend."

Aaron is next. Paul says, "You're an artist" Rosalie says, "You're a good helper. I remember when we were writing on the boards and you helped the other kids." Quinn says, "You're a brother." I say, "You're a good boy."

Paul is next. Rosalie says, "You are such a good actor!" Aaron says, "You're a good kid." Quinn says, "You're a nice brother." Quinn is next. He is at first reluctant to sit in the chair but as we go with it and start to say what we think about him, he moves to the chair and sits in it. Rosalie says, "You are a good listener and a great reader and writer." Paul says, "You are a nice brother." Alex says, "You are a good friend." David, who is just finishing his drafts, is reluctant to come to the chair. He is visibly exhausted from all the writing work he has done. We address him from where he is sitting. Quinn says, "You are nice." Alex says, "You are funny."

I show them the *I am* response sheet, which follows the format of the other response sheets, and they go to work. They are all focused and writing. It is helpful for Aaron to have his responses available for copying from the list on the chart paper. He copies the ones that he added to the list. They rewrite their drafts onto a final copy and are ready for the final binding of their books. They choose a front and back cover from a variety of construction paper colors. We read through their books with them, and then the students create and write a title along with their names and dates on the front cover.

Quinn's title is *How My Feelings Come Out!* Alex's title is *My Happy and Mad Story.* Paul's title is *My Book.* Aaron's title is *Aaron's Adventures.* Overworked David just writes his name on the cover for now. Each student practices reading his or her book from the author's chair in preparation for next week's publishing party. They are all enthusiastic and focused. We have a few minutes left so Rosalie reads aloud some of the books we created as a class. As she goes through the texts, the boys listen intently and excitedly shout out, "That's mine!" when we come across a page that they wrote.

Quinn's mother comes up to me as we dismiss and says that Quinn came into her room the other night and proceeded to tell her and her husband about why he had such a bad day. She said it was something that he had never done before, and he expressed his frustrations in a mature, appropriate manner.

All of the students transferred their ideas about who they are onto the page of their books. Quinn and David included the observations and comments from others about who they are. Everybody constructed a title that communicates a sense of ownership of the ideas, feelings, and experiences represented in the book.

LESSON 15: *Author's Celebration*

Purpose

- To provide students with a public forum through which they can read their auto-biographical writing projects and affirm an emotionally intelligent sense of self-awareness and empowered response to personal challenges and experiences.

Concept

- Empower students to have their perspectives heard and positively responded to at a publishing party attended by family members in which students take turns reading their autobiographical writing projects and receiving written affirmations from the audience.

Goal

- Each student will read their autobiographies and receive affirming responses from the audience.

Procedure

1. After an initial period in which any unfinished business or project is addressed with the class, guests, parents, and family members are invited in to assemble in a part of the room set aside for an audience.
2. For *Proclaim It*, students take turns sitting in the author's chair and reading their books out loud. For *Affirm It*, audience members are given slips of paper and pens.
3. After each student reads, audience members write a quick personal response on a piece of paper that is collected in a baggie and given to the student to take home, along with their books and face masks of the five feelings.
4. After all students have read their books, healthy snacks such as muffins and juices can be served while students show their parents their pages and work from earlier class books and projects.

Evaluation

Were the students able to read their books? Did they seem comfortable and proud showing the parents their work?

Materials

- Slips of paper, pens
- Clipboards for leaning on
- Baggies
- Snacks

It is the last morning of our program. David's father arrives to give me David's homework journal and tell me that David is at home throwing up. Makenna is not here either. I will mail them their books and face masks. I think it was hard for the parents to understand the process, the fact that each session is connected to the previous and successive sessions, comprising a whole, rather than fragmented way of learning.

Alex and Aaron sign *mad* while Paul, Cordell, and Quinn sign in *happy*. In the homework journal Aaron's mother writes *Mom feels giggly when she is happy. The sunshine makes me happy. When my children are well I am happy.* Aaron wrote *Ashley makes me happy. Jesus makes me happy.* For another homework, Aaron's mother writes *Aaron has begun using more words than using hands negatively. He is expressing himself with words more. Mr. Lee's class was very helpful. Mom uses power feeling words more also.* Aaron wrote *I am good at math. I want to read better.*

Alex's mother wrote a two-page letter to Alex citing his improvements with reading and writing and his use of self-aware language to express what he is feeling. She wrote *It is great to hear you say "I feel angry when you yell at me."* Alex then writes *I am good at nothing.* Then, with his mother doing the writing, he dictates, *Dear Mom and Dad, I am good at riding my bike. I am good at reading in front of the whole entire class. I am good at playing with my Playstation. My handwriting is improving thanks to my great mommy.*

The students are practicing reading their books for accuracy and fluency before the guests come in. Quinn is anxious and says that he doesn't want to read when the parents come in. We tell him Rosalie can read it. I set up the snack area for later. Aaron had said that he wanted cheese and crackers for the party. I show him that I got what he asked for along with some cookies and muffins. There is more anxiety in the air than excitement. I explain how the process will work, with each child taking his turn reading his book in the author's chair while all the parents write comments about the book on a piece of paper provided to them. As the next student prepares to go, I will collect the comments and place them in a baggie for each student to take home.

Also contained in the baggies will be their sets of faces that we used in previous sessions and evaluation sheets for the parents to fill out and bring in next week. After everybody reads their books, they can get some snacks and look at the comments that audience members wrote with their own parents. They will then bring their books, comments, and faces home.

Aaron is pretty shut down. I ask him to do a practice read through. He stares at me blankly with a flat affect. I encourage him some more. No response. I sincerely ask him whether he thinks he can read the book. He shakes his head no. I tell him that's why we've got to practice. Rosalie says, "Remember when we read it together last week? We'll do the same thing." I ask the group what order they want to go in, whether anybody wants to go first. Paul raises his hand. I say, "You want to be up first?" Quinn says, "I want to be up last." Alex says, "I want to be up last." Cordell says, "I want to go second."

We do our *Power Message* for the last time. Paul says, "I am happy because we're having a party." Alex says, "I am mad" and I didn't catch the rest of what he said. I ask Aaron about where he is at. He shrugs. I say, "It's hard to know where you're at today, right? We don't really know." I ask Cordell how he is. He says, "Mad!" I say, "Mad because…?" He shrugs. I ask Quinn how he is and he says he doesn't know. In an aside, I laughingly say, "Great culmination we're having here" to Rosalie, noting the irony that the students not knowing how they feel. They were anxious…a new one to try and verbalize.

We open the door and invite the parents and siblings in. They sit down and I give them each clipboards with paper. I ask the parents to respond to each reading by writing any comments down about what they hear. I tell them that we encouraged the children to be honest and to try and not worry about being embarrassed by anything their children wrote. Rosalie sits next to the author's chair to provide any necessary support.

Paul reads first. His voice is very quiet but he is reading with one-to-one matching, not from memory. His book, entitled *My Book,* reads *I want to be a doctor. I am six. I am a brother. I am an artist. I am mad when the bully hits. I feel it in my mouth. I push. I can say I am mad. I am scared when I go in haunted houses. I feel it in my stomach. The scared feeling comes when I scream. I can say I miss mom. I am sad when my dad goes to work. I feel it in my stomach. The sad feeling comes out when I cry. I can say, "I miss you." I am frustrated when I get a nail in my foot. I feel it in my heart. The frustrated feeling comes out when I cry. I can say I never should have stepped on that nail. I am happy when my mommy gets me a toy. I feel it in my stomach. The happy feeling comes out when I hug. I can say thank you.* Everybody claps. I collect the comments they wrote into the baggie and set it aside.

Aaron is next. Aaron's voice is shaking. I realize how anxious he is. Rosalie and Aaron read together: *Aaron's Adventure. I am 7. I am a boy. I am a football player. I am a skier. I am mad when I cannot go outside. I feel it in my hands. The mad feeling comes out when I say curse words. I can say this is not fair. I am scared when my sister breaks the TV. I feel it in my legs. The scared feeling doesn't come out. I can say be careful. I am sad when my sister goes to college. I feel it in my heart. The sad feeling doesn't come out. I can say call me. I am frustrated when I can't go to play. I feel it in my legs. The frustrated feeling comes out when I say I feel like hitting. I am happy when I do the dishes. I feel it in my legs. The happy feeling comes out when I am done. I can say I am happy I am done.* Everybody claps. I collect the comments.

Cordell is next. He sits in the author's chair and reads: *My Book. I am mad when I get scratched. I feel it in my belly. The mad feeling comes out when I scream. I can say leave me alone. I am scared of nothing. I feel it in my eyes. The scared feeling comes out when I scream. I can say I am scared. I am sad when I am sleepy. I feel it in my eyes. The sad feeling comes out when I don't want to do any-*

thing. I can say I am sleepy. I am frustrated when my brother bites me. I feel it in my eyes. The frustrated feeling comes out when I squeeze. I can say stop it. I am happy when I open my presents. I feel it in my arms. The happy feeling comes out when I smile. I can say I am happy. Everybody claps and I collect the comments.

Rosalie reads for Quinn as he stays in the audience. She reads, *How My Feelings Come Out! I am happy. I am a boy. I am a basketball player. I am nice. I am mad when my teacher yells at me. I feel it in my hands. The mad feeling comes out when I yell. I can say I am mad. I am scared when it is dark. I feel it in my heart. The scared feeling comes out when I run away. I can say put the lights on. I am sad when my sister pushes me. I feel it in my hands. The sad feeling comes out when I cry. I can say I am sad. I am frustrated when I flip off the swing. I feel it in my hands. The frustrated feeling comes out when I cry. I can say stop. I am happy when I bake cookies. I feel it in my hands. The happy feeling comes out when I bake. I can say I like baking.* Everybody claps and I collect the comments.

Alex is next. He quietly tells Rosalie that he is scared. She tells him that they will read it together. They read, *My Happy and Mad Story. I am a boy. I am 6. I am in the first grade. I am a computer fixer. I am mad when I don't get the red keyboard. I feel it in my hands. The mad feeling comes out when I throw things. I can say I don't like it. I am scared when I see the green face. I feel it in my mouth. The scared feeling stays in. I can say nothing. I am sad when my mommy yells in Armenian. I feel it in my head. The sad feeling comes out when I go to my room. I can say what are you talking about? I am frustrated when my teacher makes me do my dittos 100 times. I feel it in my head. The frustrated feeling comes out when I write sloppy. I can say give me the eraser. I am happy when I have to do the dishes. I feel it in my hands. The happy feeling comes out when I say yippie.* Everybody claps and I collect the comments.

I offer some affirming, supportive words about the students' and parents' participation and tell everyone to get a snack, look over their comments in the bags, and then look at the other books, which were displayed around the room, we published during the fifteen weeks. I tell the students to show the parents and siblings the pages that they wrote in the class books. As people mill about, I ask Aaron whether he was scared and he nodded. I say, "Oh! That's what was happening this morning!" He nods again. I tell him that saying the words about it really can help, even if it's just a little.

David's book, which I gave to his father at 9:30, reads *I am a boy. I am a nice guy. I am a baseball player. I am six years old. I am mad when my friends don't listen. I feel it in my belly. I can say stop. The mad feeling comes out when I cry. I am scared when I can't find my mom. I feel it in my heart. The scared feeling comes out when I call my Ellen! I can say don't leave the house. I am sad when I trip. I feel it in my heart. The sad feeling comes out when I get quiet. I can say I got hurt. I am frustrated when my friends come in my house and don't listen. I feel it in my heart. The frustrated feeling comes out when I say get out. I can say listen to me. I am happy when I am going to my cousin's house. I can feel it in my heart. The happy feeling comes out when I laugh. I can say stop.*

Makenna's unfinished book that I mail to her along with her faces reads *I am mad when my mom yells at me. I feel it in my heart. The mad feeling comes out when I yell. I can say no mom. I am scared when my mom yells at me. I feel it in my foot. I can say I'm scared. The scared feeling comes out when I yell. I'm sad when I go to my room. I feel it in my foot. The sad feeling comes out when I hold it in. I can say I'm sad. I am frustrated when my mom yells at me. I feel it in my foot. The frustrated feeling comes out when I yell. I can say I'm mad and sad.*

Everybody is snacking and checking out the other class books. The initially quiet, even tense atmosphere that the morning started with finally has fallen into more relaxed tones. The parents and the children seemed to mirror each other's anxiety before the reading.

The final autobiographical independent writing projects were a result of collaboration between verbal, dramatic, and written forms of expression that empowered students' access between and within each of the expressive forms. As "whole" texts, they integrated and documented the process from the previous fourteen lessons, facilitating communication of personal experience with emotionally intelligent language.

During reassessment and evaluation we were impressed with how much the students' writing composition had improved. Their ideas, represented by meaningful text, had become clear and comprehensive, comfortable and fluent, with full sentences and thoughts. They wrote independently and with confidence. Paul's mother shared with us that Paul took initiative and wrote and performed a five-page story with his friend, for fun.

Summary

From the first lesson, I believe that the students responded positively, enthusiastically, and successfully to the program because every task strove to reflect each individual's identity, authentic emotion, and real-life experience. Throughout the fifteen weeks, the students eagerly identified sights, sounds, and situations connected to emotions. Their emotionally intelligent oral and written responses were evident in the structured and spontaneous responses to the activities of the program. Their homework responses reflected development of emotionally intelligent communication skills, according to the parents, at home and in other areas of their lives.

The students expressed personal emotional responses to various fantastical and real-life scenarios with self-aware, independently constructed language. A range of responses facilitated by the activities of the program—from identifying a specific emotion of a character from a book, to choosing between the five feelings, to considering multiple perspectives of an emotional situation, to making an open-ended choice of emotion for role, to expressing empathy toward their peers and the real-life situations that they presented—were consistently expressed by the students with focus and enthusiasm.

Educational drama techniques engaged the whole person, unified development, deepened the experience, and integrated connections between oral and written emotional expression. By operating within the "as if" guidelines, educational drama provided a symbolic form that accessed personal, real-life emotional content, and facilitated its expression in a safe and acceptable, fictionalized context. This process of opening emotional feeling and then containing it within dramatic forms of expression allowed a full range of emotion, including primal and regressed, to be expressed. This integration facilitated deeper understanding and connection between personal, subjective experience and shared, objective learning tasks.

This deeper understanding and connection served as a tool to help process the development of reading and writing skills. The sign-in chart, *Center* activities, *Check-In*, and main activities all facilitated this integrated connection between emotional intelligence and meaningful text. The abstract codes and symbolic forms of the letters, words, and illustrations of class books, and the word problem solving skills used to create them, became symbolic extensions and reflections of the students' deeper understanding of their unique experiences. This form of personal reflection motivated the students to pursue expertise with deciphering and applying those codes and skills in order to represent and express themselves in the clearest, most empowered way. In this mutually enhancing relationship, reading and writing skills also served as tools to help process the development of deeper emotional understanding and connection.

For some students, relative comfort and ability with written language helped to organize, manage, and express emotion verbally. For others, verbal expression of emotion helped to organize, construct, and compose written text. Each form of expression—dramatic, written, and oral—prompts the safe containment and healthy release of emotional experience. Each form functions as a container and vehicle for further development in the other.

Perhaps most importantly, these troubled students, experiencing marked difficulties with learning and appropriate behavior in their regular classrooms, really seemed to enjoy the experience. The oral language of emotional intelligence, the process of educational drama, and the approach of balanced literacy functioned as connected parts of a whole integrated system of learning. Within this system, personally relevant subjective information interacted with objective forms to bring enhanced awareness, understanding, and skills to both domains. By unifying development in one whole process, meaningful authentic experience guides and empowers learning, generating a dynamic educational experience where personal meaning expressed through shared contexts, and objective understandings acquired through subjective experience, are inseparable components of learning.

PART III

Building Community, Character, and Social Skills

An Integrated Approach to Social Studies Instruction

CHAPTER 10

Constructs of the Approach

The social studies program for elementary students establishes and studies the experiences of three communities, *classroom, research,* and *virtual,* to facilitate understanding of community history, geography, economics, civics, and citizenship, while students simultaneously learn to effectively function in the communities they are studying.

Through educational drama and emotional intelligence techniques, students research and interact with the tools, materials, and concepts listed in *New York State Standards for Social Studies,* including time lines, map skills, and flow charts, and create procedures for community management such as charters and voting, to gain understanding of how a particular community functions. By integrating emotional intelligence skills within the social studies curriculum through thematic ensemble enactment, students, in addition to gaining greater access to objective information required by curriculum standards, are empowered to explore, assess, and develop their own character and social behavior as it manifests in the communities they are studying.

As in the *Literacy Express* program, educational drama provides students with the opportunity to access and explore a greater range of emotional expression and social behavior without fear of reprisal for content that might otherwise be deemed inappropriate or unacceptable in the setting. As previously stated, students are not held responsible or judged for enactment that occurs within the boundaries of the drama, as long as safe, appropriate, and respectful standards for general classroom behavior are upheld during the enactments. If a student chooses to be an angry or sad farmer, for example, the teacher does not look to pressure the student to make a more "positive" choice or imply that it would be better to be a happy farmer. The students' choice of how to play a role within the thematic enactment is seen and facilitated as an opportunity for deeper understanding regarding the objective and subjective topics being studied.

Educational drama establishes the connection between authentic subjective emotion and otherwise meaningless objective information that fuels, as discussed in part I, a powerful paradigm for learning. Besides functioning as an essential element in the process of cognition, the tools and techniques of educational drama, including role, costumes, set materials, props, and dialogue, serve as symbols of shared meaning that simultaneously represent both subjective and objective information. The symbolic representation of dramatic enactment is able to fuse, in a sense, objective details and information about a community, time line or map skills, for example, with a deeper, already ingrained aspect of purposeful awareness, understanding and memory stemming from the students' meaningful subjective experience.

The proximity of the objective and subjective information, residing in the same representative symbol, prompts students to invest meaning and connection from the subjective into the objective, generating greater access to and deeper understanding of each source of information. Educational drama creates a dynamic in which objective information is encountered and processed by the individual's subjective experience in a manner that generates meaning, purpose, and relevance.

Moreover, the *New York State Standards for Social Studies* require that students *discuss why people in communities may have conflicts over rules, rights, and responsibilities...explain how people in communities must depend on others to meet their needs and wants...critically examine how the processes of selecting leaders, solving problems, and making decisions differ in communities*, as well as many other criteria that look at the process of social interaction. Thematic ensemble enactment of educational drama, by its very definition, allows students to experience, explore, and process these concepts firsthand, evoking subjective parallels that mirror shared meanings embedded in the objective information, the social interaction of the communities, being studied.

The statewide standards also require that students demonstrate an understanding of *values,* particularly the values of American constitutional democracy, as well as participation in the roles, rights, and responsibilities of citizenship. The 2000 SAVE Act mandates that K-12 teaching in New York State include a component on *civility, citizenship, and character education instructing students on the principles of honesty, tolerance, personal responsibility, respect for others, observance of laws and rules, dignity, and other related traits.* These concepts can be lectured about, examples can be given, and scenarios can be discussed in a manner that facilitates objective awareness, and perhaps some degree of empathy, but the more efficient path toward the actual development of values, character, and related traits is by evoking authentic, subjective experience and processing that experience with emotionally intelligent response.

Educational drama, by accessing individuals' authentic experience and applying it within the shared meaning of the prescribed theme, creates conditions in which students can develop a comprehensive sense of values on their own. Rather than imposing artificial platitudes and superficial phrases printed on t-shirts, students work with genuine models to develop substantial and comprehensive strategies for communication that value self and other. While themes and conditions of enactments are simulated to accommodate curricular concepts and materials, student responses to those conditions are constructed, as described in part I, from authentic, individual perspectives of knowledge informed by unique emotional experience.

A recent study conducted by the Yale Infant Cognition Center (Bloom, Hamlin & Winn, 2007) sheds light on how these individual perspectives, left to their own devices, naturally promote development of universally accepted values of cooperation and coexistence. Infants as young as six months old, upon being exposed to toys that were either "helping" another toy over a hill or thwarting its progress, consistently, almost unanimously, chose the helping toy to play with after witnessing the two events. Our tendency to develop positive values based on connection to community is apparently hard wired. While cultural and personal experiences certainly can mutate this natural tendency, it is likely that a majority of students will, without prompting, independently value and strive for positive social functioning and seek the greater good in structured group encounters.

Reinforcing this innate sense of social values through interpersonal classroom experiences becomes a more urgent task as communication and socialization are increasingly conducted through impersonal media masked by electronic screens. While Internet technology can promote positive social connections and new opportunities to participate in expanded arenas of global, political, organizational, and recreational communities, the expanse of the World Wide Web also provides refuge for antisocial interaction shaped by abuse and neglect, allowing individuals to vent their otherwise unheard primal rage in a setting that is relatively anonymous, with no interpersonal checks and balances other than the reinforcing presence of others who feel the same way. These conditions give rise to, along with cyber bullies and sexual predators, an increasing numbers of teenagers who, because their needs for positive social interaction are not being met, express their feelings and make themselves heard by executing violent campus massacres.

By teaching the language of emotional intelligence in classrooms, we reinforce the inherent tendency for positive social interaction and develop skills for addressing social conflict while teaching students how to take care of themselves emotionally. The need to institute such a practice is clear and pressing. Every day brings another story about an infant shaken to death, a six-year-old left home alone to take care of a two-year-old and a baby left in a car for hours while a parent indulges in a drug or alcohol binge. We know how often these situations occur because we read about them in the paper or hear about them in the news. These are the ones who get caught, usually because of random circumstances. We can conclude that many more of these situations occur, undetected, on an even more regular basis. It is possible and probable that a number of students in our classes are unknown victims and future perpetrators of these abusive and neglectful situations.

Families who casually put themselves and their children at risk in this manner, along with widely accepted name-calling and physical aggression toward children, are the result of a legacy of emotional dysfunction, handed down over the years, by a relatively young culture that does not teach us how to take care of ourselves in this manner. Students need objective models for expression that empower healthy emotional functioning to break cycles of emotional neglect and abuse. The models presented in this approach engage New York State Learning Standards of *interpersonal participation as member of a team, ability to communicate ideas and feelings effectively, understanding of social patterns and processes of group relationships* and *creative self-expression*, to empower students with the skills of emotional intelligence as a key component of the social studies curriculum.

By integrating emotional intelligence activities, in which emotions are identified, expressed, and processed accurately and effectively for personal and intellectual growth, with the concepts, tools, and materials of the social studies curriculum through meaningful subjective contexts engaged by educational drama, pathways are created for absorbing and assimilating objective information about the history, geography, economics, civics, and citizenship of communities being studied. Concurrently, students are prompted to study their own subjective social behavior, enacted in the dramas generated from meaningful encounters with objective materials, as a means for acquiring and accommodating social skills and values associated with character education.

As with the process in the *Literacy Express*, each of the interactive domains, subjective and objective, informs skills and inspires operation and further exploration in the other, generating an integrated approach to development that is whole, rather than fragmented, and creating a dynamic learning environment that holds the potential for transformation.

The Program

The *Building Communities, Character and Social Skills* program presented here is the result of a six-week process conducted in a third-grade classroom of twenty-two students. We met twice a week with the students for a total of twelve lessons that ran approximately fifty minutes each. Some of the lessons would have benefited from a full hour period. While we piloted the program in early spring, implementation in the beginning of the school year would establish early models for empowered approaches to learning, social skills, and general classroom management.

Since the criteria for third-grade social studies are grounded in the concept of communities, the students work in and study their experiences within the context of three communities, classroom, research, and virtual. The classroom community generally looks at and responds to the process as a whole in more objective and reflective terms. When constructing the smaller research and virtual community groups, Ms. Markham considered her students' learning styles, interpersonal skills, and abilities with "traditional" learning tasks such as putting pencil to paper. Her goal for each of the four groups was to have at least one student who generally takes on the natural leader role, a student who has significant difficulties with traditional learning tasks, a student who experiences difficulties with emotional interactions or conflict resolution with others, and a student who has difficulty identifying what he/she wants or feels and usually just "follows the crowd."

The four research communities, each containing five or six students, are responsible for determining what procedures will best serve their group toward accomplishing the goals of the program, researching and applying information from available texts and other sources to create their virtual communities, and analyzing information that emerges from virtual community enactments. The research community and virtual community groups are comprised of the same students.

The virtual community themes are assigned to the groups by the teacher and then constructed by the research groups based on information found in available texts and sources. The textbook in the class we worked with organizes information around four types of communities: *urban, suburban, rural,* and *movable.* The students create characters, buildings, and structures, from tables, chairs, boxes, and fabrics, which correspond to the objective information researched about their assigned virtual community. The students then participate in a series of enactments in their virtual communities, in the roles of the characters they created, which engage themes and concepts listed in the standards for social studies curriculum.

Information applied by the research groups to the virtual community enactments is used to inspire interaction and dramatic conflict relevant to the assigned virtual community, which then lends itself to building social and emotional intelligence skills. Formatted sheets for individual students and groups, the contents of which are described in the lesson plans, prompt discussion and guide the interactions. Worksheets completed by individuals can be stored in folders and maintained as individual portfolios of each student's participation. Worksheets completed by the group are tacked to a threefold research board as an ongoing tool for reference and presentation at the end of the program.

While some of the lessons and activities from the *Literacy Express* can be implemented separately from the whole program, the *Building Communities, Character and Social Skills* works as a whole process, conducted in the sequence presented in the twelve lesson plans. The program facilitates a natural progression and pragmatic development from establishing community to exploring basic wants and needs, to identifying and expressing more complex emotional needs, to dealing with interpersonal problems and conflicts resulting from everyday community life, and ultimately to addressing catastrophic conditions and a sense of values based on the entire experience.

As the process moves between classroom, research, and virtual community encounters, students interact with tools and concepts that include charter documents, group management procedures, formats for research, map skills, landforms, climate, natural resources, basic goods and services, time lines, flow charts, language models for understanding and resolving conflict, newspaper articles, historical contexts, values clarification through folktales, message boards, and self-assessment.

CHAPTER 11

Establishing Community
Government, Geography, and Citizenship

This chapter describes the first group of lessons in the *Building Communities, Character and Social Skills* program. We engage the students in investigating, gathering, analyzing, organizing, and interpreting information that will support them in identifying, locating, and mapping a specific region for establishing a community, and developing a participatory, constitutional political system that the community will be governed by.

Students research texts and collect information to gain a working knowledge of the symbols and tools of community management. Students integrate research results with personal perspective to create a character relevant to their assigned communities. Educational drama techniques of set building and character development empower students to explore needs and wants as a means for developing rules and laws that will enable them to function in their communities. Students develop and apply map and orientation skills by interacting with and creating maps to determine and describe physical and geographical characteristics and natural resources and challenges of the communities they are studying. Students also begin a process of self-assessment that continues throughout the program.

LESSON 1: *The Community of Learners*

Purpose
- To provide students with a working knowledge of how different communities function by exploring and purposefully interacting with symbols and tools of community management.

Concept
- Empower students to establish, participate in, and manage their own classroom and research communities as a starting point for studying other communities.

Goal
- Each student will have meaningful input with regard to the formation, direction, and successful function of their classroom and research communities and be able to assess their individual participation and input.

Procedure
1. The teacher begins *Establishing Community* with a mini-lesson that engages the whole class in a discussion that asks the students questions such as *Why are we studying communities? What is a community?* The students reply based on prior

and common knowledge, as well as any textbook descriptions reviewed by the class.

2. The teacher asks the following questions to further facilitate discussion: *What are we a community of?* (referring to the different roles, such as *children, learners, Americans, people,* etc., that define various possible groupings of identity and community). *What are some problems that come up when we work or play together as a community? What are some things that we need to do to be successful in communities? What are some things that we need from others to be successful in communities?*

3. The teacher asks the students to consider some *Management Tools and Strategies* that help communities to function effectively. Along with the student responses, the teacher presents the concepts of *charters* and *lists of rules, meetings, voting,* and any other pertinent procedures for further consideration and discussion.

4. Referring to the classroom community of learners, the teacher lists on chart paper students' answers to the following questions: *How do we want our community of learners to function? What guidelines should we have? What tools for management and success should we use?*

5. The teacher explains that the students will be operating within three communities: *the classroom community, research communities,* in which the students will conduct the research to create their virtual communities, and *virtual communities,* in which the students will construct and manage, through role and enactment, a type of community they are studying.

6. The students meet in research community groups previously determined by the teacher, comprised of five or six children each. The children in the research groups are the same as the virtual community group assignments. For the example presented in this text, the class was divided into four groups to represent four types of communities—*urban, suburban, rural,* and *movable*—as defined by the text *Communities Around Us* (Garcia, Gelo, Greenow, Kracht, White,1997) developed for third-grade social studies. The virtual community assignments are not yet disclosed to the research groups.

7. The teacher directs the students gathered in their research groups to establish a charter of how they might work together. A creative, formatted support sheet with relevant graphics of people meeting, a chart tablet, a pencil, a watch, and so on provide guidelines that ask the students to discuss and consider questions such as *How will we decide who reads questions like these to the group? Should we write down a charter of our ideas? How will we make sure everybody's ideas are included? Should we vote on things or just see how it works out? Who will take notes or write things down if we need to? Who will collect materials for the activities? Who will be in charge of keeping the group on time? Should we each take one job or change jobs every week? How will we solve problems that come up? What else should we think about to help our group do a good job?* After listing the

bulleted questions, the formatted sheet provides space for the groups to list their *Charter Ideas*. The teacher walks around the room, conferencing with the different groups as they develop their concepts and approach.

8. The teacher engages a discussion with the whole class on any conflicts over rules, rights, and responsibilities that may have come up in the process of establishing the research community charters.

9. Each student is provided with a formatted *Timeline Assessment Sheet*. The top section of the sheet asks them to reflect on and record their contributions to any of the communities during that day's lesson. The bottom section asks the students to consider and record how any of the communities helped or supported him or her that day. The bottom section also asks the students to find a classmate who noticed something positive about that student's participation for that day and write down their observation. The students need to interact and positively comment on each other's participation to complete this part of the assessment. The top and bottom sections are boxed and connected to a thick horizontal line across the center of the paper. At the end of the program, these sheets will be taped together, connecting the horizontal lines to create a continuous time line documenting the student's participation and process.

10. The teacher reviews the sheet and models the process with the class, which they will complete after each lesson.

Materials

- Chart paper
- Formatted response sheets
- Formatted *Timeline Assessment Sheets*
- Sticky notes

Evaluation

Did each student express ideas and participate in discussions about how the classroom and research communities should function? Did the students develop and use symbols and tools for managing their communities? Did each student successfully fill out a *Timeline Assessment Sheet*?

Math and Science Integration

- Write equations that divide speaking time minutes among group members.
- Create word problems and equations that compare the number of jobs with the number of students in the group using greater than and less than symbols.

Ms. Markham introduces Marianne and myself to the class, and the journey begins. We will be with the class twice a week, for the next six weeks, from 9:30 to 10:20 in the morning. Also in the room is a student teacher, Holly Montgomery. I jump right in and ask the students, "Why we are studying communities?" They respond, "To learn...so we can know where we're going...to know the different types of communities." I answer,

"Yes" to all and challenge further with, "Why?" After a while, Danny offers, "To make a new community." This gets closer to what I'm looking for. I ask the class, "What's going to happen in about fifteen years?" Marianne adds, "How old are you going to be? What will you be doing?" The class responds, "Twenty-three…twenty-four…graduating college." I question, "So who will be making those new communities in fifteen years?" Jared guesses, "Us…?" We respond, "Yes! You will be the ones in charge!"

We continue with, "And while there are a lot of great things about our communities, there are also lot of problems and mistakes that we've made and mistakes our parents and grandparents have made, so, why are we studying communities?" Dylan answers, "So we don't make those same mistakes…?" We enthusiastically respond, "Yes! Soon, all of you will be taking over! You'll be the ones making the rules! That's why we're studying communities! So you can know more things and have more power to make things better!"

We ask the students what they know about "community," what it is, and what it means. They respond, for the most part, that it is a place where people live and work together. We ask them what we are a community of, hoping to illustrate the various identities and connections with different community groups that an individual can have. The students respond that we are a community of people, animals, and all living things. I am surprised that they begin on such a large scale. I thought I'd have to prompt them in that direction, but they went there first. We ask them what type of community meets in this room. Sarah responds, "a classroom community." Someone else says, "a learning community." Another student says, "A community of students." They continue as we broaden the list to "neighborhood community, suburban community, Long Islanders, Americans, North Americans, New Yorkers, and 'world' community members."

We explain that we will be working with "three types of communities," the classroom community, a research community, and a virtual community, which they will build and participate in. I indicate the first community and ask the students why we are here together in our classroom community and what we might want to do together. They respond, "to learn…to learn skills and new things…to read and write…to be yourself…to have fun." We give a little extra attention and enthusiastic response to the last two responses. I ask them, "How can we make all these good ideas work? What kinds of rules might we need to make those things happen?" They respond, "work together…not fight…share…be happy…don't yell…help others…don't leave stuff lying around." I tell them they are all excellent answers but sometimes it's hard to do these things! I ask them what kinds of problems get in the way of having all these good ideas work out. They respond, "when you don't agree...when people don't want your help...when people take your things...when people don't let you play... lying...being mean...not following rules."

I challenge the students with, "What kinds of strategies or tools can we use as a classroom community to solve those kinds of problems that get in the way of learning new things and skills in a fun way?" Madison says, "Work together." I ask, "How?" She answers, "By helping each other." I respond positively and ask the class, "what if the other person doesn't like our help?" I want them to think beyond the clichés and automatic responses that have unfortunately churned substantial information into meaningless regurgitation. The students start to come up with more pragmatic answers such as "compromise...deals and agreements...walking away...ignore...talk out problems." I prompt them to think about how America tries to agree on things like new laws and ideas for the country. They respond, "Have elections and vote."

As I write down their ideas on chart paper, I explain that we are creating a "charter," a document that expresses a purpose, design, and list of rules for our classroom community with common goals and guidelines for success. I tell them that we will be dividing into four research groups, and that they will be developing, on their own, charters for each of their research groups.

We assemble the students into their research groups and give each group a formatted sheet of guidelines described in detail in the lesson plan that asks them to consider how they will make decisions and function with the various tasks, such as collecting materials, keeping the group on time, and taking notes, that each group will have to undertake throughout the program. We tell them that they will create their charters on their own and will need to come up with ways to deal with differences of opinion and disagreements. Figuring out how to communicate the information on the guideline sheet is their first task. Rather than relying on the teachers, I want them to engage and participate in their own group process.

The students, now assembled in their research groups, are tentative at first, cautiously glancing at the teachers to check whether they are approaching the task correctly. They quietly ask me or the other teachers observing the groups, "Do we write it down? Should we vote?" I shrug and say, "I don't know, ask them!" referring to the other members of their research group. They continue to respond in unsure tones with all the "correct" answers a teacher would want to hear, "agreeing...talk it out...take turns..." They again look to a teacher to see whether they are "right." I tell them, "You're running this, not me!"

As the activity unfolds, the students' confidence grows and they begin to own the process. Two groups decide that one student will read all the questions. The other two groups pass the paper around the table and have each student read a question. All decide to write their answers down. The groups independently come up with numerous tools and strategies for managing and making decisions, including hearing from each member, rotating around the table for the different job assignments, selecting tasks based on individual preference, going in birth order, and instituting voting, the twenty-first finger, and rock-paper-scissors to settle disagreements. The groups finalize their charters and tack them onto the center of their Research Group Boards, a threefold presentation board provided to each group.

I tell them how exciting it was to watch the groups develop their tools and strategies, and ask each group to tell about one they came up with. It takes a little prompting to move them beyond responding with what they preconceive to be the more "correct" strategies, and toward sharing their own creative solutions.

We move to the *Timeline Assessment* activity, which, in the top section, asks the students to reflect on and record one contribution they made that day to the classroom, research, or virtual communities. The bottom section asks them to consider how the communities helped them and to find another student who noticed that they did a good job with a certain task. I explain and model the relatively simple activity, but they seem perplexed and unsure with how to proceed. I tell them it is a way for you to know and keep track of how you did today and how any of the communities helped you, stuck up for you, or listened to you. While the technical procedure is simple, it seems as though the students get a little lost when they are put in a deeper position of ownership and reflection.

Finally, they start to warm up to the task. Many of the students write more generally about offering and sharing ideas, listening and helping each other, but some of the students offered more specific examples. Jonathon writes that the research community helped him by *teaching me more sharing skills*. Brandon writes that Katherine noticed he *read loudly and clearly to the group*. Dylan writes that the community helped him by *not making me the only one giving ideas*. Nicki noticed that Mary *added onto ideas*.

A primary goal of this program is to empower students to participate in civics and citizenship and take charge of building strong communities in a healthy, proactive way. By asking the students to take action and create their own experiences, we seek to link objective concepts with subjective processes. Upon reflection, we notice the students' initial tentativeness and dependence on a more established, institutionalized process. We wonder whether this response is more of a developmental or cultural phenomenon. One thing we know for sure though: this type of response was occurring in the classroom of an empowering and dynamic teacher in the middle of the third marking period, so we know that unsure, passive response from the students is not a product of Ms. Markham's teaching style.

LESSON 2: *Needs, Wants, Rules, and Laws*

Purpose

- To provide students with a working knowledge of how communities explore needs and wants as a means for developing rules and laws.

Concept

- Empower students to identify and express personal needs and wants in order to develop rules for optimum group functioning.

Goal

- Each student will identify and express a personal need and suggest a rule to promote successful participation in the research community group, participate in group discussions to evaluate and implement rules, and successfully complete a *Timeline Assessment Sheet*.

Procedure

1. The teacher engages the whole class in a mini-lesson to illustrate how individual and community *needs* and *wants* translate into *rules* and *laws*. A structured apparatus such as a vertical flow chart or inverted pyramid can illustrate the transition from *individual needs and wants* to *classroom rules* and *village, town, county, state, country,* and *world* laws. This can be demonstrated by using the need for a clean environment, for instance. The teacher, through discussion with the class, writes an example of an existing rule or law for each organization represented in the chart, moving from classroom rule to world law.

2. Students assemble in research groups for *Needs and Wants to Rules and Laws* activity. Each of the four groups is given a threefold presentation board. A side panel is headed with *Research Group* and divided into two columns; one subheaded with *Needs and Wants* and the other with *Rules and Laws*.

3. The teacher asks the students to consider what they need to work well in their research communities, such as the need to take turns, the need for quiet, the need to be heard, and what rule they would want to have in the research community to support that need. The students write their ideas on two separate sticky notes, one for the need, one for the rule.

4. Each student takes a turn presenting first his or her need to the group, and sticking the note on the board, and then the proposed rule, and sticking that in the appropriate column on the board. After all students present their ideas or after each student's turn, the group responds to the needs and proposed rules by voting or any other procedures the group previously agreed on in their charter.

5. The teacher engages the students in a *Whole Class Assessment* by hearing from each group and comparing and contrasting strategies for how the students developed and implemented rules from individual needs in their research groups.
6. The teacher introduces the *Power Lines Message Board*, a tool that provides opportunity for further expression of needs and wants throughout the program and the school year by modeling and prompting specific language for appropriate and empowered expression of *goal statements, conflict statements, feeling statements,* and *reflection statements.* The students respond using sticky notes.
7. Students fill out *Timeline Assessment Sheets*

Materials

-   Threefold presentation boards for *Research Community Assessment Board*
-   Foam board for *Power Lines Message Board*
-   Sticky notes
-   Formatted *Timeline Assessment* sheets

Evaluation

Did each student use the sticky notes to identify and express a need or want, suggest a rule, and attach it to the Research Community Assessment Board? Did the research community groups establish and implement procedures to consider rules that attempt to satisfy members' needs and promote optimum group functioning?

Math and Science Integration

-   Calculate the number of votes needed to "pass" an idea for a rule.
-   Using charts or tables, show the number of votes each rule received.
-   Use greater than and less than symbols to compare population between town and county, county and state, state and country, country and world.
-   Research and discuss laws that protect natural habitats, animal and plant life, and other natural resources such as water cycles.

We begin by asking the class how communities make laws. "Where do the ideas for laws come from?" They answer, "The president...the government." I indicate the top of my chart paper headed with *Needs and Wants to Rules and Laws* to prompt them. They read the words, "Needs and wants...?" We ask them, "Whose needs? Whose wants?" Someone tentatively answers, "Ours...?" We affirm the response.

To illustrate the process of creating laws out of needs and wants, and the different levels of government, local to national, that can enact such laws, we use a large inverted triangle drawn on the chart paper underneath the heading that is divided by horizontal lines. As we move up the triangle, from the point on the bottom to the wider base at top, we move from the concept of individuals to larger bodies of government. We indicate the subheading *A Clean Environment* at the top of the paper and suggest that a clean environment is an example of something that everyone can need and want. The students agree. The information within the triangle is covered by cover-up tape. We explain that there are different ways to turn that need into rules and laws. We start at the bottom of the inverted triangle and take away the cover-up tape to reveal the phrase *You and I*. I ask the students why you and I might need or want a clean environment. They respond, "so the animals won't die...so the world can be a better place...so we can be healthy." I ask, "Who has a rule for themselves on keeping a clean environment?" They answer, "don't litter... pick up litter if we see it in the park." I move up the triangle to reveal *Classroom* in the next section and ask about rules that support a clean classroom environment. They respond, "put things away after we use them...if we're cutting paper for a project, throw away any scraps."

I indicate the next level moving up the triangle and explain that now we will take a look at actual laws that are created to support the need for clean environment. I ask the students whether they know what the first level of government is that can make laws. They are not sure. I remove the tape to reveal *Village or City*. I give an example of a recycling law in our village that supports a clean environment. I move up the triangle, first asking what a community of villages would be (*Town*) and then give an example of a new green building code that was recently passed in our town. I move up the levels of government, revealing a community of towns (*County*), a community of counties (*State*), a community of states (*Country, United States*), and a community of countries (*World*), giving an example of a law from each, such as *Open Space Initiative, Auto Emissions Standards, Endangered Species Act*, and *Kyoto Treaty*, that supports a clean environment.

Other concepts for needs and wants can be used, such as *A Good Education*, to illustrate the different laws that are established by the various levels of government (*Village school board elections, Town property tax allotment, County early intervention services, State character education initiatives, Federal child labor laws, No Child Left Behind, World human rights for children initiatives*). Given the present focus on global climate issues, a clean environment seemed to be the most accessible example to illustrate the identification of needs and wants as an impetus for creating rules and laws.

We assemble into research groups and ask each student to think about something they want and/or need from the research group that will help them to participate successfully. We give each group some sticky note pads and tell them to write down something they want or need on a sticky note. Then, we ask the students to write down a suggestion for a rule that will support that want or need. The students take turns and present first their need and then their rule, sticking each to the side panel of the Research Board under the heading *Research Group* and subheading *Needs and Wants* and *Rules* divided into two columns. After a student presents his or her ideas, the research group considers the rule with whatever procedures they established in the previous lesson.

Again, as we saw with the previous lesson, the students appear to be unsure and tentative in their approach. We attribute this to the same phenomenon we noticed when we asked them to reflect on their own needs and actions. We reiterate that the rule they suggest to the group will help them to take care of the want or need they identify.

The students eventually warm up to the activity. Many of them identify needs and wants and suggest rules around the notion of being heard and included, staying focused, sharing ideas, and talking out of turn. A few of the students, most notably Katie, AJ, and Carly, seem anxious and have a more difficult time identifying their own needs, crossing out and changing their perfectly fine answers to fit in with how they see other classmates answering. Jared, looking out for his quiet classmate, Niko, as the group considers Nicki's rule, asks, "Does Niko agree? I didn't hear him say anything." Niko looks up at Jared with a small smile. After Mary suggests her rule to include all ideas, Nicki asks, "But what if we don't like all the ideas?" Mary clarifies, "Let's just make sure everybody says their ideas." Nicki agrees.

One soft-spoken boy, Seth, has a very hard time with the activity and apparently feels stuck. Having expertise in the area of autism, I notice that Seth has many of the symptoms associated with Pervasive Developmental Disorders (PDD). One of the significant factors of this delay is the difficulty with objectively "tuning in" to one's state of being and sharing it with others in an appropriate context.

Seth comes up with a need and rule that "no one should smoke." Marianne prompts him to think about the research group, what might he need from the other students in the research group to help him be successful. Jenny adds, "Seth, remember when I asked you to draw a picture for me?" Marianne says, "Do you need others to ask you for help?" Seth quietly responds with, "I don't know" and repeats, "No smoking." Kara offers, "How about if you write down 'I need people to ask me' because you don't talk a lot?" No response. Marianne gently suggests, "Seth, start with 'I need...I want.'" He puts his head in his hands and, with a pained look on his face, says, "I'm trying to think. I just don't know!" Dylan suggests, "Is that what you need? You need people to just let you think?" It's as if a light is turned on as Seth looks up in relief and exclaims, "Yes! That's what I need!" He immediately goes to write it on his sticky note.

Marianne asks her group whether they want to name their rules, like the names of the laws we went over on the inverted triangle chart. They are excited at the prospect. Dylan calls his *The People Peace Treaty*; Jenny enacts *The Helper Listener Act*; Jimmy establishes the *Work Together Act*; Kara initiates the *Safe Communities Act*; and Seth invokes *The Treat Others the Way You Want to Be Treated Law*. Some of the groups come up with consequences for breaking the research community rules, including sitting apart from the group for a time-out, losing a job they wanted to do, losing tickets (a previously established classroom management tool), and finally, having to move to another community. The question of whether or not any of these consequences would be supported by the teacher does not need to be addressed at this time. What is important is that the students are establishing their communities and agreeing on guidelines and limitations that will, according to the group members, ensure optimum functioning.

We run out of time to introduce the *Power Lines Message Board* and decide to present it at the beginning of the next lesson. During the timeline assessment, some of the students begin to move from more general ideas about sharing and helping others toward identifying more specific contributions. Jonathon writes that he contributed by sharing laws, needs, and appropriate comments. Nicki, who tends to dominate, writes that she contributed by agreeing with the group. Jimmy contributed by making a group motto. Dylan notes that the community helped him by giving him a chance to speak. Seth writes that the community helped him by giving him ideas.

The students seemed so unsure, at first, with the notion of establishing procedures to identify their own needs and actions that can be taken in their favor. The question remains; are the caution and tentativeness demonstrated by the students when they are asked to authorize a process, reflect or self-assess developmental or the result of a cultural trend toward disenfranchisement and disempowerment? They do warm up to the activity though, and the focused buzz of engagement tells us that we are successfully engaging a new skill, providing a good "work out" for the part of the brain that integrates the notion of taking care of one's self while simultaneously cooperating with others for the good of the community.

LESSON 3: *Virtual Community Research*

Purpose
- To provide students with a working knowledge of how to research texts and organize information relevant to the community they are studying.

Concept
- Empower students to develop meaningful shared contexts combining objective and subjective information to create the virtual communities they are studying.

Goal
- Each student will use the available texts to compile objective information on an aspect of their assigned virtual community, identify personal subjective contexts from

the information to create a character that could live in the virtual community, and assess the process using the *Timeline Assessment Sheet.*

Procedure

1. The teacher begins a mini-lesson with the whole class on using texts to research concepts. The students take out their texts and/or other literature that contains pertinent information.

2. The teacher asks questions such as *If I wanted to find out about a river community, how could I use the book to get information? What would I do? Where would I look? What if I wanted to find out about what a school day was like for the pioneers? What about the kinds of jobs people have in rural communities?* Along with student responses, the teacher models initial research techniques such as searching the table of contents and index, scanning and skimming through chapter headings, subheadings, and phrases highlighted in the text. Questions that use the specific language found in chapter headings and index references as well as those that don't reflect specific language found in the text headings should be used. This will challenge the students to infer and deduce where relevant information might be found.

3. The students gather in their research groups to receive their *Virtual Community Assignment and Research* tasks. As stated previously, the communities assigned for this program are *urban, suburban, rural,* and *movable.* Any category of community that is being studied—international, historical, or geographical, for example—can be plugged into this model.

4. After the teacher tells each research group which virtual community they will be studying, the teacher provides each group with six formatted research sheets, each one depicting an area of research that will help the groups to develop their virtual communities. Each research group decides which individuals will research which aspect of their assigned virtual community. The topics for research and headings of the sheets are as follows: *1. Buildings and Homes 2. Jobs and Making a Living 3. Products and Services 4. Activities and Community Life 5. Travel and Transportation 6. Communication.* These headings for research were prompted by how information is organized in the text used by the class we worked with. Key words and headings that prompt and support research can easily be adapted from other texts used in other classrooms. Each individual in the research group uses the research skills previously modeled to list findings on the provided research sheet. In addition to the objective information, the formatted sheets ask students to list more subjective responses about what they might *smell, touch, hear, taste,* and *see* with regard to their research. After a period of ten or so minutes, the students take turns presenting their findings to the research group. After presenting their findings to their research group, the sheets are attached to the threefold presentation boards as reference for developing the group's virtual community.

5. Each research group comes up with a name for the virtual community they are developing.

6. For *Virtual Community Character Development*, the teacher hands out another formatted response sheet to each student to help develop roles they will play during thematic ensemble enactment of their virtual communities. Based on information shared within the research group, students will determine and write down answers to the following questions listed on the formatted sheet: *What will your character's name be? How old is your character? What will your character's job be? Who is in your character's family? What chores does your character have to do in the morning? What chores does your character have to do in the evening? What things does your character need? What makes your character mad, angry, or frustrated? What makes your character sad? What makes your character scared? What makes your character happy? What problems or conflicts might your character have to deal with? How is your character the same as you? How is your character different from you?* Concepts chosen by the students for community and character development should all relate and refer back to information found in the texts. This can be finished as a homework assignment. Students can also make nametags for their characters, an ID badge of sorts, decorated in a way that identifies some aspect of their character's job or personality. These can be made with index cards and hung around the neck using ribbon.

7. Students fill out *Timeline Assessment Sheets*.

8. The classroom community reviews the *Power Lines Message Board* and processes any necessary information.

Materials
- Text book or relevant literature
- Formatted research sheets and character development sheets

Evaluation
Did each student successfully apply research skills to acquire relevant information about their virtual community from the available texts? Did students assign relevant subjective attributes to their virtual communities? Did each student create a character with subjective attributes that fit the context of the objective information researched?

Math and Science Integration
- Create a schedule of the character's day using time designations of hour and minute.
- Estimate how many minutes or hours a character may spend on a particular task.
- Compare the time it might take for a character to accomplish different activities using greater than and less than symbols.
- Consider different types of simple and compound machines that might be found in the virtual community.
- List plants and animals that might be found in the different virtual communities.

- Consider how the buildings, structures, and lifestyles might impact plant and animal life and habitats in the different virtual communities.

We begin by introducing the *Power Lines Message Board* to the students, a tool for modeling and prompting language that we didn't get to last time. It is clear to me that having to fragment the process so it fits into forty to fifty-minute periods is a hindrance, but we're in a public school and the pressure to cram everything in—the required curriculum, the standardized tests, and everything else—is overwhelming for all involved, teachers, students, administrators, and parents. It feels ironic, like we're all spinning our wheels faster and faster in an attempt to respond to the frustration of remaining stuck in decades of failure. Our collective spinning, of course, sinks us deeper into the rut.

Marianne explains that "power lines" are words we can say to help us be powerful and get our ideas, thoughts, and feelings out in a way that does not get us into trouble. We give examples for each category listed on the board, including *goal statements, conflict statements, feeling statements,* and *reflection statements.* We ask the students what all the power lines have in common. Sarah notices, "They all start with *I?*" We triumphantly exclaim, "Yes! They all start with *I*! A power line is when you are talking about yourself, what you notice, how you are feeling, what you like, what you don't like, and what you might want to do about it." We ask what they think will happen if we try to solve a problem by starting with the word *You.* Jared says, "You talk about somebody else." I continue, "Then what happens?" He answers, "You get in trouble." Madison says, "You can get into a fight." We are happy that the students understand this concept. We praise them and say that we will be practicing power lines throughout the program and will hopefully get used to using them so we can have more power in our classroom, our communities, and our lives.

I ask the students if they can figure out our play on words and identify what two things the *power lines* can mean. Jimmy offers, "Communities are powerful?" I laughingly say, "Okay, yes! Then there are three things it can mean!" Dylan guesses, "Electric power?" I answer, "Yes! Every community needs power! Electric power, solar power, power from gasoline, good!" Mary says, "Power in our words?" We say, "Absolutely! So as we create and develop our communities, we are going to practice becoming more and more powerful with our words!" We show them a box of sticky notes in four different shapes that match icons made to symbolize the different power statements, *goal, conflict, feeling* or *reflection,* any student may need to make. We tell them that we will leave the board out and go over any power lines that anybody might stick to the board in the upcoming weeks.

We assemble into research groups to assign each group a virtual com-munity—*urban, suburban, rural,* or *movable*—identified by the textbook this particular class uses. We give an example of a popular historical drama presently showing on television and ask the students how the directors of the show are able to build the communities so that it looks like it is from that time period. The students answer that the directors of the show have to read about the communities and study them, a perfect segue for facilitat-ing our research activity.

We give out the textbooks and ask the students what we could do if we wanted to find out about a river community. "How would we use the text-book?" Madison suggests that we look at the table of contents. We encour-age Madison to be more specific. She says we can look for the word *river.* I give them more examples prompted from information in the textbook. "What if we wanted to find out about what a school day was like for a pio-neer child?" Jared says we can look in the index in the back of the book and go by alphabetical order until we get to *p* for pioneer. Then we can check each page that's listed. He starts listing the pages in the index. I say, "So we have to read all those pages?" Sarah says we can look at titles of para-graphs rather than reading the whole page, looking for words like *school days.* Mary adds, "Or education."

We hand out six formatted research sheets, each looking at a different topic, including *Buildings and Homes, Communication, Products and Services, Jobs and Making a Living, Travel and Transportation,* and *Community Life Activities* for each research group, and tell them that this is the first step toward creating their virtual communities and characters. We describe, in more detail, how they will be getting information from their research and then using those ideas, along with the materials, to build their communi-ties and characters so we can see what life is like in those places.

We tell the students they can decide who will research the different topics based on any management strategies they came up with from previ-ous lessons and then use the textbook to find information about their topic. Under each topic heading we included hints and key words they could look for in their textbooks. Three groups give one or more sheets to each mem-ber to research on their own and then report back to the group. The Urban Community group decides to do each sheet, one at a time, as a group. This process does take a lot of time, and although I want to stay out of their decision making, I eventually suggest that they at least break down into two groups of three, with each group taking on two of the remaining four sheets.

The majority of students are focused on using the textbook to find in-formation about their topic relative to their assigned community. Some have a tough time. The Movable Community decides to go around the table and take turns reading aloud from the textbook, but AJ refuses. It is also hard for AJ to understand and visualize the context in which he would be a member of an imaginary community based on the research the group was presently conducting. Katie and Ashley are quiet during the research activity and look toward Brandon and Jonathon to take the lead. Brandon exclaims that, as members of the Movable Community, they must be "portable people."

In the Rural Community, Jimmy enthusiastically clears the space to make room for the formatted sheets but soon loses steam and proclaims, "I'm so tired" as the group starts opening the texts. He quickly loses focus as soon as the "work" begins, yawning and chatting about random things. As Marianne and his group try to keep him on track, he spots a picture of a county fair in the textbook. He asks, "What's a...*blue...ribbon...pig*?" slowly reading the caption beneath the picture. Marianne explains that it's a contest that awards a prize to the best pig in the county. He laughs delightedly and asks, "Are there sportscasters there?" She indicates the textbook and tells him, "Find out." He scans the pages, finds some information, and declares, "They have television, so there must be! What other sports are there?" interpreting the pig contest as a type of sport. Marianne again refers him to the text, "See what you can find." Jimmy finds all sorts of information about different types of farms and records sports activities like sheep shearing, dairy and corn husking contests from the results of his research on his sheet.

Jimmy connects with and pursues the seemingly meaningless objective information in the textbook by integrating it within a subjective purposeful context, prompting him to gain new knowledge. His group members join in with his newly found enthusiasm and start identifying different roles they would have in the rural community. As they research, they simultaneously develop a story about an escaped pig that tries to hide at the different farms as news reports of his whereabouts are broadcast.

Seth has a tough time with the part of the research sheet that asks the students what they might see, hear, smell, touch, and taste in the community. He tells the group that he went to Massachusetts and it was all forest, making the connection with a rural community that he had visited. Marianne asks him to think back and remember what he might have heard when he was there, and he answers, "Green." After a period of confusion and coaching, he finally sorts through the different senses and successfully identifies what he heard—streams, animals, and waterfalls—and what he smelled—trees and crops—when he was there.

We are attempting to anchor the objective information from the research in a more subjective and self-aware realm. For students like Jimmy, whose learning strengths reside in personal communication, rather than reading and writing activities, and Seth, who is strong in reading and writing but has difficulty sorting, communicating, and sharing ideas from a subjective sense of self-awareness, the technique takes on more significance. The severed processes begin to reintegrate.

We tape the research sheets to their research boards, which are headed with the names of the virtual communities being studied with an accompanying graphic taped on top while the students conduct their research. At this point, the charters developed in a previous lesson are in the central panel of the boards underneath the name, and the research sheets are lined up, three in a row, in two rows below the charter. The wants, needs, and rules on the sticky notes are attached to the side panel as described earlier.

As the students work on their timeline assessments, I challenge them to "Try and be more specific! If you want to write that you contributed by sharing ideas, see if you can say what the idea was." AJ writes that he contributed to the classroom community by becoming a researcher, and Jonathon noticed that he tried to sound out words and got them. Katie writes that Brandon noticed she did a good job with her idea about smell. Seth writes that he contributed to the research community by filling out his idea paper. Joe writes that the community helped him locate a page he was trying to find.

The research activity illustrates the reciprocal process in which objective information is sought out and anchored into existing schema as a result of inspiration from subjective experience, as in Jimmy's case, while individual expression and subjective communication are further and more clearly accessed and articulated due to the introduction of objective information, as in Seth's case. These two students have very different learning strengths and styles. The integrated activity supports and engages the natural link between subjective and objective realms, allowing each student to access the task from their cognitive comfort zone, while building skills in less developed areas.

LESSON 4: *Map It/Build It*

Purpose

- To provide students with a working knowledge of map skills, location, orientation, and the ability to determine and describe physical and geographical characteristics and challenges of various regions.

Concept

- Empower students to visualize and create their own virtual communities based on information interpreted from maps.

Goal

- Each student will use location and map skills to identify and create specific characteristics of the virtual community through a combination of objective and subjective information and assess their participation by filling out a *Timeline Assessment Sheet.*

Procedure

1. Students assemble into research groups for a whole class mini-lesson on *Map Skills*.
2. Referring to the four signs—*North, South, East,* and *West*—taped in appropriate locations in the classroom (the *North* sign on the northern wall, etc.) the teacher asks the students to indicate which direction each sign represents. The teacher also asks, *Who knows what's further east of our school…? west…? north…? south…?* to promote a general sense of orientation and direction.
3. The teacher asks the students to identify where their research groups are located in the classroom. After each group determines what part of the classroom they are in (northeast, west, southwest, etc.), the teacher asks questions such as *Raise your hand if you are (east, west, north, south) of (other groups, classroom landmarks such as the blackboard, etc.)* to promote directional and orientation skills. Groups use their location in the classroom to coordinate with a relevant map found in the text to establish a location for their virtual communities. If, for example, the suburban group is in the southwest section of the classroom, they use the maps in their texts to explore what a suburban community in the southwest of the country would be like with regard to geography, resources, and climate.
4. Each research group is provided with a formatted table to help organize possible information about their virtual community. The left column of the table lists *Location and type of community, Type of landform, Bodies of water, Natural resources, Climate, Animals,* and *Environmental Challenges* in seven separate rows. The larger column on the right provides room for the group to fill in their answers. The textbook we used offered a number of maps and examples of locations for each type of community, allowing the students to determine what their particular virtual community might be like. Otherwise, relevant maps can be found, copied, and provided to the students for the same purpose.
5. The whole class then focuses on a class map or maps of the country and/or the world. Each group takes a turn locating their virtual community on a class map, and reports on climate, topography, potential for natural disaster, and any other geographical or related findings.
6. The teacher asks the students to take out the research and character development sheets they previously worked on to begin *Virtual Community/Character Building*. Using the information from that research, the students create the virtual community

they are studying, using tables, chairs, cardboard boxes, bed sheets, and large paper and markers for signs and pictures, to build the buildings and structures of the community. Simple fabrics and colored scarves are provided for building purposes as well as costume suggestions for their characters.

7. After a period of ten–twenty minutes, the teacher directs the students, wherever they are at in the process of building and costuming, to take on the roles of the characters they developed and meet and greet the other members of the virtual community in the roles of their characters.

8. The students clean up and use the rest of the period to create *Virtual Community Maps*, one for each group, of what they just built, with large white paper from a roll or a piece of chart paper, indicating where group members live or work in the virtual community, using directions and appropriate legends and keys.

9. Students fill out *Timeline Assessment Sheets*

10. The class reviews any *power lines* that need attention.

Materials

- Signs depicting *North*, *South*, *East,* and *West*
- Texts with relevant maps
- Boxes, sheets, fabrics, and other materials for building communities and developing characters
- Large white paper from rolls or chart paper

Evaluation

Did each student demonstrate an understanding of location and orientation? Was each student able to use a map to identify an objective characteristic of the virtual community? Were students able to integrate objective information with subjective experience to create and construct part of the virtual community and accurately represent it by creating a map?

Math and Science Integration

- Come up with lengths, in miles, for the boundaries of the virtual community, indicate them on the map, and figure out the perimeter and area of the virtual community.
- Estimate what can be planted for crops or gardens based on the climate, weather patterns, and growing cycle of the virtual community's location.
- Discuss how human activity in the virtual community might impact the balance of the food chain, endangered species, and animal and plant life in general indigenous to the location.

We are feeling the constraints of time and realize that we need at least a good hour to really settle in to the deeper substance and purpose of the program. For today's lesson, we decide to forego the extended map location skills, which I really enjoy, to make sure that we have enough time for the students to develop their characters and build their communities.

I put the four direction signs in their appropriate locations in the classroom. I ask the students whether they know what's north of our classroom. They correctly name some towns and states that are north. We do the same with the rest of the directions and the students do a good job with naming local landmarks, towns, countries, oceans, and continents that are toward the direction we are discussing. This is where I'd like to take more time and develop skills, but I know we have to move on.

We assemble into research groups and ask the students to raise their hands if their community is in the western part of the classroom, as indicated by the signs on the wall. We go through the rest of the directions in this manner and explain that each research group has to look at maps in their textbook and find a virtual community that is in the same location as they are in the classroom. So, the urban group located in the western part of the classroom would need to find an urban community in the western part of the country.

The movable group has a concern because they are in the northeast part of the classroom and had decided, during the previous lesson's research, that they would want to create a movable community outside of New Orleans affected by Hurricane Katrina, which is in the south. This, of course, was absolutely fine and we make a general announcement to the class that if they have an idea they really want to go with, they are not constrained by their location in the classroom. The students' confidence seems to increase with each lesson. Also, they noticed the supplies we brought in, boxes, sheets, and fabrics for building, and this has increased their energy and excitement.

The urban group has some difficulty with deciding on a location for their western city. Half the group wants San Diego and the other half wants Tokyo. The group votes. It's a tie. They decide to break the tie with the twenty-first finger. San Diego wins. Ryan and Madison are disappointed, but they go along with the decision. After a minute, I ask the group whether they have ever heard of a place in New York City where a lot of Chinese people live. Someone says, "Chinatown!" Another student says, "There's also Little Italy!" I look at Madison and Ryan and suggest that they can create an Asian section in their city. Madison puts her finger in the air and proclaims, "Tiny Tokyo!"

We ask the students to discuss in their research groups what they might know about their virtual community based on its location on the map, what the landform and climate might be like and any challenges they might face, like blizzards or earthquakes. We ask each group to send up one member to locate their virtual community on a classroom map and tell the class about any of their findings with regard to climate and topography. Dan comes up from the suburban group, finds Australia on the map, and tells us the name of their town is *Kangaroo Babylon*, a warm and sunny suburb of Sydney. John comes up for the movable community and indicates Louisiana on the map. He tells us that it's hot with storms and hurricanes. Jared comes up for the urban community and shows us San Diego, where it's hot and sometimes has earthquakes. The rural community asks whether two members can come up, which is fine, and Jimmy and Dylan point to southern California on the map and tell us that it's hot with wildfires.

We prepare the students for building, telling them that they will be using their tables and chairs, along with the sheets, fabrics and boxes we brought in, to create the buildings and structures they learned about during their research. Before we get to that, we hand out a character development sheet (we were supposed to do during the previous lesson) to each student and tell them they will be making up their own character, again based on their research, who will live in the community they build. The sheet asks the students to consider a name, job and family for their character, along with what makes the character mad, sad, frustrated, happy or scared, the types of chores the character has to do, any conflicts the character might have to deal with in the virtual community, and how the character is the same as and different from the student who creates it.

We start with ten minutes for the activity, but find that, even though the students are focused and engaged in creating their character, they need more time. Some are using the textbooks for ideas; others are looking at their research boards to develop ideas. Marianne and I get together with Ms. Markham as the students work and decide to forego the map making and the timeline assessment, as we feel that the remainder of the time would be best served with the continued development of their character ideas and the initial building of their virtual communities.

The urban community members create characters with jobs such as pizza man, the head of KASA (Kids Animal Scientist Association), chef, car racer, baseball player and photographer. The rural community jobs include farmer, news reporter, weatherman and sportscaster. The suburban community lists soldiers, a student, a surf shop owner and a café owner. In the movable community, AJ is resistant to developing and writing about his character. Jonathon, who chooses the job of a doctor, tries to encourage him. AJ finally writes that his character builds buildings. The movable community also has an ambulance driver, a veterinarian and an animal shelter worker.

We collect the sheets and praise the students' ideas and research, which document many details about the communities they are studying. We indicate the boxes, sheets and fabrics in the front of the room and tell them it's time to create and build their communities in a way that can show all the great ideas they have come up with during their research. We tell them that we are going to use the time today to experiment and get familiar with the materials, and that we will need to practice regaining attention when it is time to transition, as the activity will probably generate a good deal of noise and moving around in the room.

As we begin, two of the communities start to move their tables and chairs, so we call up the other two to get materials first. Everyone soon has a shared amount of materials. The students come alive, bursting with a focused sense of creativity, spontaneity, possibility and cooperation. AJ is actively engaged and rebuilding structures wiped out by the hurricane in the movable community. Seth is laying green and brown fabrics on the floor to resemble the fields of crops he recalls from his visit to a rural community. He excitedly calls, "Look!" to Marianne and gives a detailed narrative about what he is doing and why it fits in to the group's rural designation. Carly, who would passively wait for her classmates before she committed to any type of response in previous lessons, takes the initiative and uses black fabric to make garbage bags for cleaning up the mess at their suburban beach community. Students who were tentative, distracted or resistant are now in their element.

The students build the urban, rural, suburban and movable communities.

By creating conditions that encourage students to use their best available tools and inherent resources to study their virtual communities, we facilitate a learning dynamic informed by research and inspired by imagination. We let them take the lead on a natural path toward empowered learning and true knowledge, rather than dragging them along on a directionless road meandering around random information.

Marianne turns out the lights, an agreed-on signal that prompts the class to quiet down and pay attention. This signal will also serve us during more extended and involved dramatic enactment. They respond immediately. We ask them to step back and look at what they created. In about ten minutes, they have used simple, random materials to construct viable representations of tools and structures employed, according to their textbooks, by their virtual communities. The suburban town of *Kangaroo Babylon* has set up a beach environment interpreted from a map. The rural community, alongside their farms, has set up a television studio modeled from information found in the text. The urban community has built a skyline of boxes, already decorated with signs announcing all the different services and activities the city has to offer. The movable community, out of the rubble of a destructive hurricane, has set up their shelter for lost and injured animals.

We lead the students in a systematic approach to cleaning up the materials and putting the classroom back together; first the fabrics, then the sheets, boxes, and finally moving tables and chairs back to where they belong. It literally takes them under two minutes. The students bring up questions and concerns about using the same materials for the next time we build the communities. We tell them that they will be able to use the same ones, and, if there is a conflict, like there are conflicts in any community, we will work together and use our power lines to say what we feel and what we need so we can solve any problems that come up.

To illustrate the point, Marianne uses the example of when, during the mapping activity, Jimmy and Dylan both wanted to go up to the classroom map to indicate where their virtual community was located, and, by using power lines, they solved the problem by asking whether they both could go up. We explain that the problem may not always be solved that easily, but there is a much better chance of getting what we need from any of the communities we are working in, classroom, research or virtual, if we use the power lines. Marianne also tells the students that over the weekend, if they have any ideas about their virtual communities and want to make something, like some type of sign, list, menu or anything else that fits in with what their character does or experiences, they can make it and bring it in. I reiterate that the students' ideas are usually the best ones.

I am happy with the lesson. The only thing that would make it better is if we had twenty more minutes, time for each group to create a map of their virtual community with legends and keys on chart paper, and fill out the timeline assessments. We see how invested the students are in assimilating and accommodating the objective information when they are defining the process through subjective experience. We do not have the luxury to continue though, as the class has to go to gym and prepare for the upcoming standardized test.

Before we go, Ms. Markham tells us that she might have some time later that afternoon to work on the mapmaking and assessment activities. She emails me the next day that they started the maps but did not get to the assessments, because she spent an hour with the class further developing their characters and building their communities. She was amazed at the focus and detail of objective information that the students translated from the text and channeled into their subjective creations. She expressed sorrow for "how little the education world allows for this type of thinking at the third grade level."

CHAPTER 12

Community Life
Economics, Civics, and Environmental Challenges

This chapter describes the next group of lessons in the *Building Communities, Character and Social Skills* program. We engage the students in investigating, gathering, analyzing, organizing and interpreting information about how different communities manage the challenges of meeting needs and wants, producing and exchanging goods and services, and dealing with social conflicts and environmental challenges relevant to the communities they are studying.

Students use flow charts, tables, diagrams, sociometry, role-play, thematic ensemble enactment, and *Director's Chair* activities to participate in decision making regarding the allocation of resources, managing problems of everyday community interaction, and dealing with geographical challenges and natural and man-made crises. Students are provided with models from which civic roles, rights, and responsibilities and social interaction can be examined, and a range of perspectives about important issues, events, problems, and ideas can be considered from an emotionally intelligent perspective, prompting the proposal of effective action plans relevant to the communities they are studying.

LESSON 5: *Virtual Community Life*

Purpose
- To provide students with a working knowledge of how different communities meet needs and wants, produce and exchange goods and services, and manage the challenges of meeting those needs and wants.

Concept
- Empower students to create, enact, and assess, individually and collectively, their own experiences of meeting needs by producing and consuming goods and services in their virtual communities based on objective information previously researched.

Goal
- Each student will assume the role of a character based on previous research relevant to the virtual community being studied, and participate in the enactment of the virtual community, attempting to meet individual needs and wants while interacting and collaborating with others in the community to establish and maintain effective community functioning and then assess their participation in the process with a *Timeline Assessment Sheet*.

Procedure

1. After a quick class discussion on the different products and services produced by the different communities, the students begin *Producing and Consuming Goods and Services* by creating representations, based on their research, of what their characters provide for the virtual community using index cards and paper with simple drawings and/or words, coupons, and any other easily attainable objects. The farmer can create bottles of milk or bushels of corn, for example, with index cards. The hairdresser can draw different styles for the customers to choose from or create receipts with the paper. The soccer coach can create schedules to hand out. These can be created as homework, at the beginning of the lesson, or during enactment as an added task for managing virtual community life, where the characters attempt to balance providing goods and services for others while meeting personal needs. If done separately from enactment, the representations of goods and services are put aside to be used later.

2. Students assemble into research groups, construct their virtual communities using boxes and fabrics, and take on the roles of their characters with costume pieces.

3. The teacher turns the lights out and directs the students, in this initial *thematic ensemble enactment* of virtual community life, to become the character they created and, when the lights come on, to move through what might be a typical day for their character in the virtual community. With the lights out to gain attention and simulate nighttime before the enactment begins, the teacher prompts activity and interaction by asking questions for the students to silently think about such as *What things will your character need to do or take care of in the community when the day begins? What will you have to do to prepare for your job? What will you need to get to live and provide for yourself and your family? How will you get it?* The teacher signals the beginning of the enactment by turning on the lights. The students use the representations of goods and services they created previously, or make them at this point, in order to trade with others and obtain goods for themselves. Students can also be provided with an amount of play money in order to produce and acquire goods and services. The students strive to find the balance between providing goods and services for the community, while also meeting the individual needs of their characters. The teacher can provide a generic *To Do* or *Chores* or *Shopping List* for the students to promote this concept, or students can reflect on the need for such tools if the teacher decides not to provide them, during the research community meeting. As indicated in the *Literacy Express* section, enactment can be managed, guided, and enhanced by simply using the lights to indicate night, when all activity ceases and directions for the "next day's" enactment can be given, and day, when the activity ensues. The teacher uses his or her judgment with regard to how long to maintain enactment. A more focused class may benefit with a period of twenty minutes, while a five to ten-minute period might be ideal for a more distracted class.

4. For the *Needs to Rules to Laws* activity, members of the virtual community can meet, if needed, to create guidelines for rules and laws to be followed during thematic ensemble enactment of virtual community life. This can be suggested during

one of the nighttime breaks. In order to curb the desire to take on a "negative" role of someone who breaks laws, the teacher can make it clear that, as with most communities of the world, anyone who chooses such a role and *continues* to break laws will, if the mechanisms of the community cannot contain the disruption, have to sit out of the enactment and observe for the remainder of the period. This allows a student to assume such a role if he or she desires, provides the community with the experience of having to deal with "lawbreakers," and also protects the intent of the lesson by imposing clear boundaries and limits to enacting this type of behavior. In other words, it's fair enough if a student in role chooses to steal an apple from the market, for example, and the community can deal with it as it sees fit. If the same student does not respect the boundaries imposed by the community and "breaks out of jail," for example, the consequence imposed by the teacher of not being able to participate for the rest of the period provides ample deterrent from enacting excessive lawlessness in the virtual communities.

5. After cleanup, students convene in research groups to reflect on how virtual community members attempted to meet their needs. The teacher can introduce the term *anthropologist* and describe how, as researchers, the groups will now be studying what just happened in their virtual communities. A formatted sheet provided to each group asks questions such as *What were some of the things people needed to do or get in your virtual community? What did people have to do to take care of those needs? How do things like location, types of buildings, jobs, transportation, products, communication, and climate of your virtual community make it easy (hard) to meet those needs? How might taking care of needs in your virtual community be different from taking care of needs in the other virtual communities or the community you live in? Was your community able to work together to meet everybody's needs? What problems or conflicts did the community have to deal with when people were trying to meet their needs? Did your virtual community create laws to help solve the problems? If so, what were they? If not, what laws might have helped everyone to meet his or her needs more easily?* The teacher reviews the sheet with the class, emphasizing that the students don't need to "fill up" the potentially overwhelming sheet with "answers." The questions are meant to prompt and guide discussion of ideas at the group's discretion. It is up to each group to determine which questions may be glossed over more quickly and where their responses will be more substantial, based on what happened during their enactment.

6. The teacher engages the whole class in a discussion on comparing and contrasting what the different research groups discovered, including thoughts about how people in the different communities depend on others; what different goods and services were produced and consumed; how the different communities made use of natural resources; how environmental and geographic characteristics influenced community life, and other relevant information about meeting needs and wants in the different communities being studied.

7. *Timeline Assessment Sheets*

8. *Power Lines Message Board* review

Materials
- Paper to record virtual community laws
- Index cards or manila paper and markers to create goods and services
- Building and costume materials

Evaluation
Did each student identify and create representations of goods and services relevant to their character's role and information about their virtual community? Did students interact through role in the virtual communities and attempt to meet individual and community needs and wants with those goods and services? Did students identify challenges and discuss strategies for meeting basic needs of individuals and communities in the virtual and research community groups?

Math and Science Integration
- Estimate and use multiplication to determine how many units of goods or services you need to create to meet the needs of your virtual community.
- Estimate the cost and add how much money might be needed to acquire certain needs.
- Use the estimation of how much it will cost to meet needs to determine how to price goods and services.
- Consider what types of machines could help with particular jobs and chores.
- Discuss the impact of jobs and producing goods and services in the virtual communities on the physical environment, water cycle, and plant and animal life cycles.

We assemble into research groups and ask the class, "What are some of the basic needs people have in communities?" The students answer, "water…food…shelter…clothes." I ask how the different virtual communities we are studying—urban, rural, suburban, and movable—might take care of their basic needs in different ways. Dan says the suburban community gets their water from pipes, and Sarah adds that the rural community might get it from a pump. Mary says that in the urban community people go to stores to get food and in the rural community people can buy the food at the farm where it grows. I ask how the urban people get to the stores. Jared answers, "Taxi, bus, or walking." I ask whether the suburban group can walk to the stores. Living in a suburban community ourselves, we say maybe, but people in suburban communities tend to use cars.

We explain to the students that they are going to create, using index cards, paper, and markers, the products, goods, and services of their virtual community based on their research and the job they assigned to their characters. So, a restaurant chef might make a menu. A storeowner can make price tags. A farmer might make bushels of corn or other crops to sell. We model some examples we put together earlier. Sarah asks, "What if you're a kid and you have no job?" I suggest that kids have a big job and that maybe she could make a homework sheet. Marianne asks, "What about the movable community where they might not have jobs right now?" I respond that they could make labels of medicines for the animals they are helping at the animal shelter. Joe suggests that they could make nametags for the animals and Sarah suggests the index cards could be the actual animals being taken care of.

We hand out the supplies and the students start making their goods, services, products, schedules, menus, tickets, price lists, and other items based on their research and character development that reflect the possible needs and wants in their virtual communities. After about five–ten minutes, I announce that we will have another couple of minutes to finish making the items, and then we will build our communities and get into character. I tell the students that they can continue to make items once we are in our virtual communities and that continuing to make the items and produce goods will become part of their character's activities and story for the day.

Ms. Markham reminds the students that, after the last lesson, they practiced setting up and then cleaning up their virtual communities within thirty seconds. She turns the lights off and the students quickly transform the space and get their costume pieces for their characters. When all the communities are built and the students are in character, I get their attention and explain that we will begin our stories with the lights out, pretending that it's nighttime. During that time, the students need to listen for direction about what might happen in the communities when the lights are turned on and the day comes. I tell them that for today's story, the characters will have to find a way to take care of their own needs and their families' needs, while also doing their job and providing goods and services to the rest of the community so that other people will be able to take care of their needs as well.

I turn the lights on and the students, in their roles as virtual community members, "wake up." The sportscasters and news reporters at the television station in the rural community start planning their programming schedule for broadcast. Kara visits the station and suggests a show called "Farmer Time" that can showcase her latest crops and livestock. In the suburban community, members are dropping in at Carly's Café and Surf Shop and looking at the menu to get some breakfast before taking the bus to school and driving to work, but Carly's supplies are running low. Some urban community members visit the zoo and buy souvenirs at Mary's gift shop while others tend to the afternoon lunch crowds at the restaurant. In the movable community, AJ takes the lead making lists of all the neighborhoods damaged by the storms so the ambulance driver, animal rescue worker, and construction worker can see who needs help and coordinate their efforts. The construction worker also notes that repairs are needed at the hospital. Back at the shelter, the veterinarian starts listing the animals that need treatment and what their sickness is.

Mary makes tickets from index cards for visiting the zoo in the urban community.

After about ten minutes of activity, I turn the lights out and call for nighttime. The students hurry back to their homes. I narrate that, on the last day of the story for today, the virtual community members are going to think about any problems, conflicts, or frustrating things that come up as they try to meet their needs. I suggest that they may need to meet as a group to come up with any laws that might help their community address problems or conflicts.

When the lights come up, the suburban community members become increasingly concerned as they run out of food. Members of the urban community continue to get frustrated because too many people from other communities are visiting the zoo and overcrowding the restaurants. Meanwhile, members of the rural community attempt to bring some food over to the emergency workers in the movable community, but they are abruptly told to leave by movable community members, who are dealing with an ambulance that needs new parts and keeps breaking down. I tell the students that in another minute, nighttime will be here, so they should find a way to end their story for the day. I turn out the lights and transition them into clean up.

The students assemble into research groups after the room is put back together. I tell them that they will now be anthropologists, scientists who study people and the communities they live in. I explain that they will be thinking about and discussing what they noticed about how their characters tried to do their jobs and take care of their needs in the virtual communities during the enactment. I show them the formatted sheet I prepared, which asks a lot of questions (listed in the lesson plan procedure), and tell them I don't want them to get overwhelmed and stuck in feeling like they have to answer every question with so many words. I read through the questions to the class and say they don't have to answer in any particular order; they can jump to any question they might have an idea about.

In the suburban research group, Sarah suggests that the members reach out and "team up" with the rural community, so they can get more food when supplies are low. They note that it will probably be easy for them to get what they need because they are close to the rural areas. In the rural research group, Jimmy shares that he saw stories on the Internet about how two farms went out of business because animals ate all the crops at one, while another shipped food that arrived at its destination rotten. The group decides to make a law supporting purchase of food from their local farmers. They also discuss their concerns about being ordered out of the movable community after attempting to deliver some food. The urban researchers, while noting the convenience of having so many products and activities available in their urban community, acknowledge the members' frustration about the crowds. They are not sure what they can do about it. The movable group documents the difficulty its members had with managing emergency services in the wake of the hurricane. They agree on the need for special communication devices as well as acquiring the latest, most advanced technology that can help them to prepare for impending storms. The students are engaged and animated throughout the process, and we are sorry to have to bring the research meetings to a close. Together as a classroom community, we discuss their observations, frustrations, and strategies with producing and consuming goods and services to meet basic needs.

We hand out the timeline assessments and the students get right to them. We don't know whether it's because of familiarity or the support of the enactment, but it seems as though it's easier for the students to do them this time. Carly writes that she contributed to the virtual community by getting food for her family. Katie writes that the community helped her by helping her spell some words. Ashley writes that the community helped her by adding on to what she had to say. Jimmy writes that Dylan noticed he did a good job with telling about what he found on the computer. Kara writes that the community helped her by buying her food. Seth writes that he contributed to the virtual community by making the news camera.

We collect their sheets and tell the students how impressed we are with their work. Through enactment, the students are able to experience, first-hand, some of the difficulties, problems, and solutions that arise when attempting to meet the needs and wants of different community members. By integrating subjective experience, the new information is able to be organized and established within a much broader schema. Studying their subjective participation and social behavior in the virtual communities they created, accurately represented by their research, brings an expanded awareness and deeper understanding to the realities of crowded cities, the need for equipment and technology in response to emergency situations, and the problems and solutions that come with making sure basic needs such as food and shelter are met.

LESSON 6: *Conflict and the Language of Emotional Intelligence*

Purpose
- To provide students with a working knowledge of how to effectively address conflict with the language of emotional intelligence through specific models and experiences.

Concept
- Empower students to identify, express, and construct purposeful emotionally intelligent language relevant to challenging individual and social circumstances they encounter.

Goal
- Each student will identify and express a range of emotional experience using emotionally intelligent language and assess participation with a *Timeline Assessment Sheet*.

Procedure
1. The teacher begins a mini-lesson with the whole class on emotional intelligence by asking the students to vote, with a show of hands, whether they think it is *good* or *bad* to be *mad*. The teacher can record the vote on the blackboard and ask the same question for *sad*, *scared*, *frustrated,* and *happy*. With the likelihood that a majority of students will vote that it's *bad* to have the more difficult feelings, the teacher presents the surprising information that it's actually good to feel these things. The teacher can illustrate this point with the following example, also described in part I.

2. The teacher asks the students how their parents would feel if they saw an older student bullying them on the bus or the walk to school. The students hopefully answer that their parents would be mad at the bully. The teacher describes how this would be an appropriate reaction that would protect the student and start a process that would help solve the problem. The distinction is made of *how* the anger is expressed that determines whether it is helpful or harmful to the situation, prompting the presentation of the terms *Super Power* and *Sour Power*. While any expression of anger generates power, if the parents are physical with the bully or call denigrating names (*Sour Power*), the parents would get in trouble, but if they expressed their anger at the bully with strong and clear statements like from the power messages (*Super Power*), it would be a good thing that would help to solve the problem.

3.   Referring to five signs placed on different walls of the classroom, each one printed with *mad*, *sad*, *scared*, *frustrated*, or *happy*, the teacher explains how scientists, doctors, and researchers are all finding out that knowing about emotions and being able to say what they are is as important as any other subject and learning that takes place in school.

4.   For *Choose It/Move It*, the students are directed to move to the sign that best describes how they feel about the following things that the teacher calls out, one phrase at a time: *How does it feel to go to school? To be in your research group...? Saying what you need...? Researching from the text...? Building the communities...? Making the map...? Filling out the sheets...? Doing the timeline...? Having meetings...? Being your character...? Working with classmates...? Things that happened in your virtual community last time...?* More child-friendly terms can be used at first, such as *bedtime, eating pizza, roller coasters,* and so on, to warm up the concept before moving to more complex ideas. After each phrase is called and the students move to the sign, the teacher asks them to make a face and strike a pose that portrays the feeling, and randomly points to different students, asking them to make a *power statement* about why they chose the feeling beginning with the words *I feel...* The teacher can ask the students for any other criteria they would like to measure.

5.   The students return to their seats and the teacher presents the *Emotional Intelligence Cause and Effect Flow Chart* that provides a model for resolving conflict through emotionally intelligent *super power* expression. Examples of *Super Power Statements* that begin with phrases *I am, I feel, I know, I will, I need, I can, I think* are highlighted above the flow chart. Under the heading *Turn a Sour into a Super*, the flow chart starts with a box that says: *Problem: A classmate is not cooperating with a project.* That flows into a box that says *Sour: You're ruining everything!* The next step, shaped like a stop sign, says *Stop and Think*. The next step reads *What am I feeling?* that flows into *Speak out with a Feeling Statement: I feel frustrated!* and then *Think: What do I need or want?* Finally, the chart ends with *Speak up with a Super Power Statement: I want our project to look good!* We go through the flow chart with the class.

6.   The teacher asks the class to suggest conflicts that exist among the students. The conflict should be based in reality and can either represent something that is presently occurring or has previously occurred between classmates or with other friends.

7.   The teacher asks for volunteers, students who are willing to come to the front of the room and "work" their conflict using the language modeled in the *Power Dialogue* approach on the other side of the flow chart, or role-play a conflict suggested by another student using the approach. Examples of the power dialogue model can be found in the narrative following this lesson plan.

8.   The students assemble into their research groups for *Research Group Encounter* and use the power dialogue and *Super/Sour Power* model to explore conflict that exists

within the group and/or in the school environment. The whole class hears from each research group with regard to their dialogue.

9. *Timeline Assessment Sheets*

10. *Power Lines* review

Materials

- Five pieces of paper printed with *mad, sad, scared, frustrated,* or *happy*
- *Emotional Intelligence Cause and Effect Flow Chart*
- *Power Dialogue* model

Evaluation

Did each student identify and express a range of emotion based on personal and social encounters? Did students demonstrate an understanding of the super power/sour power model? Did students use the models to construct emotionally intelligent language when addressing conflict in the research groups?

Math and Science Integration

- Use tables, graphs, and charts to show patterns of expression, such as differences between boys and girls, for certain criteria.
- Use greater than and less than symbols to compare responses of emotion to different criteria.

Much of this lesson, for purposes of modeling, will be presented in dialogue form.

Teacher: Today we are going to start with a vote...Do you think getting mad is a good or a bad thing? Who votes that getting mad is a bad thing? Raise your hand (80 percent raise hands). Who votes that getting mad is a good thing? Raise your hand (the remainder raises hands). It looks like the majority voted that it's bad, but some people voted that it's good. Gianna, why did you vote that getting mad is a good thing?

Gianna: You can get it out?

Teacher: Great. Why else? John?

John: It feels good to let it out.

Teacher: Yes! Sarah?

Sarah: Being mad is OK.

Teacher: It *is* OK and even a good thing to be mad! Most kids and most adults vote that getting mad is a bad thing. We want to show you that getting mad can be a good thing. I know that sounds weird, but here's why. What if you were walking to school or getting on the bus and some mean fifth grader came up to you, took your backpack, pushed you, and your mom or dad saw, how would they feel?

Students: Really mad!

Teacher: Yes! Really mad! And that would be a good thing because their mad feelings would stick up for you and help to solve the problem. It's a very important idea that getting mad, sad, scared, or frustrated actually can be a good thing! It depends on how it comes out of us though. If it comes out in hits, kicks, or hurtful words, then it makes a bigger problem, and we call that *sour power*. Unfortunately, that's how a lot of people's anger and mad feelings come out, and that's why so many people think that getting mad is a bad thing. We are going to play a game to practice saying the different feelings in a *super power* way, ways to say emotions that will make us stronger and more in charge. Take a look at the signs I have on the wall. What does that one say?

Students: Mad!

Teacher: That one?

Students: Sad!

Teacher: That one?

Students: Scared!

Teacher: That one?

Students: Frustrated!

Teacher: And that one?

Students: Happy!

Teacher: Good. Guess what? In the past ten years, doctors, scientists, college professors, and brain researchers have found out something very important. They have figured out that being able to say these feelings, knowing about how they are inside of you and telling about them with super power words make you just as smart as getting the best grades on all the tests in math, spelling, science, and social studies. So, I'm going to say something that you might have a feeling about. If the thing that I say makes you feel sad, then walk to the sad sign (we go through each of the remaining signs—mad, scared, frustrated, happy—in this manner). There is no right or wrong answer. Whatever is true for you is the right answer. So, let's start with going to school. How is it for you to go to school? (The class moves to the different signs. They start to giggle and act a bit alarmed when they see some classmates go to *mad*, *sad*, or *frustrated*.) If I point to you, I want you to make a super power statement about why you chose that sign. Start with *I feel*, say which sign you are at, and then tell us why you picked it. (Ms. Markham coaches a reluctant Seth to make a choice.) Ready? Kara! (the only student who chose *mad*).

Kara: I feel mad when I go to school because I don't like to do school work (anxious giggles from the rest of the class).

Teacher: Yes! It makes you mad! That was a smart answer! Next, Bedtime…! (The students move.) If I point to you I want you to say the whole sentence…I feel…because…Mary?

Mary: I feel frustrated because when it's time for bed I want to watch TV shows that are on.

Teacher: Yes! Jared!

Jared: I feel mad because my mom won't let me play video games in bed (more anxious giggles, as if expressing feelings in this manner, speaking in a way that goes against the established "right" thing to do, is taboo).

We hear from each student at least once, moving from more general childhood themes to more specific criteria regarding the program we are working on. The students freely and openly express fears, anxieties, and frustrations as I ask about what it's like to be in their research groups (a mix), to say what they need (lots of scared), building the virtual communities (lots of happy), making the map (a mix), researching with the texts (a mix), and filling out the time lines (a mix). Everyone sits and we introduce the *Emotional Intelligence Flow Chart* and the *Power Dialogue Chart*.

Teacher: All communities, whether you are in an urban, suburban, rural, or movable community, have problems and conflicts. How do the people in communities try to solve problems? (The students answer with all the patented responses that generally reflect docile, polite submission.) Yes! A lot of people think that turning sour power into super power means being nice and polite, and that's a terrific way to be, but if we feel angry or frustrated or scared, we need to make strong, even loud statements that may not be so nice and polite! We've just got to make sure that the words don't hurt anybody and they make people want to listen to us. I noticed that a lot of you went to *scared* when I said, "saying what you need." A lot of us don't know how to do it without getting other people mad at us! We weren't taught how! It's really scary to say what we need and stick up for ourselves!

Jimmy: There's a saying that says, "sticks and stones may break your bones but names will never hurt you."

Teacher: I saw that sign in your hallway!…Do you think that's true? Do you think that names and nasty words don't hurt? I know that words have hurt me! It's hard to ignore or just walk away from those things! (murmur of agreement from the students). We are going to teach you how to say and solve problems with super power words, and if you learn this, you are going to be very powerful people! Most adults don't know how to do this. It takes a lot of power to say words that tell how you feel without hurting anybody. It takes a lot of strength to handle problems with these kinds of super power words (indicating the chart). It's easier to say, "You stink! You ruined everything!" That's sour power, when you talk in a hurtful way about somebody else. (We go down the column on the top of the flow chart listing the sour power phrases, which start with *You*.) When you try to tell people what's bothering you by starting with the word *You*, it gives *them* the power and control because they have their own ideas about themselves, and your idea and feeling about what's happening can get taken over by the other person. When you start with *I* (we go down the list of super power phrases), then you stay in charge of your ideas and feelings. Now, you all had very polite things to say earlier about how we can express anger, but does anger sound so nice? How can we express anger and mad feelings in a super power way that is loud, clear, and strong?

John: I feel *so mad*!!! (in an angry tone)

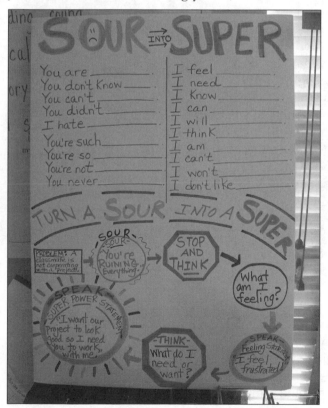

Sour into Super Chart.

Teacher: Awesome! That's super power! (We give random examples of situations that could evoke frustration and anger and ask the students to try some super power phrases.) This is the challenge! For the rest of the year, we want to make you the super power class. In order to do that, you've got to be able to take the sour words and turn them into super, so, for example, a classmate is not cooperating with a project and you feel like they're messing everything up. Sour words like (indicating the phrase written at the beginning of our *Turn a Sour into a Super* Emotional Intelligence Flow Chart) *You're ruining everything!* might come out. Why is that sour?

Students: Because you're saying *you*!

Teacher: Yes! You're blaming them. As soon as the sour comes out, the first step is (indicating the next information on the flow chart).

Students: (reading) *Stop and think.*

Teacher: Yes, because those sour words come out too easily. What do you think you should stop and think about?

Students: (reading) *What am I feeling?*

Teacher: Yes! Instead of getting stuck on the other person, you've got to think about what you know about your own ideas and feelings first. So what do you think this person (hypothetically saying *You're ruining everything*) might be feeling?

Student: Frustrated!

Teacher: Yes! How could they say that in a super power way?

Student: I feel frustrated!

Teacher: Yes! What else might they be feeling?

Students: Maybe mad or sad or confused…?

Teacher: So you think about and say what you are feeling. Then there's another part. This is a big one! And it goes back to what we did in our research communities last week. Saying what we need and what we want in the situation. Who can think of what this person might need or want?

Student: I need my group to work with me so we can build the community.

Student: I want everyone to listen.

Student: I want everyone to cooperate.

Teacher: Great answers, but here's the tricky part. We can say, "I want everyone to listen" and "I want everyone to cooperate," but can we control everyone?

Student: No.

Teacher: No, we can't. So, if I want everyone to cooperate and nobody's cooperating, then I just feel stuck in my frustration, but, if I say, "I want our project to look good," it gives me more power to say what I need and want, and maybe it will cause the other people to agree and cooperate so I can get what I need and want. Who wants to volunteer? Jenny. What if we were in the same group and I said to you (agitated tone directed at Jenny) "You're ruining everything!" what would it make you feel?

Jenny: Sad.

Teacher: Yes! And what would it make you want to say back at me?

Jenny: You're not the boss of me.

Teacher: Yes! And then it starts a little fight! If I said, "I want our project to look good!" does it make you want to fight with me? What does it make you want to say?

Jenny: Me too.

Teacher: Yes! It's a big difference! Both ways of talking to Jenny held the same idea: one way was sour and started a fight; the other way was super and made it more likely that we would cooperate and get what we want. Thank you, Jenny. And I have to tell you again, the doctors, the scientists, all the people who study and do experiments on the brain have found out that if we can have this kind of super power and say how we feel about things, it will make us so much smarter in every other subject and everything else we do.

Jared: It's weird!

Teacher: It is weird, Jared! But here's how the scientists found it out. They looked inside brains and saw that in order to get smarter about something, the thing you are learning about first needs to move through a part of our brain that figures out how we feel about it. If we don't know how we feel and we don't know how to say it with super power words, the new stuff we are learning isn't as strong in our brains as it could be (we flip the chart over to the *Power Dialogue* side). Let's try some! Maybe we can look at a situation that happened in our communities or our research groups, or even on the playground, and we'll try to turn the problem into a super power dialogue where both people can feel powerful and get what they need. I remember something happened yesterday when we were building our virtual communities (looking at Madison and Kara). Remember when you both wanted the same scarves, girls? Want to try it? (they nod). Come on up! (to class). This is the situation. Yesterday, when we were building our virtual communities, Kara and Madison both went for the same scarf, and Kara said, "You're taking my scarf!" Then Madison said, "No! I had it first!" And then they were stuck. Is that about right? (they nod). Ok, so one of you will be "A" (indicating the chart) and the other will be "B." Kara, think about how you were feeling when you had the scarf in your hand, and Madison went to take it. You're going to (reading from the first box on the dialogue chart) *Think about how you are feeling* and tell Madison by saying (reading) *I feel* blank *because I* blank...and you're going to fill in the blanks. And you can say it loud and strong!

Kara: I felt mad because I had the scarf first and then I went to get another one and I put this one down.

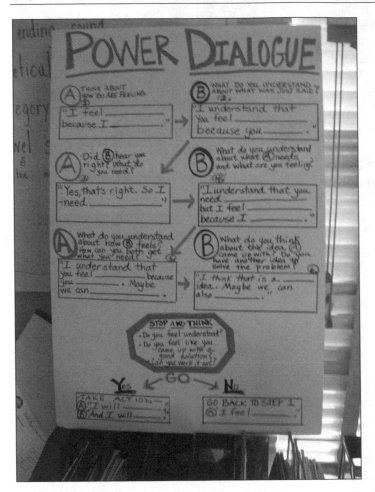

The Power
Dialogue Chart

Teacher: Now your job Madison, is to think about (reading next box to the right) *What do you understand about what was just said?* That's your first step. This is very important, boys and girls, because most of the time we don't listen to what the other person is saying because we're thinking about what we want to say. So, what did you understand about what Kara just said? (reading) *I understand that you feel* blank *because you.* Let's take it together. I understand…

Madison:…that you feel…

Teacher: Do you remember what she was feeling?

Madison: (looking at teacher) She was mad because…

Teacher: Tell her.

Madison: I understand that you were mad because…

Teacher: Do you remember? Do you need her to say it again? (Madison pauses) This is OK! Sometimes we need to hear it again! It gives us a chance to listen. So ask her, why were you mad again?

Kara: (jumps in) I felt mad because I put the scarf down because I needed another scarf and when I got it you took the scarf I had.

Madison: I understand that you were mad because I didn't know you had the scarf first.

Teacher: Awesome! We're jumping a few steps ahead but that's great! Kara (reading the next step) *Did* (Madison) *hear you right?* That's why you were mad? (nods) (reads) *What do you need? Yes, that's right. So I need...*

Kara: Yes that's right, so I need you to listen to listen to me from now on.

Teacher: Wow, that may be a big hard job! What do you need Madison to listen to you about?

Kara: I need her to...

Teacher: Tell her.

Kara: I need you to listen to me when I tell you about what happened.

Teacher: Great! An even more powerful way to say it would be "I need to tell what happened!" Now Madison (reading the next step) *What do you understand about what* (Kara) *needs and what are you feeling? I understand that you need...But I feel...because I...*How did you feel, Madison? Did you feel like Kara was just arguing with you? What was it like for you?

Madison: (tentatively) I felt sad because...(a little stuck)

Teacher: (to the class) It really is hard work, boys and girls! (supporting Madison) Why did you feel sad, Madison?

Madison: (clear and strong) I felt sad because it was the only one that would actually fit my box!

Teacher: Exactly! Now your job, Kara, is to tell (reading the next step) *What do you understood about how* (Madison) *feels? How can you both get what you need? I understand that you feel* blank *because you* blank. *Maybe we can* blank.

Kara: I understand that you were sad because it was the only one that fit your box.

Teacher: Wow! Kara (who has substantial learning disabilities and struggles with reading and writing) is good at this! And now it's solution time! (reading again) *Maybe we can...*

Kara: Share it, or you can use it one day and I can use it the next?

Teacher: (reading the next step to Madison) *What do you think of the idea* (Kara) *came up with? Do you have another idea to solve the problem?* (Madison shakes her head) No? That one works for you? (Nods) OK (reads) *I think that is a* blank *idea. Maybe we can also* blank. Once you have come up with an idea and it works for both of you (reads the next step) *Stop and think. Do you feel understood? Do you feel like you came up with a good solution? Can you work it out?* Do you feel like Kara understood you? (nods) Do you feel like Madison understood where you were coming from? (nods) Do you both feel like you came up with a good solution? Can you work it out? OK, if yes, then you (reads final step) *Take action. I will* blank. Kara, start with you.

Kara: I will share the scarf.

Teacher: Madison, how about you? (reads) *And I will* blank.

Madison: I will listen to what happened.

Teacher: Great! Now let's say you couldn't find a solution. Then you have to (reads) *Go back to step one.* You know what? All I knew about what happened yesterday between these girls is that they were fighting over the scarf. If we left it that way, Madison, you might have thought, "Kara always has to get her way!" and Kara you might have thought, "Madison saw I had the scarf and tried to take it from me!" What I learned was that Madison took the scarf because she thought it would fit her box and she didn't even know Kara wanted it. Neither of these girls was purposely being mean to each other. This could have blown up into a bigger problem, but you girls did a great job resolving it! OK, let's get into research groups.

Jimmy: Can we do one?

Teacher: OK, one more. What happened?

Jimmy: Well, I went over to AJ's community to give them some pizza yesterday, and Jonathon said, "Get out of here!"

Teacher: So who is it between, you and Jonathon? (nods) Come on up, boys! Let's take it through the steps. Start with *I felt.*

Jimmy: I felt sad because I brought your community pizza and you wouldn't take it.

Jonathon: I understand that you felt sad because I said get out of here I don't want your pizza.

Teacher: Did you feel more sad that he didn't want your pizza or that he said get out of here?

Jimmy: That he said get out of here.

Teacher: Was that right? Did he get it?

Jimmy: That's right, so I need you to do what I say and not say no when I bring you something.

Teacher: Mmmmm…That's hard! A lot of times, our first idea tells us to try and control the other person. Maybe you need him to know something…something about you?

Jimmy: I need you to treat me fairly like everyone else.

Teacher: Great! An even more powerful way to say it would be "I need to be treated fairly like everyone else." Do you understand that, Jonathon?

Jonathon: I understand that you need to be treated fairly like everyone else, but I felt like I needed to get some work done because we had to fix the buildings in our community and find the animals that needed help.

Teacher: So you were feeling stressed at the time! Jimmy, what do you understand about what was happening for Jonathon?

Jimmy: I understand that you needed to do things in your community. Maybe if we all get our work done we can have some fun in our communities.

Jonathon: I will try to get work done so we can have more fun.

Teacher: (laughing) Awesome! (to Jimmy) So did you feel understood? (he nods) (to Jonathon) And do you feel understood? (he nods) Can you work it out? Let's see…(reads) *I will…*

Jimmy: I will ask you if you are ready for something.

Jonathon: And I will try to treat you with more respect.

Teacher: Great job! Now this is what I got from these two guys. (to Jimmy) You might have thought that Jonathon was mad at you or annoyed with you, but what did you learn about Jonathon?

Jimmy: He was just trying to get his work done.

Teacher: Right! It wasn't about you! That is very important! How about you, Jonathon?

Jonathon: I was just mad about what was happening in our community but it came against Jimmy and he got upset.

Teacher: Thank you boys! Everybody into your research communities! I noticed that when we were playing the game, many of you went to *scared* or *frustrated* when we called *being in your research communities*. This is your chance to talk together as a group, use the *Sour to Super* and *Power Dialogue* charts (we hand out a smaller version to each research group), and see if you can deal with any problems that are happening in your research groups, your virtual communities, anything else in the classroom or playground.

The students get right to work in their research communities. As I walk by the suburban group, Carly excitedly shares that Gianna sat in her seat as they got into their group, and they used the power dialogue to solve the problem. AJ writes *I feel mad* and tells the other movable research group members that he is not getting to build as much as he wants to during virtual community enactment. Brandon and Jonathon, while trying to show understanding for AJ's position, express their frustration with having to sift through the existing rubble of buildings destroyed by the hurricane to find injured people and animals, while AJ wants to start rebuilding. Neither party feels satisfied enough to offer any solution at this point.

In the rural research group, Jimmy and Dylan express their frustration with Kara's tendency to monopolize materials and act unilaterally. They struggle to move through the dialogue and finally transition from "You take everything!" and "You don't listen" to "I want our whole community to look good. I need some stuff too!" and "I need you to be part of our team." A resistant Kara finally "breaks" as the language becomes less accusatory. She tells the group, "You're right, I don't share and I try to get everything." She continues, "I do it at home too because my little brother takes everything and no one listens to me." The group expresses its understanding and Kara pledges to share materials and work more with the group. The urban research group couldn't think of any conflict that occurred, so they made up a story about a problem at the playground and used the dialogue chart to solve it, writing things like *I feel frustrated, I need people to take turns,* and *I know how you feel.* As the time for the lesson draws to an end, we praise their work and hand out the timeline assessments.

The students continue to get more capable with filling out the timeline assessments, offering more specific observations and reflections. Dan writes the community helped him by using dialogue as power, and Sarah noticed that Dan used the power words to try to help people in the group. Mary writes that the community helped her by getting her feelings out. Nicki writes that she contributed to the community by saying what she really felt. Ms. Markham sternly tells Ryan, who has reached his limit and is off task (as he often is) that he can fill it out now or during recess. He looks frustrated. I ask him to try using some power words to say how he feels. He says, "I'm frustrated! I don't know what to write!" I tell him that he just contributed to the classroom community. He writes that he contributed to the classroom community by using power words to say he is frustrated. Jonathan wrote that Brandon noticed that he did a good job with working out a problem with Jimmy. AJ writes that he contributed to the research community by being honest. Seth writes that he contributed to the classroom community by making a choice. Kara writes that the community helped her by telling her how to share.

We collect the papers, praise their work, and say goodbye for today. Although their encounter with the "new language" is a bit awkward at first, the students become confident and competent with it as the lesson progresses. Their natural tendency to surrender personal empowerment by accusing or blaming the other will continue to challenge them, as it does all of us, but their initial foray into learning and practicing the language of emotional intelligence nets some early successes.

LESSON 7: *Addressing Interpersonal Character Conflict*

Purpose

- To provide students with a working knowledge of how different people in different communities reflect a range of perspectives about important issues, events, problems, and ideas.

Concept

- Empower students to explore and express different perspectives, through role and enactment, of challenging emotions and social situations that cause conflict.

Goal

- Each student will express an emotional perspective within the enactment and explore its effectiveness in addressing and resolving conflict.

Procedure

1. After a brief discussion and listing of examples of the types of problems that may occur in the different communities, students begin *thematic ensemble enactment* of their virtual communities by retrieving and constructing the boxes, signs, sheets, and other materials previously used to build the community. Students assume the role of their characters through costume pieces and other props previously used.

2. For *Character Encounters*, the students are given the direction, during "nighttime," to consider the research they did and think about their characters' feelings and conflicts, what might make them mad, sad, scared, frustrated, and happy, and if their character is the type to express those feelings with super power or sour power. Whether the students enact their characters with super or sour power is their choice. When the "morning" comes, each student will decide what problem or conflict their character will deal with as they move through their day in the community, and if they will use super power or sour power to attempt to resolve the problem. The students are reminded that characters who choose to use sour power may not use actual physical aggression or inappropriate language. Stage fighting techniques, where no contact is made and substitute language may be used for otherwise inappropriate sour power behaviors that some children may wish to exhibit. The students are reminded that excessive sour power behavior that does not respond to the rules and laws established by the community will be pulled out of the enactment.

3. The teacher uses the lights to represent night and day, control the action, quiet things down when necessary, and further develop the plot. For the last "day" of the enactment, the teacher can suggest, during the night, that the students can end the story however they want. Perhaps their character will, after using sour power and getting a negative response from the community, try to respond with super power to solve the problem. Maybe the character is frustrated with not getting any results with super and resorts to sour power. It is up to each student to determine, as long

as their actions remain within appropriate boundaries, how their characters will respond to the conditions presented during the enactment.

4. The students clean up and meet in research groups to analyze the virtual community dramatic enactment using two formatted sheets. The first one, *My Character's Day*, asks the students to respond by completing the following sentences: *Today, in the virtual community, my character felt...My character felt that way because...My character showed how he or she felt in the community by...I think it was a (super or sour) way to show feelings because...I am (the same as or different from) my character when I show feelings because...*The students fill these sheets out on their own. As a group, they respond to another sheet, *Character Conflicts*, that asks them to *Talk about some of the problems or conflicts the characters had to deal with in the community. Talk about which characters handled problems by using super power. What did they do that made it super? Talk about which characters handled problems by using sour power. What did they do that made it sour?* There is also a section underneath the talking points that asks them to write in a character's name and suggest a super power phrase the character could have said during the enactment. The students consider the actions of their characters and explore how power statements and other super power approaches may have contributed to strategies for conflict resolution in the virtual communities.

5. *Timeline Assessment Sheets*

6. *Power Lines* review

Materials

- Building and costume materials
- Formatted *My Character's Day* sheet for individuals
- Formatted *Character Conflicts* talking points and super power chart for the group

Evaluation

Did each student express an emotional perspective through role in the context of the enactment of virtual community life? Were the students able to examine the emotional content of their character in the enactment and formulate emotionally intelligent *super power* responses from expressions of *sour power*?

Math and Science Integration

- Estimate how many times super power was used during the enactment and how many times sour power was used.
- Create word problems around the use of super versus sour power during the enactments.
- Discuss which conflicts during the enactments might impact or disrupt the physical environment and natural life cycles indigenous to the virtual communities.
- Discuss which conflicts in the virtual communities were the result of how the physical environment and life cycles function.

We begin by telling the students, "We are going to get right to it! Let's do our one-minute set-up of our virtual communities and characters." After a minute I turn the lights on, then off again and tell the students, "It is night-time in your community. Listen for directions on what today's story will be about. I don't want any more busy-ness with set-up. When the lights go out, we're silent and still, waiting for the day to come. You've done your research. You know what your community looks like. You know about what life is like in your community. You know about working with your other community members to try and get the things you need and want. As you get ready to become your character, think about the job your character has and what your character has to do during the day. I want you to also think about a problem, a conflict that your character might have in the community during the day, something that makes your character mad. sad, scared, or frustrated. Think about how your character shows those feelings. Is it more super power or sour power? It's your choice.

I continue, "So when the lights come up, it will start a new day in your community, you might go to your job, you might take care of some errands or chores, you might get some things you need, but there is going to be a mad, sad, scared, or frustrated problem that your character is going to have to deal with. Get ready, because here comes the day!" I turn the lights on. The students get to their business. The students in role interact for a few minutes in what feels to be a calm and cooperative atmosphere. I want to warm them up to engaging conflict. I call for nighttime.

I narrate, "On the first day, I saw a lot of people in the communities getting their work done and taking care of things, and that's important. When day two comes through, we are going to start seeing and hearing about some of those conflicts and problems. Think about how we've been practicing with the super and sour power words and dialogue. Let's see which characters are frustrated, angry, and scared. What will the conflicts be in the communities? Will the characters deal with the problems with super power or sour power? Here comes day two!" I turn the lights back on.

This time, the buzz in the room conveys a bit more agitation. In the suburban community, Carly says, "I'm so angry!" because she can't find the sign for her café. Gianna wants Sarah to come and play after school but Carly wants her to come to the café and help out. Sarah is also afraid that she might forget her lunch as she gets ready for school. In the urban community, Mary accuses Ryan of stealing some items from her gift shop. He adamantly denies it. Madison is frustrated that she can't get things set up right in her car dealership.

Meanwhile, bugs that are eating crops and getting into all the town's equipment are plaguing the rural community. The cameras aren't working at the television station, so Jimmy leaves to find a job as a policeman in the city. Jenny, whose hair salon has been overrun by the bugs, blames Kara for not controlling them on her farm. Kara threatens to shut down her farm and move. In the movable community, the animals have escaped from the shelter and are hiding in a condemned building, causing a tense standoff between the rescue workers and AJ the construction worker, who does not want to stop his work to let them retrieve the animals. Also, Jonathan the doctor is angry with the ambulance driver who went the wrong way and was not able to reach the patient. The ambulance driver is incensed with the doctor for speaking to him in such a sour way and will not accept his apology. I turn the lights out and call for nighttime.

For the last day of the story, I tell the students that it will be up to them to end their part of the story in any way that they want. "Maybe you started out angry and will use super power to solve the problem. Maybe you were happy, but things happened that made you feel frustrated and you end up being more sour. It's up to you. If you have handled the problems with super power so far, you might want to see what it's like to have a sour power response. So, here comes the last day." I turn the lights on.

Ryan is becoming increasingly uncomfortable with the accusation of stealing from Mary's gift shop at the zoo in the urban community. His discomfort moves from the role of his character into his role as Ryan. I try to support him by role-playing with the ever-compliant Mary, who is experimenting with sour power through her character. I challenge her with, "You don't have any evidence on him!" She persists. After denying the allegations once again, Ryan says, "I want to quit. I'm too stressed!" Nicki "saves" him by saying, "Look! The things were in Rusty's (the red panda at the zoo) cage!" I praise him for how he used power words to let everyone know what is going on for him. Mary insists that Ryan must have put them there, but he now has allies in the community and is able to hold his ground. She relents and apologizes for accusing him. He brightens up, tells her he will help her catch whoever stole from her store, and offers her a free corn dog from his restaurant.

In the rural community, Dylan tries to kill the bugs with insecticide and ends up poisoning the water supply. The group insists that he go to the city to buy pipes so that they can hook up with a clean water supply. He sees Jimmy in the city and convinces him to come back and help. The suburban community ends their day calmly and peacefully, with all the characters finding solutions to their problems. It is another story in the movable community.

The doctor and ambulance driver remain angry at each other, and the construction worker refuses to work with the veterinarian and animal shelter rescue worker. He ignores their pleas to let them in the building so they can save a dog. I call for one more minute to finish up whatever the characters need to do or say in the communities before the story comes to a close for the day. The lights are turned off and the students are instructed to put their communities and supplies away, and assemble into their research groups.

I hand out the formatted *My Character's Day* sheet described in the lesson plan that asks the students to think about and write down their answers to how their characters felt about and handled the conflict and whether they are the same as or different from their characters. Mary writes that her character felt disappointed because she thought Jackson (Ryan's character) stole things from her gift shop. She showed how she felt by blaming it on him and that it was a sour way to handle it. She is different from her character because in real life she uses super power and in the story she used sour power. Ryan felt frustrated because he wasn't the thief. He showed how he felt by telling the truth and that was a super power way to handle it. Ryan writes that he is different from his character when he shows feelings because he doesn't use super power. Nicki writes that her character felt sad because her sister Jane (played by Mary) was blaming her partner (Ryan, in the restaurant they run) for stealing her stuff. She showed how she felt in a super way by saying that he didn't steal it after she found the things in the cage. She writes that she is different from her character because when she gets mad she says sour things.

In the suburban community, Carly writes that she showed how she felt by saying she was angry because her sign was stolen. It was a super way to show her feelings because then people knew how she felt. She writes that she is different from her character because when she gets angry she just holds it in. In the rural community Dylan felt mad because he had to fix everyone's problems. He showed his feelings in a super power way because he did not say any bad words when he told everyone. He is the same as his character because when he is mad he just says it and gets it over with.

In the movable community, AJ writes that his character felt angry because people were trying to save a dog when he was working. He showed how he felt by yelling at them and that it was a sour power way to show feelings because it can hurt them. He is the same as his character because sometimes he yells. Jonathan writes that his character was mad because he got in a fight with the ambulance driver for something he did. He showed his feelings by taking it out in sour power on the ambulance driver and blaming him for everything. He is different from his character because he takes out his anger in a nice way. Brandon, the ambulance driver, writes that his character felt sour/mad because the doctor was yelling at him for his own mistakes. His character showed how he felt by being sour back to the doctor who wouldn't stop yelling at him. He is different from his character because he doesn't yell at people who blame him.

I hand out the *Character Conflicts* sheet described in the lesson plan that asks the students to now talk as a group about how the different characters handled the problems and what super power phrases they could have said to help with resolution. I go over the sheet and the research groups begin their meetings. The discussions are lively and focused as the students analyze their characters' actions and discern between acts of super power and sour power and how it affects the problems that came up during the virtual community enactment.

The urban community writes that Jane (Mary) could say *I want to know where my stuff is!* Jackson (Ryan) could say *I did not steal your stuff! I don't like being blamed!* Cassy (Nicki) could say *I don't want to be yelled at!* The suburban community writes that Sarah could say *I need someone to take care of me!* The rural community writes that Chuck (Seth) could say *I am so annoyed! The bugs are in my camera!* Bailey (Kara) could say *I need to say my side before people get so mad at me!* The rural community writes that Susan (Katie) could say *I need to get that dog out!* Tom (AJ) could say *I'll try to get the dog only if I hear him crying!* Jonathan could say *I feel sorry and this is all my fault!*

AJ makes the point during the discussion that "It's easier to be sour. It's easier to talk sour." We agree and try to explain how it may seem easier at the time, but then it gets harder when you're sour because people won't listen to you and you might get in trouble, instead of getting what you need. He agrees with us but says that he learns about being sour from his dad and that his dad teaches him sour words, so he doesn't think he'll ever be able to have super power. We tell him that he is already getting stronger with super power by using sour words during the enactment and then understanding the difference during the discussion in his research group, and that helps everybody to learn and get stronger.

On the timeline assessment, AJ writes that he contributed to the virtual community by *being angry* and that Katie noticed he did a good job today with *sour words*. Ryan writes that he contributed to the virtual community by *telling the truth* and that Mary noticed that Ryan did a good job with *using super power*. Nicki writes that she contributed to the virtual community by *helping Ryan* and that Mary noticed she did a good job with *staying out of problems*.

In hindsight, we realize that we could have integrated more objective information into the process by having a quick discussion or mini-lesson about the various problems and conflicts that the different virtual communities might experience based on the research the students have done on location, transportation, jobs, communication, products, and general way of life. Their conflicts, though, did end up being relevant to the communities they are studying.

The students' abilities with applying the language and using the skills of emotional intelligence, along with their analyses of their behavior in and out of role, indicate a broadening skill set that engages the established standards of *ability to communicate ideas and feelings effectively, understanding of social patterns and processes of group relationships, creative self-expression,* and *interpersonal participation as member of a team.*

LESSON 8: *Addressing Virtual Community Conflict*

Purpose

- To provide students with a working knowledge of how to make decisions and resolve conflict stemming from the different people, events, problems, ideas, and perspectives that make up different communities.

Concept

- Empower students to explore, express, analyze, and resolve, through role and enactment, challenging emotions and social situations that cause conflict.

Goal

- Each student will participate in an examination and analysis of a challenging social situation, explore strategies for intelligent emotional expression to address and resolve conflict, and assess their participation in the process with a *Timeline Assessment Sheet.*

Procedure

1. The students prepare for *thematic ensemble enactment* by building their virtual communities and taking on the roles of their characters with costumes and any props they have been using.

2. The teacher announces, during "nighttime," that each virtual community will conduct a *Town Meeting* during the "day" in which all community members, in role, will attend to voice any complaints and concerns with what has been occurring in the virtual community. The teacher directs each group to develop and manage their own approach to conducting and documenting the "minutes" of the meetings, using the skills and tools they have been employing thus far to function effectively in the different community settings they have been managing.

3. The groups incorporate the tools so that each member is able to assert an *Emotional Intelligence Power Statement*, using *super power*, documented by a formatted version of the power dialogue model, in order to be heard by the virtual community members and engage a process toward potential resolution.

4. After the teacher determines that each student in role has asserted a *power statement* to their virtual community and received a response, the students clean up their virtual communities and assemble back into their research groups.

5. Research groups report on how the process went, or, as a lesson extension, the teacher can use the *Director's Chair* technique described in parts I and II and ask each group to come up with a situation, from their research group, virtual community enactments, or other social encounter, that either was resolved with super power statements and dialogue, or remains conflicted and problematic to present to the class. The teacher tells the groups that one student will be the director and the others will be actors. A director's chair is set up near a more open area of the classroom in which a scene can take place.

6. Each group chooses its director, who then sits in the chair when it's his or her turn, and describes the situation. The director then casts the show, from students in their research group or any of the students in the class, depending on the size of the cast. The teacher or another student can say "scene one take one" and clack the scene marker, and the director calls *"action"* with the megaphone to begin the enactment. At the end of the scene, the director calls *"cut"* and all the students are asked what they think it would feel like if they were involved in the situation. After the students respond, the director reworks the scene, infusing the dialogue with power statements where appropriate, calls "action" and runs the scene again using the power statements.

7. *Timeline Assessment Sheets*

8. *Power Lines* review

Materials

- Building and costume materials
- Formatted *Power Dialogue* models
- Director's chair
- Megaphone and scene marker (available at party discount stores)

Evaluation

Was each student able, through role, to make an emotionally intelligent statement during the enactment? Did each student participate in and demonstrate an understanding of emotionally intelligent expression during the *Director's Chair* activity?

Math and Science Integration

- Have each student use a small memo notebook to keep track of and tally numbers of super power and sour power incidents observed around the school for a day or a week.
- Compare students' findings using charts and tables.
- Use simple fractions to compare data of how often students and school officials use super or sour power to address conflict.

We direct the students to assemble into their research groups. I tell them, "In every town and city, in any type of community, people have town meetings to try and deal with problems that come up for them so they can make their communities better. That's what we are going to be doing today.

You're going to have a town meeting in your community. We are going to build our communities and hold town meetings that will look at some of the problems and conflicts you were playing with yesterday. In the town meetings, there is usually a person who runs the meeting and asks the people to say their problems and opinions, and there is someone who takes the minutes. Does anyone know what that is? The minutes are the notes of what happened during the meeting so the community can have a record, or proof, of what people said."

I continue, "For your town meetings, we are going to give you this (formatted model of the *Power Dialogue* chart) so you can keep the minutes and fill in what people are saying. It's what we used the other day (indicating chart on the wall) to help us find super power words that can solve problems and get us what we need. Use your tools that you came up with in earlier meetings to figure out how you are going to manage your town meeting. Who is going to be in charge? Will you take turns? How are you going to decide? Vote? Who will keep the minutes? Use the meetings to try and solve problems that came up in your communities yesterday. You can also make up new ones. Even if you solved all the problems yesterday, you can think about them and talk through them using the power dialogue sheets." We turn the lights out and tell the students to set up their communities.

During nighttime, we tell the students that when the day starts, they are going to go right into their town meetings. The community will decide where, on which side of the town the meeting will take place. Who will take charge? Who will keep the minutes? Which conflicts will be brought up? I remind them about some of the conflicts that occurred yesterday. I recall that the ambulance driver and the doctor had a confrontation in the movable community; the gift shop owner accused the chef of stealing in the urban community; there were some problems between friends and sisters in the suburban community and all sorts of calamities were occurring in the rural community.

We turn the lights on and they spring into action. We coach them as they interact, speaking over their activity for the groups that need more guidance with organizing their meeting place, leadership hierarchy, and structure for proceeding. For the most part, the students take the initiative electing leaders and determining which "cases" will be heard. The urban community pulls their chairs into a circle and chooses Madison, thanks to her twenty-first finger, to conduct the meeting.

In the rural community, Dylan nominates himself as mayor and the group unanimously votes him in. He calls the meeting to order and Seth starts "filming" the proceedings for the virtual television station. The insect problem is brought up, and Kara expresses that since no one is buying her fruit, it's going rotten and that's what's causing the problem. Jenny complains that bugs are all over her hair care products and brushes and she is losing business. Dylan tells Kara that she is responsible for the infestation and cleaning up Jenny's hair salon, although the town will make more of an effort in the future to sell her fruits and vegetables. Jimmy agrees and adds that she should pay for the new water supply too since the spray for the bugs poisoned the wells. A frustrated Kara says, "Can we *please* start the power dialogue?"

Before they begin recording on the sheet, Dylan asks Seth the cameraman what he thinks about the problem. Seth says, "Let's go organic." Dylan chimes in with, "Then, if the stuff gets rotten, we could have a special place to dump them!" Jimmy says, "But who is right and who is wrong? Someone has to lose!" Dylan says they have to solve the problem and not say who is right and who is wrong. Jimmy, who's more interested in stoking the conflict, leaves in frustration and goes back to the city as Kara the farmer and Jenny the hair salon owner come to a balance of expressing their frustration regarding their own situation, along with an understanding of the other's position. They come up with a solution that satisfies both.

We give a two-minute warning and instruct the students to clean up and come back to their research groups. I tell them that I noticed the different ways the communities had their meetings. Some were very focused on one issue while others moved across a wider range of topics. Some were quieter while others were more lively. I point out that this is how it is in adult town meetings too. I recall for them a recent news story about a government meeting from another country where everybody started fistfighting and jumping all over each other in their official meeting place.

Someone asks whether we have town meetings in our town. I tell them that we have town meetings when people want to do things like build onto their houses, start a new community program, understand new laws, or make a new park. Town meetings are scheduled and then notices are sent out that lets everyone know when it will be. Someone asks whether we have town meetings when someone does something bad and they have to tell the truth. We talk a little about courts and those types of structured meetings.

We ask to hear from each group about any problems they solved and what was easy or hard about having their meetings. Kara reports from the rural community that she was almost put in jail for the bug problem. Dylan added that it was hard to keep the meeting under control because everybody was frustrated and had different opinions. I said that it seemed hard to solve problems in the meetings because people wanted to say who was right and who was wrong. I noticed that the urban community was stuck in the problem of who stole from the gift shop and who was right and who was wrong, but it seemed as though the power dialogue helped to find a solution. The town meeting "minutes" from the urban community read as follows:

Ryan: *I feel really frustrated because I wasn't the thief of Jane's gift shop!*
Mary: *I understand that you feel frustrated because you say you didn't do it.*
Ryan: *Yes, that's right, so I need you to know I was not the thief!*
Mary: *I understand that you need me to know that you were not the thief, but I feel frustrated because I don't know who put it in Rusty's cage.*
 Ryan: *I understand that you are frustrated because you think I put it in his cage. Maybe we can find out who did.*
Mary: *Maybe we can figure it out together.*
Ryan: *I will help you find who did it.*
Mary: *And I will let it go since I got my stuff back.*
Ryan: *How about if everybody comes to the restaurant for pizza?*
The suburban group notes that their group is small today so their meeting was quiet. Their conflicts involved theft, as well as a more domestic issue. The minutes from the domestic conflict presented at the town meeting read as follows:

Gianna: *I feel frustrated because I wanted them to come home for dinner.*
Carly: *I understand that you feel frustrated because you bought food for the family.*
Gianna: *Yes, that's right, so I need you to eat at home instead of going out.*
Carly: *I understand that you need me to eat at home but I feel sometimes we can go out.*
Gianna: *I understand that you feel angry because I bought food you didn't like. Maybe we can take turns buying food.*
Carly: *Maybe we can make plans to go out.*
Gianna: *I will ask you what kind of food you want.*
Carly: *And I will ask you if we can go out.*

The movable community reports that they confronted a couple of contentious issues at their town meeting. The group explains how AJ would not budge with regard to rescuing the dogs in the buildings under construction, until Jonathan asked him what he would do if it were his dog that was stuck. For the most part, AJ held his ground, complaining that it was too dangerous and that it would cost him money to have to stop working while they rescued the animals. Finally, Jonathan entered a motion that would give him the authority to override the construction worker's objections and the group approved. We comment that laws are often enacted out of frustration and the need to take action. Their minutes read:

AJ: *I feel mad because I was trying to fix the building and you came along.*
Katie: *I understand you feel mad because you were trying to work.*

AJ: *Yes, that's right, so I need to work without anyone bothering me.*

Katie: *I understand that you need to work, but I feel frustrated because there is a dog trapped inside the building and we need to save it!*

AJ: *I understand that you feel upset because you need to save the dog. Maybe I can try to find him.*

Katie: *Maybe we can work together.*

AJ: *I will try to find the dog.*

Katie: *And I will try to watch the animals so they don't escape.*

We feel very impressed with the level of engagement, passion, and commitment to the process demonstrated by the students. We hand out and collect the *Timeline Assessment Sheets*. Brandon writes that he contributed to the classroom community by listening to each group when they were talking. Mary contributed to the virtual community by getting everyone focused. Sarah writes that the community helped her by solving problems with power talk. The community helped Dylan by not going crazy in court. Seth contributed by making a camera and Ryan contributed by telling the truth to solve the problem.

The students are becoming increasingly able to authentically transform their subjective responses to the objective conflicts brought about by the researched information on the geography, economics, civics, and citizenship of their virtual communities. Subjective learners are using personal experience as a strategy for interacting with and acquiring objective information, and objective learners are using the materials and concepts of the academic curriculum to engage expressive and interpersonal skills.

As we get ready to leave, Mary mentions that she sees so many other students handling everyday conflicts on the playground and in the cafeteria in a sour power way. We mention to Ms. Markham how great it would be if students were trained to be *Super Power Rangers*, in the same manner that students in some schools are trained to be peer mediators. As a *Super Power Ranger* though, the students with that responsibility could wear a cool cape and mask during their tenure and "fly" around the school with a copy of the power dialogue model and facilitate the process whenever and wherever one of these problems emerges. Something to think about.

LESSON 9: *Virtual Community Challenge*

Purpose

- To provide students with a working knowledge of how different communities are affected by geographical challenges, natural disasters, and environmental crises, and how community members organize and adapt to their environments to manage consequences from these types of events.

Concept

- Empower students to effectively respond to catastrophic conditions through role and enactment

Goal

- Each student will experience, through role and enactment, some hardship brought about by natural disaster or environmental challenge, organize and work with other virtual community members to address individual and collective hardships, and assess participation in the experience with *Timeline Assessment Sheets*.

Procedure

1. The students assemble into research groups and, based on the location of their virtual communities assigned by them in Lesson 4: *Map It/Build It*, decide on a *Natural Disaster/Environmental Challenge*, such as a hurricane, tornado, blizzard, drought, volcanic eruption, earthquake, wildfire, pollution, encounter with hazardous or toxic materials, that could inflict their virtual community. Other texts may need to be provided for this research. The students, in role, will need to work together to respond and adapt to a natural or man-made disaster relevant to their geographical location using tools and skills available to them within the confines of their virtual communities.

2. When the students decide which disaster or challenge they will encounter, they build their virtual communities and assume the roles of their characters to prepare for enactment.

3. The teacher explains to the students that their virtual communities will have to deal with the disaster or challenge they have decided on. Facilitated through three phases, *Anticipation and Preparation*, *The Hit*, and *The Aftermath*, the enactment begins with the virtual community members anticipating and preparing for whatever disaster they choose to encounter. Community members might, for example, hear weather reports, notice volcanic activity, watch the news about dangerous pollution levels in the water supply, or find out about a toxic spill on the Interstate. During "nighttime" the teacher suggests the following for the students to consider: *How will you need to prepare or respond...as an individual...as a group? Do you know it's coming? How do you know? Can you prepare for it? Are there special tasks people can do? How will you work together? How will it affect providing for needs, products, and services, communication, transportation, buildings and homes, activities and community life?* Even if there is no opportunity to know beforehand that the disaster will occur the next day, as in the case of an earthquake or hazardous spill, virtual community members can discuss and lobby for and against laws and regulations regarding the potential for disaster with regard to the community's location and history.

4. After a "day" of anticipation and preparation, the students are told during night-time that the next day will be *The Hit*, when the disaster or challenge strikes their community. This will likely be a somewhat chaotic enactment, but, as long as students have been respecting the boundaries of enactment with regard to physical contact and utilizing the tools provided for communication and management, the loud and volatile dramatizations that are likely to come with this enactment will be manageable as well.

5. After the disaster hits and the students in role respond to the ramifications, night is called and the community members prepare to deal with the *Aftermath* the next "day," including cleanup and any other business that needs to be taken care of. During this phase, the teacher or students can act as news reporters, visiting the various communities and interviewing members about the disaster and how the community dealt with it.

6. Along with *News Reporting*, the teacher instructs each community to create a *Newspaper* using formatted response sheets in which members can contribute *Articles* about the disaster, highlighting personal stories, life-changing events, the damage and impact on products and services, communication, transportation, buildings and homes, activities and community life, as well as positive *Character Responses* and acts of heroism, demonstrated throughout the ordeal. The format for the newspaper sheets can include a name for the paper such as *The Times Gazette*, the date, a fifty-cents price, and a headline such as *Extra Extra! Disaster Strikes!* above the space for the article title and then five or so lines for information. Underneath, a space can be provided for an illustration.

7. The students clean up and meet in research groups. The teacher hands a formatted sheet, headlined with *Disaster Strikes!* that asks the students to *Talk with your group about the disaster that struck your community* and discuss *How did you feel about how the community handled the emergency? How did the community do during the Anticipation and Preparation, the Hit, and the Aftermath? When did you and other community members show super power? When did you and other community members show Sour Power? How did you and other community members handle the problems caused by the disaster and any sour power that came up?*

8. Lesson extension: Each group reads one or more of the newspaper articles to the class, and one conflict from each community is processed with the power dialogue

9. *Timeline Assessment Sheets*

10. *Power Lines* review

Materials

- Building and costume materials
- Formatted *Disaster Strikes* discussion sheet
- Formatted paper for newspaper articles

Evaluation

Did each student experience, through role and enactment, a hardship brought about by natural disaster or environmental crisis relative to the geographic location of their virtual community? Did the students work together to address consequences of the catastrophic events? Did they use the newspaper article to reflect on and communicate their experiences?

Math and Science Integration

- Calculate losses in money terms brought about by the disaster.
- Create word problems for addition, subtraction, and simple multiplication and division relative to the damage brought about by the disaster.
- Use simple fractions to compare damaged and stable structures.
- Discuss how the disaster might impact plant and animal habitats and resources and how they might adapt.
- Discuss which disasters might have changed the layers of the Earth.

It is 9:10 AM. We are about to leave our house to teach our 9:30–10:15 lesson when we get a call from Ms. Markham. News 12, a television news network that reaches over one million households, is coming to the class at 10:15 to do a story on our program. I go back upstairs and change my shirt. As we drive to the school, we decide to do the lesson as planned, and then extend the lesson by adding a piece at the end that would tie in to the lesson, showcase the power dialogue, and give the students more experience with the procedure.

We arrive at the classroom and the students are excited and restless about being on television, interesting conditions to execute and manage environmental crises. Before we begin, we talk with the students about the news crew coming at 10:15 and explain what will happen until then and once they arrive.

I ask the students to tell us about different types of natural disasters that occur around the world. They come up with hurricanes, tornados, earthquakes, tsunamis, droughts, and floods. We also talk about environmental disasters that occur because of people and pollution. Dylan raises his hand and says, with a sense of importance, "In the rural community we had to spray to kill bugs and we poisoned the water supply!" We empathize with their tragedy.

We assemble the students into their research groups and tell them that they are going to think about and choose a kind of environmental disaster they will need to deal with in their virtual communities based on their location, landform, and climate previously determined from their research. I explain that a community in the middle of the country would not be directly affected by a hurricane since it gets its energy from the ocean, and it would be very unlikely for a city on the Gulf Coast to get hit by a blizzard since it is in the deep South. I do leave room though, in this age of climate change and uncertainty, for a range of weather possibilities, as long as the event is shown to be highly unusual within the context of the enactment. We make sure that the groups are on the right track and accurately corresponding location, landform, and climate with potential disasters before we build the virtual communities.

After the students have set up, I explain that the event will occur in three stages. First will come the anticipation and preparation for the event. I ask the students, as they "sleep" in their communities, "How will you find out about the disaster? What will you need to do to prepare and make yourself and your family safe when you hear about what's going to happen?" I look toward the urban and rural communities, both "located" in Southern California, who are planning on dealing with an earthquake and continue, "Even if you don't know it's coming, you do know that you live in a community where those things can happen, and you can spend the first day of the story thinking about if you have enough supplies or if you need any new laws to deal with the disaster that *could* happen in the near future. Some things we can know about, like a storm (looking toward the movable and suburban communities), because of weather reports, but some things we don't know about until it happens, like earthquakes. On day one, you are going to find out that a disaster is coming, or you are going to talk with your community members about how you can prepare for disasters that will likely come in the future." I turn the lights on and the students wake up.

Jane (Mary) is very alarmed by the behavior of the animals in her zoo. She calls to her neighbors: "Rusty (the panda) is freaking out! The animals are trying to tell us something!" The urban community members gather around Rusty's cage. Jane continues, "I read in an animal translation book that this could mean some kind of danger might be coming!" Cassie (Nicki) says that maybe an earthquake will hit! The group starts stocking supplies in their specially constructed shelter.

In the movable community, worried members meet to discuss the weather report, which is predicting another direct hit by a major hurricane just when the community was starting to get back on its feet after the last storm. Katie the animal rescue worker expresses concern for all of the animals that will likely be killed and hurt. Would there be enough space for them at the shelter? Would there be enough medicine? AJ feels worried about the safety of his family and friends. Brandon the ambulance driver is worrying about how he will get the sick and injured to the hospital if the streets are flooded. Jonathan is sad and scared at the prospect of another storm.

In the rural community, Kara also points out that her animals are acting strange and that something may be coming. The rest of the community dismisses her, but Seth the cameraman says he saw that show on the animal channel too, and he teams up with Kara to convince the others that the animals' behavior means that disaster is coming. Finally, they convince every one to go to the highest ground in the community. Meanwhile, the suburban community works together to prepare for the impending hurricane, stocking supplies and reinforcing buildings.

The lights are turned off. The students scramble to their resting places, waiting in silence for the next day to arrive. I narrate that when the day comes, it will be the day the disaster hits, and while it may be chaotic, we have to keep safety in mind. Furniture may shake and buildings may crumble, but nothing can be thrown, and no one may actually grab onto anyone else to express anger or fear. I turn the lights on. The hits are dramatic and even intense, with two earthquakes and two hurricanes occurring simultaneously, but the students balance their enactments of destruction and chaos with appropriate containment and care. After a minute or two of catastrophic conditions, I turn the lights out.

When the lights come up for the next day, we find that, besides the physical damage to the communities brought about by the disasters, relationships among some community members suffer as well in the aftermath. After the earthquake, the mayor (Dylan) and the policeman (Jimmy) in the rural community have a (staged) fistfight because, in the chaos, the mayor ordered an evacuation and the policeman didn't know what that meant. One accusation and insult lead to another and soon they both have broken bones, held together by makeshift slings. In the suburban community, Sarah's family is mad because Sarah almost drowned when the army didn't respond to her calls for help. Meanwhile, the army was frustrated because they didn't get the necessary support from the local police and firemen. Bad feelings prevail in these communities in the immediate aftermath of the disasters.

Meanwhile, in the urban and movable communities, relationships were able to be repaired as a result of working together to face the catastrophe. Jane and Jackson (Mary and Ryan) became friends again after helping each other and surviving the earthquake together. AJ the construction worker reached out to the animal workers and offered his help with rescuing animals before he starts demolishing and reconstructing damaged buildings. Instead of the begrudging acceptance he assumed at the town meeting regarding the new law that protects the animals, he expresses an empathetic concern for the safety of the animals in the wake of the damage done by the hurricane.

I switch off the lights for nighttime and tell the students that, when the next day dawns, they will be writing newspaper articles describing their experiences in dealing with the disaster. They may choose to write about the physical damage to their community, their own personal story of what happened to them, how their lives may now change, acts of heroism, or any leftover issues that remain to be dealt with as a result of the catastrophe. I hand out the formatted papers described in the lesson plan. Our plan at this point would have been, after the students finish, to collect the newspapers, get into research groups, and hand out the formatted talking points sheet and then the timeline assessments, as the allotted time for the lesson was coming to a close, but, since the news crew was arriving any minute and we had another period of time, we told the students we would choose one article from each community to read, and one conflict from each community to work through using the power dialogue model.

When the news crew arrives, the students are ready. The reporter interviews me, Marianne, and Ms. Markham, and then the crew films the lesson we prepared. The rural community goes first. Dylan reads his headline *Earthquake Strikes Farmerfield California!* and then his article: *During the aftermath news partners Lucas* (Dylan, the mayor) *and Ron* (Jimmy, the policeman) *are in one big fistfight. When the earthquake hit Mayor Lucas told Cop Ron to evacuate, but he did not know what that meant. After the fistfight, Lucas and Ron will still do news but they will maybe never work together again. Many trees and buildings are knocked over. Only the news station stayed up. We still might have aftershocks.* The boys come up to the power dialogue model chart and do a great job expressing a balance of anger, frustration, and understanding and authentically coming up with a solution.

The urban community is next. Cassie (Nicki) reads her headline *Where is the Stuff?* and then her article: *An earthquake came and all the stuff in the stores was destroyed. It was horrible! We need supplies! People and animals are getting very sick!* Jane (Mary) and Jared successfully use the power dialogue model to deal with a conflict about where the community would get the money to repair the zoo.

Doctor Jonathon from the movable community reads his headline *Disaster in West Bush!* and then his article: *A hurricane just rolled into West Bush! It's a fight for survival! People and animals vs. Hurricane Katrina. Thousands will be injured! Who will win? People and animals or the Hurricane?* They work the now-familiar conflict between the animal rescue workers and AJ the construction worker. They express their positions with strength and conviction and then find common ground.

Sarah from the suburban community reads her headline *10 Year Old Sarah Almost Drowns!* and her article *Innocent Sarah is trying to get to safety on her house when Hurricane Cindy washed her down the street! The army tried to save her but they couldn't. She had to save herself.* Sarah's family (Carly and

Gianna) confronted the army men (Danny and Joseph) with their frustration about how Sarah had to fend for herself. After each side vented their frustrations with the challenge of the storm, all parties committed to improving communication and coordinating strategies in times of emergency.

The presentations by the students filmed by the news crew are terrific and concise, offering substantial examples of what we are trying to do with the program. Their responses are spontaneous and on target with none of the contrivance or superficiality that all too often permeates these types of representations. They speak strongly and confidently, transforming their sour power responses to conflict into viable and mature solutions that are simultaneously self-aware and cooperative with others. The reporter interviews us again after filming the students. Some students are interviewed as well. Jonathan says that the program teaches him "how to work with words." Sarah says that acting in the communities helps her to know what life is like for people who live in other communities and the acting helps the ideas to stick because she's living them rather than just reading words. They ask the students to reenact some of the disasters. The news crew spends an hour and a half in the classroom. We don't have time for the timeline assessments.

That night, as we anxiously watch the evening newscast, we are incredulous at how our program is portrayed. The anchor says something to the effect of "A program at JFK Elementary in West Babylon is teaching the children some important life lessons! They even show the students what to do if they find money!" Literally, those two sentences introduce the program. The screen then switches to Jared, who, responding to some extraneous information regarding the conflict with Mary about how to fund the reconstruction of the zoo after the earthquake, says, "If I find some money I should give it back." Switch back to the anchor who says, "That's some good advice! The program is run by Dr. Lee and Marianne Chasen, Directors of Kid Esteem." That was it. The story was maybe ten strange seconds in which one completely out of context sentence was used to represent the entire program. It was meaningless.

I vow to explain the irony to the students the next day.

CHAPTER 13

Community History
Traditions, Values, and Timelines

This chapter describes the final group of lessons in the *Building Communities, Character and Social Skills* program. We engage the students in investigating, gathering, analyzing, organizing, and interpreting information about how different communities acknowledge and celebrate accomplishments, achievements, contributions, and important historical, technological, and cultural events, eras and milestones from the near and distant past.

Students use art, music, legends, folktales, oral histories, and historical narratives developed through role and thematic ensemble enactment to transmit the ideas, values, beliefs, and traditions of the communities they are studying. Timelines are used to analyze and compare differences in community life between the present and past time periods, and to understand the varying factors that justify and influence settlement in different communities being studied. Students present their research findings collected over the course of the program to the rest of the class.

LESSON 10: *Virtual Community History/Anniversary*

Purpose
- To provide students with a working knowledge of how different communities acknowledge and celebrate accomplishments, achievements, contributions, and important historical events and eras of the near and distant past.

Concept
- Empower students to create and participate in, through role and enactment, an official event or celebration marking some significant anniversary or historical milestone in their virtual communities.

Goal
- Each student will participate in an enactment depicting a particular historical era significant for their virtual community, use time lines as a means for analyzing and comparing the difference in community life between the present and past time periods, and then assess their participation with *Timeline Assessment Sheets*.

Procedure
1. The teacher engages the whole class in a mini-lesson on *Founding Communities* and *Historical Anniversaries*. Students discuss why communities are founded and how establishing new communities can address people's needs and wants and re-

solve conflict. The founding of the United States as well as the local community can be used as examples.

2. The teacher makes the connection to the power dialogue and super power words by pointing out the first words of the Preamble to the Constitution, *We the People* (1787). The class discusses different ways to celebrate historical events and anniversaries, using examples such as Independence Day on July 4, or a recent school, town, or city anniversary in which community events like parades, reenactments, time capsules, and other rituals celebrate the passage of time and accomplishment within a community.

3. Students assemble into their research groups. The teacher instructs the groups to determine and create a *Founder's Day* anniversary celebration marking historical passages of time and accomplishment within their virtual community.

4. The teacher provides each group with a formatted *Founder's Day Celebration* sheet that lists eighteen events or inventions, such as the first steam engine in 1698, the bicycle in 1818, the telephone in 1849, the television in 1932, and the video game console in 1968, to give them a reference for creating their own virtual community events. The sheet also guides the groups to 1. *Think about and decide when and why your virtual community was founded. What year was your community first settled? What need was met by the first settlers in your community? What did they want? What conflict was solved by founding the community? 2. Create your Founder's Day banner by filling in a time line of important events in your virtual community's history. Write down the name of your virtual community, and a community "Super Power" motto that your research group comes up with. 3. Prepare a small presentation or skit that will show the rest of the class the super power words your founders said that solved the conflict and established your community. Show how life was different in your virtual community at the time when it was founded.* (The teacher provides each group with a piece of poster board formatted in this manner.)

5. The teacher can give examples of possible *Virtual History/Anniversary Events* that can be included on the banner's time line, such as the construction of the community's first factory, the discovery of gold or oil, rebuilding after an earthquake, or the passage of important laws that changed its course of development. While the historical events recorded on the timeline for the virtual community will be fictional, the events need to accurately reflect earlier research conducted by the students and coordinate with the geographical location and social conditions for the virtual communities originally determined by the research groups.

6. The teacher instructs the students to prepare for *thematic ensemble enactment* in a manner that will celebrate a historical period in their virtual communities. The students need to build their communities and interact as if they were in the earlier time period, at the outset of the historical event.

7. After the students clean up, the research groups meet and discuss how *buildings and homes, jobs and making a living, products and services, activities and community life, travel and transportation, communication and general quality of life* were different for the virtual community in the earlier time period.
8. *Timeline Assessment Sheets*
9. *Power Lines* review

Materials

- Building and costume materials
- Large white paper or poster board formatted as a *Founder's Day* banner

Evaluation

Were students able to respond to the context of historical inventions to create their own virtual community time line? Did students construct a type of ritual or event to celebrate or acknowledge some significant occurrence in their virtual community's history? Did students identify differences of community life between the time periods and use time lines to illustrate those differences?

Math and Science Integration

- Estimate the population of the virtual community at the time of its founding and compare it to an estimation of its present population.
- Calculate how many times the virtual community population has doubled and tripled over the time span.
- Calculate what a future population might be at the same rate of growth.
- Determine how many years have passed since certain events have occurred.
- Use the time line to determine how many decades are represented, and how many inventions were created in each decade.
- Compare the different types of machines that were available during the different eras and how they may have progressed from simple to compound.

We start the lesson by talking with the students about yesterday's news program. They are disappointed with what was shown in the broadcast. I tell them that this is why we are doing our social studies project. It was great to see and hear Jared, but the news story showed a little piece of something that really didn't explain about what we are doing. It didn't make sense. In our research and virtual communities, we are trying to find the bigger meaning from the information that's in the textbook. The news story showed that us grown-ups are not so great at getting the bigger meaning. Lots of important things we need to know are shrunk into smaller meaningless pieces. That's what happened with the news story.

Jonathan says, "When I was watching it, I didn't get why they showed Jared saying he should give money back because that's not really what they were talking about." I answer, "Exactly Jonathan, it didn't make sense. We know you made sense, Jared, because we know the whole story. Lots of you said important things that could have shown people what we are doing. The news people weren't so good at finding those things from all the filming they did." Other students voice similar responses. I check to see that Jared is okay with all this criticism of the story highlighted by his otherwise extraneous comment. He seems fine and chimes right in with the rest of the class. We move on.

I ask the class whether they remember, back when they were in first grade, Founder's Day, the celebration the school had for its fiftieth birthday. Some hands go up. I call on Sarah, who says, "It showed the day the school was built." She is on the right track. I ask the students what they hear in "founder." Danny says, "Found?" I answer, "Yes! It was the day people came together and 'found' their ideas together to begin JFK. It's a term that's used to describe the beginning of a community, the founding of a community."

I continue, "I bet you all know something about the founding of the United States. Does anybody know the year we started as a new country, a new community of Americans?" The students offer some guesses in the 1800s. Mary asks, "Wasn't it in the 1700s?" I answer, "We're getting closer!" After a few more guesses I say, "1776. 1776 was when the people in the colonies got together and said, 'You know what? We've had enough! We need our own country and we're ready to start it!'"

I connect to "Boys and girls, we've been talking about how communities help people with the things that they need and things that they want and conflicts they need to solve. Does anybody have any ideas of what some of things were that people needed or wanted that inspired them to make America?" Kara answers, "They wanted to be free and they didn't want to be slaves." We affirm and reiterate the correct information. "Yes! They wanted to be free from England. Mary?" Mary offers, "I think they were a British colony then and George Washington helped them to be free?" I answer, "Yes! George Washington is called a 'founding father' because he was one of the first men who found the ideas to create America!" Danny asks, "Wasn't that the Revolutionary War?" I respond, "Yes! They had to have a war to get what they needed from the British. Does anybody else know what other things they needed?" Jenny says, "More money?" I affirm, "Yes. They wanted more money for themselves." Sarah says, "They didn't want to pay taxes." I answer, "Yes and they were very annoyed because they had to pay the tax money to the British government, but they didn't get to vote like all the other British people. There were a lot of things that people needed and wanted that made them decide to start a separate country called the United States of America."

After a few more exchanges about wanting to vote for the president and having their own religion, I ask the students whether they know what the

Constitution is. They respond appropriately that it's a paper that shows the rules and laws of the country. Someone says that they take it out on Independence Day. I say that we have been talking about our super power words and ask what the super power words start with. The students respond, "*I*." I say, "Great! Who knows what the first word of the Constitution is? Does anybody know?" I figure it's a stretch but Sarah answers "We?" I say, "Yes! *We*! *We* is all of the *I*'s coming together, and that's another kind of super power! So, there are the needs and the wants and the conflicts of America, and the *We* power words that helped them to find and create their ideas about building a community of the United States."

I transition, "How about your school? Does anybody have any ideas about the needs and wants and conflicts that inspired people to create JFK Elementary fifty-three years ago?" Katie says, "They wanted a place for children to learn and get an education?" I respond, "Yes, but why not stick with what they already had?" We explain that fifty years ago, many people moved from the city into suburban communities. They make the connection that it got too crowded in the existing schools, so people needed to make new schools because they wanted a better education. I ask who knows the super power motto of their school and what it starts with. They respond, "We're on our way with JFK." Even though it's caught up in the contraction *we're*, we bring attention to the *We* power word that begins the motto.

We talk about how communities celebrate events like Independence Day in America and Founder's Days in local communities. The students list events like fireworks, parades, flag saluting, and parties. I add the idea of re-enactments, when people role-play, in costumes, a time from the community's history. I tell the students that, in their research groups, they are going to create a celebration for a Founder's Day in their virtual communities and come up with a date the community was founded and the events they will be celebrating.

I show them the banner format, a large piece of poster board, that each group will receive. On the banner is a place to fill in the community's name, the date it was founded, a community motto beginning with *We*, and a blank timeline with spaces for four dates that document important events that occurred in the community's history. These events can be fictional, or they can parallel real events written on a timeline format I provide them with.

I hand out the formatted *Founder's Day Celebration* sheets with the timeline of historical inventions and events described in the lesson plan and the students get to work coming up with their own dates and contexts for why and how their virtual communities were founded. The rural community town of Flowerfield, California, was founded by explorers looking for fertile land to feed a growing nation in October 15, 1885. Their motto is *We are growing together as one!* Their timeline uses a mix of fact and fiction, showing the founding in 1885, the population surpassing one thousand people in 1888, the first airplane seen flying over the town in 1903, the first museum built in the community in 1943 and they extended the timeline to include a fifth event of the earthquake in 2008.

The urban community of San Diego documents their founding date as 1886, when a group of people fled to escape the wars that were occurring in the east. Their motto is *We have a dream to make peace.* Their timeline shows the zoo being built in 1888, the First Annual Grand Pogo Stick Contest occurring in 1980, video cameras arriving in 1983, and the earthquake hitting in 2008.

The West Bush movable community lists July 15, 1903 as their founding date. Their town grew from the need of traders to have a place to rest before they shipped their goods between the Mississippi River and the Gulf of Mexico. They originally had a motto of *We are here to help and trade.* They later changed it to *We are here to help and we are here for you.* They list 1903 as the year the Town Hall was built and 1915 as the year the port was built.

Suburban Kangaroo Babylon was founded in 1885, when a stagecoach traveling between the city and the rural areas broke down and a group of people became stranded. As travel became easier, especially with the invention of the automobile in 1885, the town grew. Their motto is *We stick together.* In 1903 the army fortress was built and the first laws were made. In 1904, houses were built for the army's families and in 1913 the first schoolhouse was founded.

Some of the timelines are not completed because we run out of time. We tell the groups that have begun planning their presentations that they will be able to use their ideas when we do the commercials for the communities in a couple of days. Although we are rushed, we hand out the timeline assessments because we were not able to get to them the last time. Gianna writes that Sarah noticed that she did a good job with trying to make things fair. Dylan writes that he contributed to the research community by giving lots of dates for the time line. Seth writes that he contributed to the research community by voting. Mary writes that she contributed to the research community by making up a song and dance for the community's town.

We tell the students that we love the work they are doing and we have two more lessons to do with them. We are inspired with how they have come to own the process of visualizing and implementing their ideas and engaging in the tasks of the curriculum while analyzing their own participation and social behavior in the virtual communities created from their research. By providing the students with the tools and contexts that empower them to "own" the process, they eagerly and enthusiastically invest in the acquisition of new knowledge, historical perspective, and analysis, by integrating and applying subjective experience.

On our way out of the school, the principal stops us in the hall and tells us that an apparently longer version of the News 12 story aired later at night and early this morning. Anything, I think, would be an improvement.

LESSON 11: *Virtual Community Life*

Purpose
- To provide students with a working knowledge of how different communities transmit ideas, values, beliefs, and traditions using legends, folktales, oral histories, and historical narratives.

Concept
- Empower students to express, through role and enactment, values they have developed in the context of their virtual community experiences.

Goal
- Each student will participate in the creation of a folktale, legend, or historical narrative depicting some common value experienced by the virtual community group.

Procedure
1. The teacher engages the whole class in a discussion about community gatherings and asks the students to consider types of social events that bring communities together, using examples they have likely experienced in their schools, neighborhoods, towns, and cities.
2. The students assemble into research groups and discuss the types of social gatherings that could occur in their virtual communities and which one they would like to use for enactment. A formatted sheet facilitates the process by prompting the students to 1. *Talk about some of the experiences your characters have had in the virtual community stories. 2. What important or valuable things happened to your character and neighbors when you: —developed your laws? —built your communities? —took care of your needs? —managed conflict and problems? —survived the disaster? —attended the town meeting? 3. Which experience from your virtual community can tell the story of how the characters try to live by your super power "We" motto?*
3. The students are asked to consider events during the previous enactments that were important and valuable to their characters. A class discussion can explore the meaning of *value* in this context.
4. The teacher instructs the students to prepare for *thematic ensemble enactment* by building their virtual communities and getting into the roles of their characters.
5. During nighttime the teacher facilitates a *Virtual Community Social Encounter* by telling the students that, when the day comes, the communities will gather at their social event and reflect on memorable moments that have occurred during their

past encounters. Students in role will participate in *Oral Tradition Narratives* by sharing important and valuable experiences that occurred for their characters during previous enactments.

6. After hearing from all community members, the group will decide on one of the reflections or a combination of experiences that had particular meaning or value for all members, an encounter in which something important was learned. Using the ladder method, in which paper and pen are passed around the group so that a story is created with everyone's input, the community members create *Virtual Community Folktales and Legends* to transmit values that became clear during the course of enactment. Formatted and structured approaches can include starting each story with *Once*, or suggesting that one of the community members play the role of a child, if one doesn't already exist, who can prompt the storytellers by asking "And then what happened?"

7. *Timeline Assessment Sheets*

8. *Power Lines* review

Materials
- Building and costume materials
- Formatted response sheet for creating and sharing stories
- Paper for documenting folktale, legend, or historical narrative

Evaluation
Did each student share, through role and enactment, a valuable experience that emerged from participation in virtual community life? Did each student contribute to the virtual community folktale, legend, or historical narrative?

Math and Science Integration
- Calculate how many years are represented by the story.
- Determine how many seasons have passed during that time, how many times the Earth has rotated, and how many times the Earth has revolved around the Sun.
- Discuss how many life cycles may have been completed for certain animals during that time.

We jump right into the lesson by asking the students to name some different places that people go to in communities to get together and meet for social gatherings and events. The students respond, "Town square...town hall...the street for a parade..." I ask them to think about the community they live in. Where do they go with their families for community celebrations and fun social events? They respond, "The school...the town pool...block party...church..." I tell the students that, when they get into research groups, they will discuss where people in their virtual communities might meet for social events. Would they meet in a school? Town Hall? A restaurant? We assemble into research groups.

I tell them that after their discussion, they are going to decide where their virtual community members are going to meet for a fun social gathering. Then, after we build the communities and arrive at the social gatherings, "You are going to share stories about what happened to you as your character in the virtual communities over the past six weeks. What things were important or valuable to you? What does that mean? Valuable?" The students respond, "Precious...expensive...worth a lot." I respond, "Yes, so what you are going to think about, is what happened in the community that was worth a lot to you. Not worth a lot in money, but worth a lot how?" Mary says, "Important to you, like someone helping you?" I answer, "Yes! You are going to remember and talk about things that are worth a lot to you, things that you value, like someone helping you, making new friends, solving problems, or working together to make something good happen. Maybe it helped you feel good, or you learned something, or it made a positive change. What was important and valuable to you?"

I give each group the formatted sheet described in the lesson plan to help them organize and talk about their ideas. As I hand out the sheets, I bring up the notion of folktales, how communities develop tales about the folks who live there, by sitting around and telling stories about things that happened to them, to communicate valuable messages and experiences about what life is like in their community. "After people tell the stories," I continue, "Someone writes them down, and that's how folktales are created. So you are going to create a folktale in your virtual community. Think about your super power *We* motto. What happened in your community that was important and valuable to all of you? You're going to turn it into a story when we get into our virtual communities."

The students shift into research mode. They have become extremely focused and efficient in these small groups of five or six. Students who needed prompting and redirection earlier in the process are consistently engaged and invested. They pore over the talking points, offering ideas, listening to each other, and working toward consensus.

We get a sense, after about ten or so minutes, that the groups are ready to transition. We tell the students that, if they have decided on where they will meet and what the topic of their story is, they can begin setting up their virtual communities. When the groups are ready and the students are in costume, I get their attention and say, "When the lights come up and the day starts, you are going to go to the meeting place in your community, and you're going to take turns telling your part of the story about what happened in your community that was important and valuable. I will leave some paper here for each group. See who wants to write down the story or the ideas for the story. You can take turns or just have one person write it. However your group wants to do it is fine. You can start your story with, 'Once upon a time.' You can pretend, if there are no children characters in your virtual community group, that you are telling it to a group of little children. This is how communities tell the important and valuable stories of their lives. This is how folktales are made."

I turn the lights on. The rural community meets out in the open, around a bonfire. The urban community meets in the shelter that protected them from the earthquake. The suburban community has a picnic outside their town hall. The movable community meets at a block party. The groups document their stories through different methods. Some are taking turns so all members can participate in writing it down; others choose one person to write. After ten or so minutes, I collect their papers. Some of the stories are written in outline form. Some are full prose. I can dress them up and edit them later, if needed, into more of a story format.

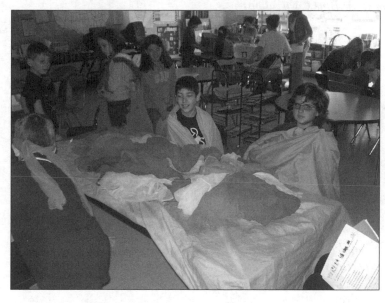

Members of the rural community tell tales around a "bonfire" of colored fabrics piled on the table.

The completed drafts, ready to be read during the next day's final presentation on the last day of the program, read as follows:

Rural Community
Once in Farmerfield, fruit flies took over the town. They were everywhere. They started on the farm because no one was buying the fruit. All the fruit got rotten and then the flies came. More and more flies came every day. The farmer tried to kill them but she couldn't. The Mayor tried to spray poison on them but they didn't die and the poison polluted all our water. The cameraman came to report the story but

his camera blew up from a bug that got inside it, but that's another story. So, the fruit flies even got into the beauty shop. The hairdresser went to get her supplies and she saw fruit flies everywhere! She lost all her customers and she was angry! She blamed the farmer. The farmer blamed the Mayor. The cameraman blamed the police men and the police men left for the city. Everyone was fighting! Finally the Mayor called a meeting at Town Hall. Everyone told what was happening. We decided to work together to get rid of the fruit flies. Then came the giant compost! We built it then and it is still there today. We dump all our rotten fruit and garbage there and the fruit flies love their new home far away from the town. The Mayor has made a law to clean our water and never to use poison again! It was that conflict that helped us have the motto We all grow together as one. We learned that working together is better than working against each other!

Other Rural Legends:
How Shipwreck Lake Got Its Name
The Legend of the Blue Corn Monster

Urban Community

We knew something was coming. Rusty the panda was acting strangely in his habitat at the zoo. And then it hit. The earthquake was so strong. Some of us had forgotten what it was like since it was such a long time since the last earthquake and we didn't know what was happening! Our city was destroyed! Many of us were injured. Thanks to two of our community members, we remained safe and kept to our motto of having a dream for peace! A long time ago, Cassie and Jackson, after hearing stories of the big earthquakes of the past, decided to dig out and build a shelter underneath their restaurant. At the time, people laughed at them and said it was a waste of time and money. But Jackson and Cassie kept going, stocking the shelves with food and supplies. And now, every year, at the anniversary of the great quake of '08, we have a pizza party in our underground shelter and tell the tales of how we handled that disaster without any yelling or screaming! We survived and became better friends by fulfilling our dream of peace!

Suburban Community

Everybody, especially the animals, seemed restless because they knew what was coming. But nobody expected it to be so strong! When the hurricane hit, it almost ripped our town apart, but we stuck together, just like we stick together today. No one had ever seen a storm like it. It swept through our streets with strong winds and heavy rain. Buildings were falling down everywhere! Our town was falling apart! A wave crashed right through downtown and carried some of us away as the waters rose! But then, as the winds started to calm, an army helicopter appeared looking for people who needed help! As they lowered into position, a wave hit the rescue workers and knocked them to the ground! Colonel Joe broke his arm! One girl

had to save herself! We definitely had some problems with communication and pre-
paring for this storm, but in the end, we did stick together and we survived! We
came together and rebuilt our town and our lives to be even stronger!

Movable Community

One evening, in the large town of West Bush, Louisiana, a community of people
worked like never before! The waters were rising. The rain was coming down like
bricks from the sky, heavier and heavier! No one could stop it. The wind was blow-
ing! Suddenly, the water from the Gulf of Mexico raced down the streets! The wa-
ter was rising higher and higher! People began to panic as their houses fell down
and flooded. Soon, help arrived. Helicopters lifted stranded people. Boats picked up
people and animals. The water was too deep for anyone to stand in anymore. It
was up to us! An ambulance driver and doctor saved patients that were stranded.
They were heroes saving others! The animal shelter worker and veterinarian saved
countless animals. The construction workers of the town worked to rebuild the hos-
pital and other buildings that were destroyed by the hurricane. Many families
moved into trailer homes because their homes were gone. To celebrate their survival
and their community of heroes, the people of West Bush held a large celebration in
the streets of their new movable community.

For the timeline assessments, most of the students write about contributing to the storytelling process. Seth writes that he contributed to the virtual
community by making a campfire. Jenny affirms, by writing on Seth's paper,
that he did a good job with building the fire for everyone. AJ writes that
Brandon noticed that he did a good job with sharing his ideas for the story
even if other ideas got picked. Madison, who is often distracted and somewhat sullen, writes that Mary noticed that she did a good job with having
fun.

The students were able to express and transmit a sense of values within
the context of the objective information they researched and applied to create
their virtual communities. Most importantly, they did this organically, in the
absence of a didactic, prescribed lecture about acquiring values or what types
of values need to be adhered to. It occurred in a meaningful context that integrates objective and subjective information, anchoring the experience in
both realms of awareness.

We tell the students that tomorrow, for the last day of the program, we
are going to be presenting all our research and making commercials for our
communities, and then we'll show the tape of the much improved extended
news story we got a copy of over the weekend.

LESSON 12: *Virtual Community Research Presentation*

Purpose

- To provide students with a working knowledge of factors that justify and influence settlement in certain communities and how those factors vary in different communities.

Concept

- Empower students to create their own presentations and research findings to the rest of the class around their experiences in their virtual communities.

Goal

- Each student will participate in presenting an aspect of research and findings about their virtual community, observe presentations from other groups, and assess their participation in the process.

Procedure

1. Students assemble into research groups to create a *Commercial* or *Slogan* highlighting the positive aspects for travel, doing business, or settling in their virtual communities.

2. Along with their commercial or slogan, each research community prepares for a *Presentation* of all *Research, Charters, Maps, Newspapers, Folktales,* and *Timelines* created over the course of the program, to the rest of the class. Using the available management and communication tools that the groups have worked on, each group decides how they will present and who will present the different documents and materials of the project. A formatted sheet headlined with *Tell us about your community!* helps the students organize the process by providing sentences they can complete with a space before each sentence to write in the name of the student name who will be reciting it. The incomplete sentences read as follows: *We studied a...community. We named our community...Our community is located in...It is a...landform. Our climate is...Our homes and buildings are...People communicate by...People travel around mostly by...Our laws include...People make a living by...Some of the goods and services include...Some of the problems our community has to deal with are...Our community is special because...*

3. Each group makes their presentation to the rest of the class. Students respond by noting similarities and/or differences with their experiences in their communities.

4. During a final enactment, students can create and present a commercial to promote life in their community.

5. Final thoughts/closure for research community

6. *Timeline Assessment Sheets*

7. *Power Lines* review

8. Final thoughts/closure for classroom community

Materials

- All previously created materials and representations of research

Evaluation

Did each student participate in presenting information about their virtual community to the rest of the class? Did students attend and respond to presentations by the other groups?

Math and Science Integration

- Divide and represent pieces of information to be presented by students using simple fractions, charts, and tables.

We start the lesson with, "Boys and girls! It's our last day! Here's what we are going to do. First, you are going to do a research presentation with your research community. Then, you are going to make a commercial about your virtual community that would make people want to visit or live there." We bring up an example of a commercial on cable television that promotes the local town where the students live.

I show them the formatted information sheet headed with *Tell Us about Your Community!* described in the lesson plan and explain how they will organize their presentations by completing the sentences about the research information and filling in the names of the people who will read the sentences. I go over all the incomplete sentences on the sheet and bring out the research boards, where all their research group papers from previous lessons are, for reference. The students, assembled in their research groups, get to work.

When they are finished filling out the formatted sheet, the research groups take turns presenting their research by standing in front of their tables with their boards in the background. Each group presents by having one student read a sentence and then passing the paper to the next student in the group, who reads the next sentence. In true third-grade fashion, each group, unbeknownst to the others, chooses to read the last statement, *Our community is special because...* in unison. The presentations read as follows:

We studied a rural community. We named our community Farmerfield. Our community is located in California. Our climate is sunny, hot and dry. Our homes and buildings are farms and small buildings. People communicate by news stations on television, computers and phones. People travel around mostly by cars, busses and tractors. Our laws include no hunting, no polluting, no stealing. People make a living by farms, police, news reporters, hairdressers, teachers and bankers. Some of the goods and services include fruits, vegetables and sports. Some of the problems our community has to deal with are earthquakes, pollution and getting people to buy our farm products. Our community is special because we all grow together as one.

We studied an urban community. We named our community San Diego. Our community is located in California. Our climate is dry, hot and sunny. Our homes and buildings are tall skyscrapers, zoos and restaurants. People communicate by cell phone. People travel around mostly by walking and busses and trains. Our laws include listening and focusing and looking at the speaker. People make a living by working together doing lots of different things. Some of the goods and services include health care. Some of the problems our community has to deal with are earthquakes and crowded places. Our community is special because we help each other.

We studied a suburban community. We named our community Kangaroo Babylon. Our community is located in Australia. Our climate is hot and humid. Our homes and buildings are average size for a suburban town. People communicate by phones and in person. People travel around mostly by cars, boats and bikes. Our laws include work together, help your neighbor, don't steal, respect each other. People make a living by running their own small businesses. Some of the goods and services include protection, safety, clothes and handbags. Some of the problems our community has to deal with are hurricanes and floods. Our community is special because we stick together.

We studied a movable community. We named our community West Bush. Our community is located in Louisiana. Our climate is hot and wet. Our homes and buildings are trailers and RVs. People communicate by phone, email, visiting people. People travel around mostly by boats and cars. Our laws include listen when someone is talking, don't fight with fists, only words. People make a living by building, providing medical care, and helping animals. Some of the goods and services include protection and food. Some of the problems our community has to deal with are storms and flooding. Our community is special because we worked together to survive Hurricane Katrina.

After the presentations, the research groups set up their virtual communities and rehearse their commercials. I give them their banners they made in the previous lesson and encourage them to incorporate any ideas they were developing for the Founder's Day presentation since we didn't have enough time to see them. I tell the students, in the roles of their virtual community characters, that Marianne will read one of the stories they created from yesterday's lesson, and then that virtual community will then go right into their commercial.

The groups, although they only had a ten–fifteen minute period to create and rehearse their commercial presentations, are, for the most part, amazingly well done. We are tapping into what they do best. The group work they have accomplished from previous lessons empowers their free-range creative minds with focused efficiency. Each group presents with a choreographed song singing the praises of their community that truly seems like they rehearsed for a day or more.

We tell them how much we enjoyed their work and hand out the last timeline assessment. Carly writes that she contributed to the virtual community by working out a conflict. Seth writes that he helped with the commercial. Mary writes that she contributed by singing a song. Jonathan writes that he contributed to the research community by helping to come up with a catchy phrase. AJ writes that Brandon noticed that he did a good job with noticing that he needed help with ideas.

Summary

As with the *Literacy Express*, the students responded positively, enthusiastically, and successfully to the program because every task strove to reflect each individual's identity, authentic emotion, and real-life experience. During the twelve weeks, students approached, explored, and interacted with the objective information of the third-grade social studies curriculum from an established base of knowledge generated by meaningful subjective experience. Their unique emotional and social perspectives were evident in their responses to and management of the academic materials and concepts.

Educational drama techniques engaged the whole student, integrated emotional intelligence skills, facilitated multiple, multifaceted approaches to connect with a range of learning styles, and provided a system of shared symbols that fused objective information with subjective experience. The structure of educational drama provided a fictionalized context that accessed personal, real-life emotional content and facilitated its expression in a safe and acceptable manner.

This deeper connection to the whole student served as a tool that processed information and prompted understanding of the skills and concepts defined by the learning standards for social studies. Students learned about the history, geography, economics, civics, and citizenship of communities around the world because the concepts of culture, governmental procedures, research, maps, landforms, climates, resources, needs and wants, decision making, goods and services, conflicts, adaptation, history, and values functioned as symbolic extensions of the students' unique emotional and social experiences.

The reciprocal and mutually enhancing manner discussed in part II in which these two realms, the academic object and the personal subject, interact and integrate, was evident throughout the course of the program. For students like Ryan and Seth, both of whom are considered gifted yet have somewhat of a tough time with interpersonal skills, relative comfort and ability with processing objective information helped them to access, express, and interact from a more personal subjective perspective, which in turn prompted deeper involvement with the information being studied.

Other students, like AJ, Kara, and Jimmy, all of whom receive extra help and tutoring for a range of academic related disabilities, were able to use their relative strengths with expressing subjective emotional perspective to help organize and construct a more systematic approach to understanding the objective information being studied, which in turn prompted more skills and expertise with interpersonal communication.

Perhaps the most gratifying result is that the students really seemed to enjoy the experience. The actual construction of and participation in the virtual communities appealed to the whole range of learners, inspiring them to apply their imaginations to more mundane academic tasks while studying their own social behavior in a manner that brings a higher order, rather than chaos, to the process, which functioned as a whole and integrated system of learning.

Realizing an American Approach to Education

A Pledge of Allegiance

America does not have a cultural tradition backed up by thousands of years of literature and history upon which an approach to education may be built. We are, however, the ideological heirs of the founding fathers' vision, which originated the cutting-edge notion to incorporate free will, freedom of expression, individuality, independent thought and way of life, liberty, and the pursuit of happiness, as a rationale for creating a nation. These historical concepts that put America on the map are, for the most part, the common denominator of our cultural identity, and, although they may be interpreted differently, are philosophically embraced by the many divergent wings of our political schools of thought.

Emotion, at the core of individuality, informed the hearts, minds, and souls of revolutionary men and women during colonial times that established our cultural identity. Our country was founded because people were able to acknowledge and articulate feelings of anger, betrayal, neglect, and oppression, and then take action in a collective context based on their understanding of those emotions. Their desire and ability to establish a greater good that would empower individual life and liberty emerged as a result of their emotional intelligence. The concept of emotional fulfillment, the *pursuit of Happiness*, is a fundamental construct put forth in the Declaration of Independence (1776).

The approach in both programs presented in this text, the *Literacy Express* and *Building Community, Character, and Social Skills*, integrates the skills of emotional intelligence through educational drama, providing specific structures through which individual emotional experience is accessed and integrated with objects of shared meaning in a collective context. The unique subjective experiences of the students who participated in these programs generated knowledge and understanding about objective skills and concepts pertaining to the academic curriculum, creating a powerful and focused learning environment, with the individuality of the whole student functioning as the primary learning tool. As stated by educational drama pioneer Brian Way (1967), "Education is concerned with individuals; drama is concerned with the individuality of individuals" (p. 3).

American values of independence, freedom of expression, creativity and individuality, although hotly debated when it comes to cultural accommodation of how different individuals choose to pursue happiness, still manage to abound in many shapes and forms in our culture. Yet we have not been able to create an approach and action plan for our classrooms that can engage our unique American values in a way that inspires academic excellence and visionary thinking. We seem to have created, as indicated by all the reports and studies, the opposite of that ideal, an educational system that continues, as indicated by the title of John Taylor Gatto's (1992) book, to "dumb us down."

Why has our approach to education fallen so far short of these ideals? How does a society based on individuality and freedom of expression perpetrate a system that ends up functioning not as an affirming vital force for those values and ideals but as a "fundamental betrayal of the American Revolution" (Gatto, 1992, p. 15), "repugnant to our founding myths and to the reality of our founding period" (pps. 100–101)? Why, in a society that flourished as a beacon of freedom for an oppressed world, have we reached the dark milestone where one out of every hundred Americans is in jail (Pew Center for the States, 2008)? How did the original intent of what we say we stand for go so far astray in our approach to education, an institution so key to the future and ongoing revitalization of our American culture?

In his book *The End of Education: Redefining the Value of School* (1995), Neil Postman discusses how commercial interests have pervaded and compromised meaningful, emotional connection to important cultural symbols, eroding their value to our public education system and general cultural identity. Postman identifies a sense of "skepticism, disillusionment, alienation...and loss of meaning" when Abraham Lincoln's face "is used to announce linen sales," the Statue of Liberty is used to "persuade potential customers to fly to Miami," Moses "is depicted in a poster selling kosher chickens," "the infant Jesus and Mary have been invoked to promote a rock-music television station," "Uncle Sam [is used] to sell frankfurters [and] Martin Luther King Jr.'s birthday is largely used as an occasion for furniture sales..." (p. 25). This degradation of meaningful, emotionally connected cultural symbols, according to Postman, affects "every social institution, not least the schools" (p. 24).

The cycle deepens as the commercial interests that profit by compromising our cultural symbols and the values they represent, then seek to further capitalize on our biological and social need to register and give form to emotional experience. A deluge of objects, masquerading as emotionally meaningful in order to deceive our compromised value system, are peddled for the sole purpose of commerce and profit. As people attach themselves to objects and experiences in an attempt to invest meaning and fulfill these emotional needs, items of commercial culture such as fashion, video games, and the latest cellular phone gadgets, quietly accompanied by the more sensationalized social pariahs of substance abuse, sexual promiscuity, and other addictions rush to occupy the void left by depersonalization and emotional disconnect originally perpetrated by corporate driven, commercial interests.

Ironically, these objects, presented as a meaningful panacea to individuals frantically searching for emotional connection, are all too often dangerous and unhealthy. A full-page advertisement for a popular hamburger chain claims, "America's favorite fries will make you feel '*WONDERFUL*' inside!" (2000, May 4, *Newsday*, p. G11). America's "favorite fries" have recently been found to cause cancer. That's not very wonderful for our insides. A coupon for a video pizza chain reads, "You've given your kids love, affection and a home, now give them what they REALLY want!" Corporate interests create a commercial culture that unfortunately seeks to capitalize on our emotional dysfunction by providing often unhealthy objects and experiences that claim to clarify and fulfill those very same connections that they have systematically disrupted.

Many of these corporate media encounters that coerce us into purchasing the objects of our alleged desire, even when they are not directly detrimental to our physical and emotional well-being, deter us from intelligent emotional awareness and expression. This sets up an addictive cycle in which we feel the need to consume more objects and experiences in a futile attempt to fulfill and satisfy our otherwise mismanaged and increasingly dissatisfied and unfulfilled emotional schema. The commercial nature of our culture encourages us and depends on us to function in this manner.

Have our schools become mere cogs in this cultural aberration that seeks to depersonalize our unique values system in order to make a profit? Does our approach to education merely promote an endless cycle of meaningless economic consumption, perpetrated by herding our children toward an increasingly limited number of choices for self-expression that, according to Postman (1995), only functions to serve the "gods of economic utility [and] consumership" (p. 24)? Gatto (1992) plainly asks, "Should we continue to teach people that they can buy happiness in the face of a tidal wave of evidence that they cannot?" (p. 67).

Rather than feeling helpless in the face of cultural decay and corporate control, we need to educate, in the spirit of our founding fathers, free-thinking, independent individuals who can make emotionally intelligent, empowering choices for themselves and their communities. This contradiction that exists, the discord between traditional American values and our approach to American education, is at the core of our academic and ultimately social dysfunction.

An American approach to education that reflects these values and concepts should promote independent thinking, individuality, and the pursuit of happiness. A cornerstone of the approach, emotional intelligence, for these reasons and those discussed earlier, supports and strengthens individual thought and expression by accessing unique subjective experience. Then, as exemplified by the founding fathers in the first three words of the Preamble to the Constitution, *We the People*, these unique subjective experiences are processed in a collective context in order to create shared meanings that benefit the general welfare of the community in a manner that further strengthens, rather than compromises, individuality.

Educational drama facilitates these processes that naturally occur in students as whole, integrated operations. In the absence of such an approach, we compartmentalize the curriculum and train students to respond in a manner that is disconnected from personal, meaningful emotion-based experience, contorting their natural processes and causing thought patterns to become equally disconnected, fragmented, and compartmentalized. Educational drama empowers an integrated curriculum and restores a "whole" cognitive process by connecting students with materials and concepts through personal, emotion-based experiences that are uniquely meaningful rather than mass-produced.

A Pledge of Allegiance

I pledge allegiance to the values and ideals that this country was founded upon, and to teach in a way that empowers freedom of expression, independence, individuality, and the integration of whole and creative thought processes for each student I encounter.

Dylan was right. We teach to make our community better, to ensure that we don't make the same mistakes, to progress, *in order to form a more perfect union* (U.S. Constitution, 1787). For what other purpose should we undertake any teaching? What could be a more practical, pragmatic, and valued mission than that? And, if we are teaching from a foundation of American values, then we are beholden to facilitate the process in a manner that empowers liberty and justice for all.

In order to teach from this position of strength, we need to move past the insecure and immature notion that any criticism of America is unpatriotic. It is an indisputable, historical fact that this nation, along with all of the great and unique values that have been discussed, was also established on a foundation of genocide and slavery that still affects the way our country does business. And we need to be grown up enough and patriotic enough to acknowledge, if we want to continue to uphold America's greatness, the indisputable fact that our present-day systems for managing education, commerce, air, water, food, industry, military activity, medicine, government, religion, and a host of other social mechanisms, are fraught with approaches that are at best impulsive and short-sighted, and at worst pathological and self-destructive.

So many of the basic things we need to do to nurture and take care of ourselves, like eating, breathing, managing waste, and pursuing health, operate in a manner that actually leads us more quickly to our own demise. Our children react accordingly to this social dysfunction, and we address the problem by medicating them with antipsychotic drugs and passing laws that encourage teachers (1995, July 27, *Newsday*, p. A8) and parents (1999, June 11, *Newsday*, p. A22) to paddle and spank them into submission.

I pledge to do my duty as an American citizen and operate from this patriotic stance of shedding light on our mistakes, flaws, and fundamental dysfunctions and not be deterred from this noble mission of education by those who insist that patriotism is best expressed through lapel pins, waving the flag and general compliance with the status quo as prescribed by the powers that be. While expressing pride in our unique American values, we must remain vigilant of those who would use such rituals as a means for placating and manipulating us into abeyance, keeping us from actualizing the American values we are pledging to, as long as profit can be made from denying liberty and justice to some.

An American approach to education needs to reflect purpose and materials that facilitate freedom of expression, independence, individuality, and the integration of whole and creative thought processes in every aspect of the curriculum. The activities and materials of classroom instruction need to ask students *who are you?* This needs to be the primary objective in every lesson we teach. If we do not specifically direct students to respond personally in relation to the objective content we are teaching, then we are not responding to the cognitive, social, or cultural needs of the American student.

In reaction to myriads of health problems and chronic obesity, our society is attempting to structure a more comprehensive approach to physical fitness. Let's start a movement for a more comprehensive approach to emotional fitness. Emotionally intelligent functioning is a critical and key component of cognitive processing and academic success. Competence with the skills of emotional intelligence is crucial to stemming the tide of emotional crisis and social decay, characterized by violence, depression, anxiety, drug addiction, and other antisocial behaviors increasingly exhibited by children. Educational drama, because of its ability to integrate, unify, and empower cognitive and emotional development and transform individual experience, can and should play a central role in addressing the chronic clamoring for educational reform that can address these concerns.

While Gatto (1992) concludes that public school teaching is ultimately "destructive to children" (p.19) and "even in the best schools a close examination of curriculum…turns up a lack of coherence, full of internal contradictions" (p. 2), we have not begun to tap the potential of an American approach to public education. Hopefully, some of the ideas presented in this text will help to remediate the contradictory nature of how we teach and restore some coherence to the curriculum.

Text for *I Have Feelings. How About You?*

By Marianne Franzese Chasen

I have feelings.
How about you?
Sometimes I am happy.
Sometimes I am sad.
Sometimes I am frustrated.
Sometimes I am mad.
Sometimes I am scared, and that's hard to be.
But whatever I am feeling, it is a part of me.

Mad
I feel in my belly a big tight scream.
Should I hold it in or let my words come out mean?
My face feels hot and my teeth want to growl.
If I were a wolf I would just start to howl!
Then my Mom comes in with her loud "No!"
That's it for me! I just want to punch, hit and throw!
My Mom keeps talking but I can't hear
Because right now, my mad feelings are here.
These are the things that make my mad feelings come.
When I want a new toy and my Dad says "No!"
When I want to play longer and it's time to go,
When I have to get in bed but I want to stay out,
When I have to talk in a whisper but I want to shout!
When my sister takes my octopus and won't give it back,
When I want peanut butter crackers and my brother ate the last pack,
I feel mad. How about you?

Sad
I feel in my heart a quiet kind of pain.
It's all gloomy in me like a day full of rain.
My face is getting red.
My eyes just made a tear,
Because right now, my sad feelings are here.
These are the things that make my sad feelings come.
When my Mommy and Daddy both go to work,
When my big brother calls me a baby and a jerk,
When the sign on the roller coaster says I'm too small,
When my mom stops reading to me because she gets a phone call,
When I watch the tape where the lion's daddy dies,
When my sister is sent to her room and she cries and cries,
I feel sad. How about you?

Scared
I feel all shaky and I just want to run.
I hold myself tight. This feeling's no fun.
My eyes are closed. I could scream with fear,
Because right now, my scared feelings are here.
These are the things that make my scared feelings come.
When I think of a witch, a ghost or a ghoul,
When I think that my mom won't come get me from school,
When I dream that a monster is chasing after me,
When I wake up at night and it's so dark I can't see,
When I hear my parents start to fight and shout,
When my doctor takes the needle out,
I feel scared. How about you?

Frustrated
I want to scream and I want to cry.
I just can't do it no matter how hard I try!
Again and again I can't get it right.
I stamp my feet with my fists closed tight.
I start to cry "It's just not fair!"
Right now, my frustrated feelings are here.
These are the things that make my frustrated feelings come.
When my socks are crooked and I can't get them straight,
When my mom yells "Hurry up! We're going to be late!"

When I can't tie my shoe or make the letters in my name,
When my sister won't let me play with her game,
When I don't know the words to say how I feel,
When Dad yells, "Now stop making such a big deal!"
I feel frustrated. How about you?

Happy
I feel tickly inside and out.
All I want to do is laugh, sing and shout.
My face has a smile from ear to ear,
Because right now, my happy feelings are here.
These are the things that make my happy feelings come.
When I walk on the beach or play in the sand,
When I see a plane in the sky or I'm holding a hand,
When I ride on Daddy's shoulders or get a hug from Mom,
When I take a trip to the zoo or pick zucchini from Grandma's farm,
When I eat spaghetti for breakfast or run through the park,
When I get a book from the library or find my teddy in the dark,
I feel happy. How about you?

My feelings come because things happen each day.
They show on my body in their own special way.
I'm just learning the words to tell how I feel.
My feelings are mine. They make me real.
I have feelings. How about you?

REFERENCES

America's favorite fries will make you feel wonderful inside (1998, April 5). *Newsday*, p. G11.

American Medical Association (2000).

Associated Press (2008, May 5). More kids in U.S. get meds. *Newsday*, p. A6.

Beaumont, K. (2004). *I like myself*. San Diego: Harcourt.

Blackford, H. (2007). *Tiger's story*. New York: Boxer Books.

Bloom, P., Hamlin, K. & Wynn, K. (2007). Social evaluation by preverbal infants. *Nature*: 450. 557 – 559.

Bolton, G. (1979). *Towards a theory of drama in education*. Essex, England: Longman Group.

Bolton, G. (1999). *Acting in the classroom*. Portland, Maine: Calendar Island.

Centers for Disease Control and Prevention (2008).

Chasen, L. R. (2003). *Linking emotional intelligence and literacy development through educational drama for a group of first and second graders*. Doctoral dissertation, New York University.

Chasen, L. R. (2005). Spectacle and ensemble in group drama therapy treatment for children with ADHD and related neurological symptoms. In Haen, C. & Weber, A. M. (Eds.), *Clinical applications of drama therapy in child and adolescent treatment* (pps.153 – 170). New York: Brunner-Routledge

Clay, M. M. (1991). *Becoming literate: The construction of inner control*. Portsmouth, NH: Heinemann Educational Books.

CNN Television (November 3, 2003). *America's failing education system*. Cable News Network.

Courtney, R. (1980). *The dramatic curriculum*. London: Heinemann Educational Books.

Courtney, R. (1995). *Drama and feeling: An aesthetic theory*. Montreal, Canada: McGill-Queen's University Press.

Cowley, J. (1983). *The monsters' party*. Bothell, WA: Wright Group.

Damasio, A. R. (1994). *Descartes' error: Emotion, reason, and the human brain*. New York: G. P. Putnam's Sons.

Damasio, A. R. (1999). *The feeling of what happens: Body and emotion in the making of consciousness*. San Diego: Harcourt Brace.

Declaration of Independence (1776).

DePaola, T. (1979). *Oliver Button is a sissy*. China: Voyager Books.

Dorn, L. J., French, C., & Jones, T. (1998). *Apprenticeship in literacy transitions across reading and writing*. York, Maine: Stenhouse.

Duffy, T. M., & Jonassen, D. H. (Eds.). (1992). *Constructivism and the technology of instruction: A conversation.* Hillsdale, NJ: Lawrence Erlbaum Associates.

Eggleton, J. (1988). *Now I am five.* New York: Wright Group.

EPE Research Center and America's Promise Alliance (2008).

Erikson, E. H. (1968). *Identity: Youth and crisis.* New York: W. W. Norton.

FBI (2006).

FBI Uniform Crime Report (2007)

Fine, B. (1957a, October 11). Educators upset by Soviet stroke. *New York Times*, pp. 1, 11.

Fine, B. (1957b, October 12). Satellite called spur to education. *New York Times*, p. 1, 3.

Fountas, I. C., & Pinnell, G. S. (Eds.) (1999). *Voices on word matters Learning about phonics and spelling in the literacy classroom.* Portsmouth, NH: Heinemann.

Fox, J. (Ed.) (1987). *The essential Moreno.* New York: Springer.

Fox, J. (Ed.) (1999). *Gathering voices: Essays on playback theater.* New Paltz, NY: Tusitala.

FOX Television. (2003, November 23). *Education crisis in America.* FOX Broadcasting Company.

Garcia, J.R., Gelo, D. J., Greenow, L. L., Kracht, J. B., White, D. J. (1997). *Communities Around Us.* Morristown, NJ: Silver, Burdett & Ginn Inc.

Gardner, H. (1983). *Frames of mind: The theory of multiple intelligences.* New York: Basic Books.

Gardner, H. (1999). *Intelligence reframed: Multiple intelligences for the 21st century.* New York: Basic Books.

Gatto, J. T. (1992). *Dumbing us down the hidden curriculum of compulsory schooling.* Philadelphia: New Society.

Goleman, D. (1996). *Emotional intelligence: Why it can matter more than IQ.* New York: Bantam Books.

Henkes, K. (1991). *Chrysanthemum.* New York: Greenwillow Books.

Henkes, K. (2000). *Wemberly worried.* New York: Greenwillow Books.

Jennings, S. (1999). *Franklin's neighborhood.* New York: Scholastic.

Kann, E., & Kann, V. (2007). *Purplicious.* New York City: HarperCollins.

Kirwan, W. (2007). *Nobody notices Minerva.* New York: Sterling.

Kraus, R. (1971). *Leo the late bloomer.* New York: Simon and Schuster.

Landy, R. J. (1994). *Drama therapy concepts, theories and practices* (2nd ed.). Springfield, IL: Charles C. Thomas.

Lester, H. (1994). *Three cheers for Tacky.* Boston: Houghton Mifflin.

Mayer, M. (1983a). *All by myself.* Racine, WI: Western.

Mayer, M. (1983b). *I was so mad.* New York: Random House.

McCaslin, N. (1980). *Creative drama in the classroom* (3rd ed.). New York: Longman.

Moreno, J. L. (1978). *Who shall survive?* New York: Beacon House.

National Drug Intelligence Center (2008).

Nayer, J. (1994). *My five senses: A lion's tale*. New York: Newbridge Communications.

Neelands, J. (1984). *Making sense of drama*. Oxford, England: Heinemann Educational Publishers.

New York City Board of Education (1999). *The district two balanced literacy program 1999: A handbook for teachers*. New York City Board of Education.

Newman, J. M. (1985). *Whole language theory in use*. Portsmouth, NH: Heinemann Educational Books.

O'Brien, A. S. (1992). *My name is Johari*. New York: Newbridge Communications.

Penn, A. (2006). *The kissing hand*. Terre Haute, IN.: Tanglewood Press.

Penn, A. (2008). *Chester Raccoon and the big bad bully*. Terre Haute, IN: Tanglewood Press.

Pew Center for the States (2008).

Piaget, J. (1951). *Play, dreams and imitation in childhood*. London: William Heinemann.

Postman, N. (1995). *The end of education: Redefining the value of school*. New York: Vintage Books.

Progress in International Reading Literacy Study (2007).

Reuters (1999, June 11). Okla. law reaffirms spanking rights. *Newsday*, p. A22.

Salovey, P., & Sluyter, D. J. (Eds.). (1997). *Emotional development and emotional intelligence: Educational implications*. New York: Basic Books.

Schools' struggle with violence (1998, May 24). *Newsday*, pp. A21, A40.

Slade, P. (1954). *Child drama*. London: University of London Press.

Slate, J. (2001). *Miss Bindergarten takes a field trip with kindergarten*. New York City: Penguin Putnam.

Snowball, D., & Bolton, F. (1999). *Spelling K–8*. York, Maine: Stenhouse.

Tinsley, B. (2004, April 27), *Mallard Fillmore*. Kings Features Syndicate.

Trends in International Mathematics and Science Study (2003).

UNICEF (2003).

U.S. Constitution (1787).

U.S. Department of Education (2008).

Wagner, B. J. (1998). *Educational drama and language arts: What research shows*. Portsmouth, NH: Heinemann.

Way, B. (1967). *Development through drama*. Atlantic Highlands, NJ: Humanities Press.

Weaver, C. (1988). *Reading process and practice from socio-linguistics to whole language*. Portsmouth, NH: Heinemann.

Wells, R. (1984). *Noisy Nora*. Ontario, Canada: Scholastic.

Wells, R. (2008). *Yoko writes her name*. New York: Hyperion Books.

INDEX

Studies in the Postmodern Theory of Education

General Editors
Joe L. Kincheloe & Shirley R. Steinberg

Counterpoints publishes the most compelling and imaginative books being written in education today. Grounded on the theoretical advances in criticalism, feminism, and postmodernism in the last two decades of the twentieth century, Counterpoints engages the meaning of these innovations in various forms of educational expression. Committed to the proposition that theoretical literature should be accessible to a variety of audiences, the series insists that its authors avoid esoteric and jargonistic languages that transform educational scholarship into an elite discourse for the initiated. Scholarly work matters only to the degree it affects consciousness and practice at multiple sites. Counterpoints' editorial policy is based on these principles and the ability of scholars to break new ground, to open new conversations, to go where educators have never gone before.

For additional information about this series or for the submission of manuscripts, please contact:

Joe L. Kincheloe & Shirley R. Steinberg
c/o Peter Lang Publishing, Inc.
29 Broadway, 18th floor
New York, New York 10006

To order other books in this series, please contact our Customer Service Department:

(800) 770-LANG (within the U.S.)
(212) 647-7706 (outside the U.S.)
(212) 647-7707 FAX

Or browse online by series:
www.peterlang.com